NEXT LEVEL
GAMES REVIEW 2024

First published in Great Britain 2023 by Expanse
An imprint of HarperCollins*Publishers*
1 London Bridge Street, London SE1 9GF
www.farshore.co.uk

HarperCollins*Publishers*
Macken House, 39/40 Mayor Street Upper,
Dublin 1, D01 C9W8, Ireland

Written by Ben Wilson

ISBN 978 0 00 853738 8
Printed in Dubai
001

All games have age guidance and we recommend that parents and guardians of
younger gamers are aware of these guidelines and the content of the games being
played. This book is for a general audience and therefore reviews the year in gaming,
covering a wide range of games from PEGI 3 to PEGI 18. While we have ensured
the content of this book is suitable for a general audience, discretion is advised.

Expanse & HarperCollins are not responsible for content hosted online by third parties.
Any links to websites were correct at the time of going to print. We recommend online
activity for younger fans is monitored by parents and guardians.

NEXT LEVEL

GAMES REVIEW 2024

BY BEN WILSON

CONTENTS

064

036
GOTHAM KNIGHTS

Retro

Check out the biggest games from ten, twenty and thirty years ago. Page 94, 138 and 208.

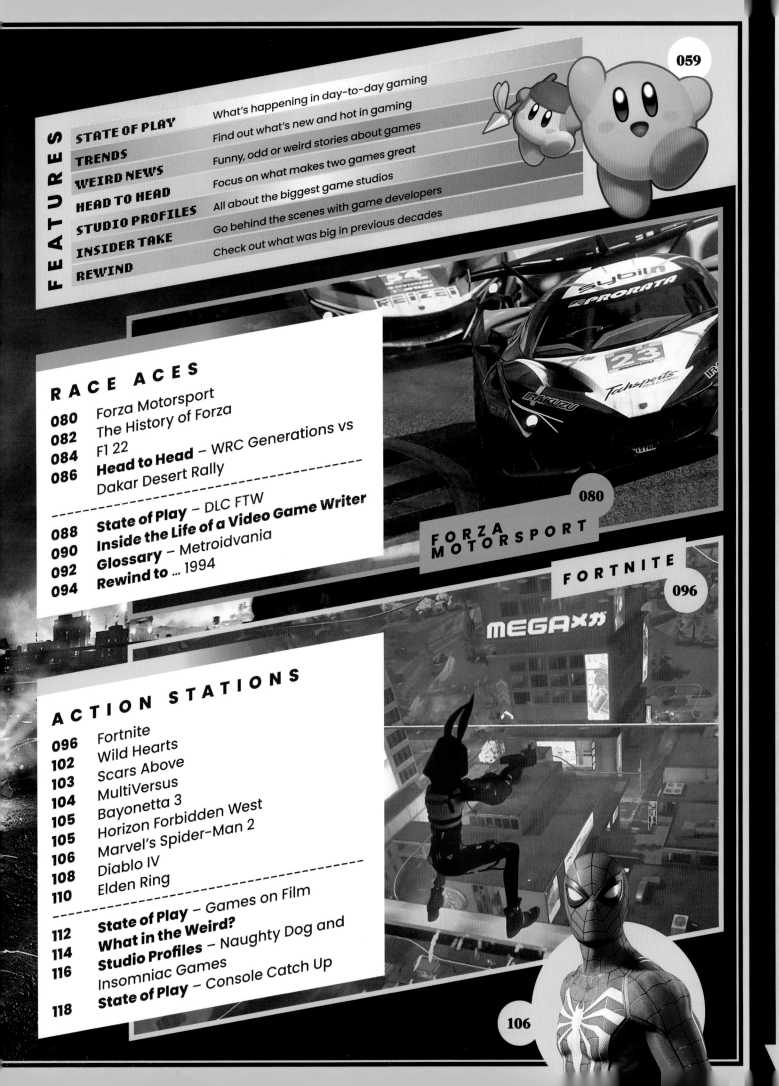

059

080

FORZA MOTORSPORT

FORTNITE

096

106

DESTINY 2: LIGHTFALL 148

122

160

143

The Insider Take

Hear from industry experts on pages 16, 74, 174 and 206.

INTRODUCTION
BY BEN WILSON

It's impossible to make a top five of the year. You'd need to squeeze fifteen games into it! Particularly for gamers who grabbed a next-gen console. PS5 and Xbox Series X shone once again, thanks to their technical abilities and growing libraries of great new games. *Elden Ring* continued to astonish players, and picked up a ton of Game Awards. Cat sim *Stray* was similarly impressive, showcasing just how good indie efforts can be. *Sonic Frontiers* and *Street Fighter 6* brought a return to form for old favourites and essential newcomers included *Hogwarts: Legacy*, *Fall Guys* and *Disney Dreamlight Valley*. They're all covered in these pages!

For those who prefer familiar faces, the 'big four' just keep on getting better. *Minecraft* delivered the very cool Trails and Tales update, and a whole new game: *Minecraft Legends*! *Roblox* added tie-ins with George Ezra, My Little Pony and fashion brand H&M. *Fortnite* kept us all hooked with the awesome Chapter 4 and essential outfits, like Captain America. As for *Overwatch* fans: they were treated to the long-awaited sequel, where teams of five fight it out across Rome and New York. Amazing!

Two of those smash hits contributed to another memorable year in eSports. *Fortnite* and *Overwatch* remain pioneers in competitive gaming, along with classics like *League of Legends* and *DOTA 2*. *Valorant*, meanwhile, is the hot up-and-comer. Our dedicated eSports section takes a closer look at those – along with seven must-know hints that could turn you into the next big thing!

For a lot of players, this incredible year in gaming can be summed up in a single word: *Zelda*! Nintendo Switch owners finally got their hands on *The Legend of Zelda: Tears of the Kingdom*, and it lived up to the hype. Link's latest adventure smashed the world record for the fastest selling Nintendo game ever. It sold 10 million copies in three days!

As well as fantastic games, it's been a year for some truly crazy news stories. We've squeezed them all into these pages. There's the Twitch streamer who figured out how to play *Elden Ring* with her brain – and the new *Sonic the Hedgehog* lore master, tasked with keeping track of the spiky one's bonkers thirty-year-history. You'll also read about the PS5 electric car, *Genshin Impact* pizza and the man who completed every single N64 game ever made!

One of my favourite elements of making this book is interviewing developers about their annual highlights. The makers of *Stray, FIFA 23, Ghostbusters: Spirits Unleashed, Destiny 2, Apex Legends* and many more talked about the games they love, and features they're most proud of. There are some really surprising answers – but I don't want to spoil them before you've got to those pages! We're also including guest writers for the first time. Writer and presenter Alysia Judge outlines how you can use gaming to aid your physical and mental health, *No Man's Sky* writer Will Porter explains how to pen a hit video game and horror expert Louise Blain shares the best games for a family audience. It's wonderful to have them on board.

The other thing I love about making this book is digging out the best games you might not have tried. Look out for *Wild Hearts* – a fun, linear adventure where you slay beasts in feudal Japan. *Two Point Campus* is an equally amusing treat. It feels like *The Sims* but set at university! Also worth a mention is my throwback favourite, *Teenage Mutant Ninja Turtles: Shredder's Revenge*. This retro beat-'em-up features ninja shenanigans to enjoy whether you're seven or seventy!

It's been a brilliant year – but there's also loads to look forward to. What upcoming games are you most excited about playing? If you can't decide, flick to the back of the book for inspiration. We peer ahead to some of the biggest new releases. Supermassive robots return in *Transformers Reactivate*, while *Kingdom Hearts IV* is shaping up to be the year's must-play action-RPG. There'll be plenty more on those in *Next Level Games Review 2025*. Until then ... enjoy!

COPYRIGHT © BEN WILSON

GLOSSARY

4K – Ultra HD! It's an even clearer picture than HD.

AAA – A big blockbuster release (also known as triple A), like *Marvel's Spider-Man 2*.

AI – Artificial intelligence. In the gaming industry, it means the computer plays a character within the game.

ACHIEVEMENT – Challenges or goals set by your platform, like Xbox or Steam, that you can complete in a game to earn points.

AMIIBO™ – Nintendo figurines and cards that you can buy. Tap them against your console and unlock new characters, weapons, actions and more.

AR – Augmented reality. A type of technology that places gaming images into the real world, like *Pokémon Go*.

AVATAR – A big blue alien. Also your playable character in a game. Usually an avatar is customisable.

BACKWARDS COMPATIBILITY – When a new console is released, studios will make them backwards-compatible so older games will work on newer platforms.

BATTLE ROYALE

BATTLE ROYALE – A giant online multiplayer game, like *PUBG*.

BETA – An early version of a game that's sometimes made available ahead of an official release, so players can test out the gameplay and mechanics.

BOSS – The big bad enemy – much tougher than regular baddies. You usually come across a boss at the end of a level or the end of a game.

BUTTONMASHER – An insult for someone who isn't very experienced at gaming.

CAMPAIGN – Long-running games, like *The Elder Scrolls Online*, often have extended quests called campaigns. These are usually the main story mode of the game.

CCG – Collectible card game. Build a deck of cards and battle other players or the computer. *Hearthstone* and *Magic: the Gathering* are CCGs.

CEL-SHADED – An animation style that makes characters look cartoon-like while still being 3D. *The Legend of Zelda: The Wind Waker* is cel-shaded.

CHECKPOINT – Get to a checkpoint to save your progress. They're usually safe areas with no enemies around and quite often look like bonfires.

CLOUD – An online storage system. If you back up your game to the cloud it has been saved online.

CO-OP – Short for cooperative game. Where several players work together to complete a quest. Sometimes this is the same as the solo (or single-player) campaign, but you can play it with your mates.

COMBO – A sequence of buttons that, when pressed in the correct order, make characters perform new or special moves.

COSPLAY – Costume play. When mega fans dress up as characters from a game, TV show, book or movie, they are cosplaying.

CPU – Computer processing unit. The engine in your computer or console that runs the game.

CUTSCENE – A short, story-led scene in a game that helps give players more background info.

DEVELOPER – The studio or company that created the game. Sometimes there is more than one developer working together.

DLC – Downloadable content. Add-ons, like new levels, characters, skins and modes, that are available after the first release of a game. *WWE 2K23* has regular DLC.

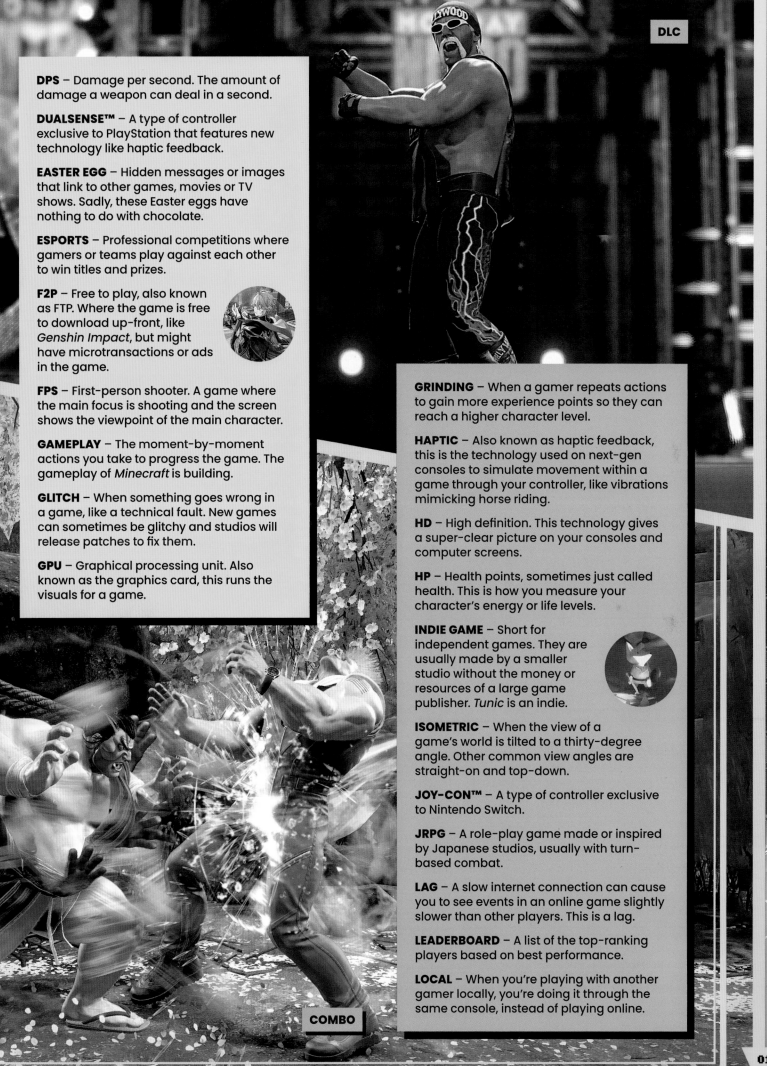

DPS – Damage per second. The amount of damage a weapon can deal in a second.

DUALSENSE™ – A type of controller exclusive to PlayStation that features new technology like haptic feedback.

EASTER EGG – Hidden messages or images that link to other games, movies or TV shows. Sadly, these Easter eggs have nothing to do with chocolate.

ESPORTS – Professional competitions where gamers or teams play against each other to win titles and prizes.

F2P – Free to play, also known as FTP. Where the game is free to download up-front, like *Genshin Impact*, but might have microtransactions or ads in the game.

FPS – First-person shooter. A game where the main focus is shooting and the screen shows the viewpoint of the main character.

GAMEPLAY – The moment-by-moment actions you take to progress the game. The gameplay of *Minecraft* is building.

GLITCH – When something goes wrong in a game, like a technical fault. New games can sometimes be glitchy and studios will release patches to fix them.

GPU – Graphical processing unit. Also known as the graphics card, this runs the visuals for a game.

GRINDING – When a gamer repeats actions to gain more experience points so they can reach a higher character level.

HAPTIC – Also known as haptic feedback, this is the technology used on next-gen consoles to simulate movement within a game through your controller, like vibrations mimicking horse riding.

HD – High definition. This technology gives a super-clear picture on your consoles and computer screens.

HP – Health points, sometimes just called health. This is how you measure your character's energy or life levels.

INDIE GAME – Short for independent games. They are usually made by a smaller studio without the money or resources of a large game publisher. *Tunic* is an indie.

ISOMETRIC – When the view of a game's world is tilted to a thirty-degree angle. Other common view angles are straight-on and top-down.

JOY-CON™ – A type of controller exclusive to Nintendo Switch.

JRPG – A role-play game made or inspired by Japanese studios, usually with turn-based combat.

LAG – A slow internet connection can cause you to see events in an online game slightly slower than other players. This is a lag.

LEADERBOARD – A list of the top-ranking players based on best performance.

LOCAL – When you're playing with another gamer locally, you're doing it through the same console, instead of playing online.

COMBO

MATCHMAKING – An automatic process that joins you up with other players online.

METROIDVANIA – A style of platforming game inspired by the classic *Metroid* and *Castlevania* series. Focusing on exploration and revisiting previously-explored areas with new abilities.

MICROTRANSACTIONS – Paid content within a game, like when you buy new skins, weapons and ammo.

MINI-GAME – Games within games! This can be a collection of mini-games, like *Fall Guys* or *Mario Party*, or a short game within a longer one, like Gut Check Challenge in *The Legend of Zelda: Breath of the Wild*.

MMO – Play together in a huge online server.

MMORPG – Massive multiplayer online role-play game. You can see why they shortened it! *World of Warcraft* and *The Elder Scrolls Online* are MMORPGs.

MOBA – Multiplayer online battle arena. *DOTA 2* and *League of Legends* are MOBAs.

MOD – Short for modification. Player-made updates or patches that give a game a new look or mechanic.

MULTIPLATFORM – When a game can be played on more than one console or platform, like PS5, Switch and PC.

MULTIPLAYER – Any game that's more than one player. They can be cooperative or combative, like *Overwatch*.

NES – Nintendo Entertainment System. A console from the 80s.

NEXT-GEN – Next-generation console. The new versions of gaming platforms, like PS5 or Xbox Series X/S.

NOOB – People who are new to gaming.

NPC – Non-player character. Any character you come across in a game that isn't controlled by another human.

NS – Nintendo Switch.

OPEN WORLD – A game without a strict path to follow, where players are free to roam around the huge world to complete their objectives.

PATCH – Downloadable updates to fix bugs and glitches or add content.

PLATFORMER – A type of game where you jump, bounce or run onto different platforms and objects across the screen to get to new levels.

PORT – A version of a game that's been moved to a new platform or console without major reworks.

PRO GAMER – Someone who plays a game professionally, in eSports competitions.

PS – PlayStation.

PUBLISHER – The company who releases the game. They don't always create it themselves, that's a developer.

PVE – Player versus environment. When it's just you and the computer AI.

PVP – Player versus player. When you're against another human or group of humans. This can be online or local.

QTE – Quick time events. These are button prompts during cutscenes that require the player to act quickly to succeed.

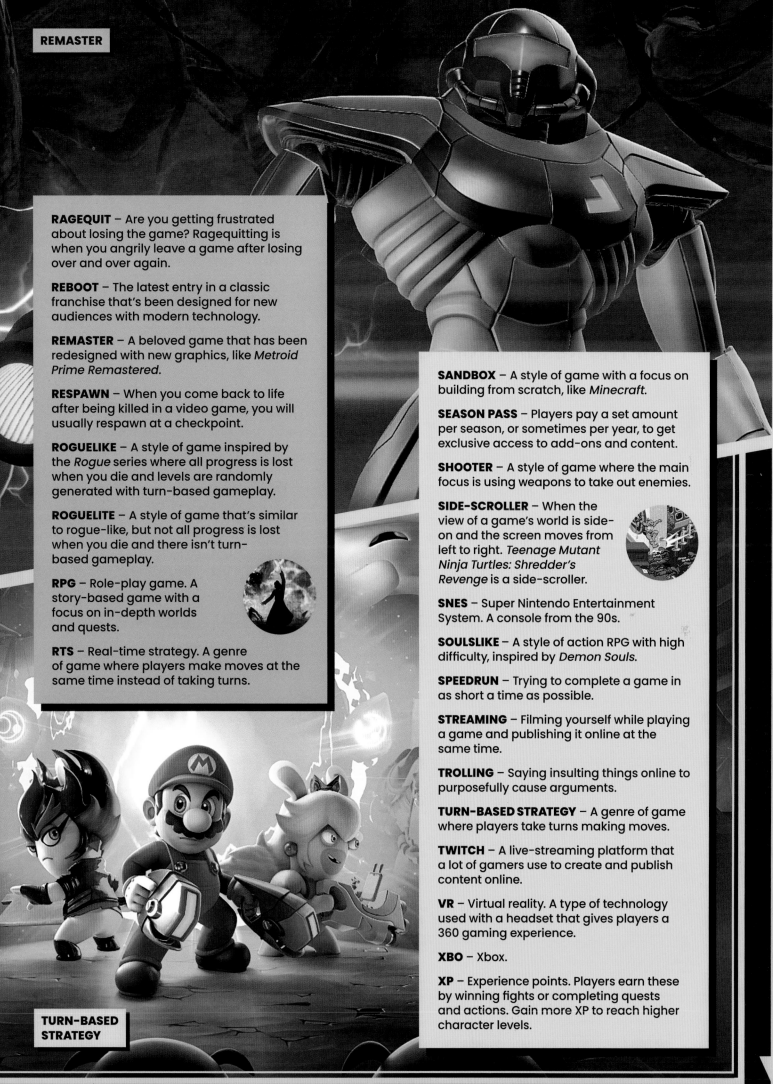

RAGEQUIT – Are you getting frustrated about losing the game? Ragequitting is when you angrily leave a game after losing over and over again.

REBOOT – The latest entry in a classic franchise that's been designed for new audiences with modern technology.

REMASTER – A beloved game that has been redesigned with new graphics, like *Metroid Prime Remastered*.

RESPAWN – When you come back to life after being killed in a video game, you will usually respawn at a checkpoint.

ROGUELIKE – A style of game inspired by the *Rogue* series where all progress is lost when you die and levels are randomly generated with turn-based gameplay.

ROGUELITE – A style of game that's similar to rogue-like, but not all progress is lost when you die and there isn't turn-based gameplay.

RPG – Role-play game. A story-based game with a focus on in-depth worlds and quests.

RTS – Real-time strategy. A genre of game where players make moves at the same time instead of taking turns.

SANDBOX – A style of game with a focus on building from scratch, like *Minecraft*.

SEASON PASS – Players pay a set amount per season, or sometimes per year, to get exclusive access to add-ons and content.

SHOOTER – A style of game where the main focus is using weapons to take out enemies.

SIDE-SCROLLER – When the view of a game's world is side-on and the screen moves from left to right. *Teenage Mutant Ninja Turtles: Shredder's Revenge* is a side-scroller.

SNES – Super Nintendo Entertainment System. A console from the 90s.

SOULSLIKE – A style of action RPG with high difficulty, inspired by *Demon Souls*.

SPEEDRUN – Trying to complete a game in as short a time as possible.

STREAMING – Filming yourself while playing a game and publishing it online at the same time.

TROLLING – Saying insulting things online to purposefully cause arguments.

TURN-BASED STRATEGY – A genre of game where players take turns making moves.

TWITCH – A live-streaming platform that a lot of gamers use to create and publish content online.

VR – Virtual reality. A type of technology used with a headset that gives players a 360 gaming experience.

XBO – Xbox.

XP – Experience points. Players earn these by winning fights or completing quests and actions. Gain more XP to reach higher character levels.

The Game Awards

All The Results from Gaming's Biggest Awards

California Love

The big show took place at the Microsoft Theater in Los Angeles. Guest presenters included Al Pacino, Bella Ramsey and Daniel Craig!

Game of the Year
Elden Ring

FromSoftware's monstrous action-adventure scored the biggest award of all. Oh, and two more to go along with it! *Elden Ring* also won Best Game Direction and Best Art Direction. The other nominees for Game of the Year were *Horizon Forbidden West, Stray, God of War: Ragnarök, Xenoblade Chronicles 3* and *A Plague Tale: Requiem*.

Complete List of Winners

Game of the Year:
Elden Ring

Best Game Direction:
Elden Ring

Best Narrative:
God of War: Ragnarök

Best Art Direction:
Elden Ring

Best Score and Music:
God of War: Ragnarök

Best Audio Design:
God of War: Ragnarök

Best Performance:
Christopher Judge in God of War: Ragnarök

Games for Impact:
As Dusk Falls

Best Ongoing Game:
Final Fantasy XIV

Best Independent Game:
Stray

Best Mobile Game:
Marvel Snap

Best Community Support:
Final Fantasy XIV

Best VR/AR Game:
Moss: Book II

Innovation in Accessibility:
God of War: Ragnarök

Best Action Game:
Bayonetta 3

Best Action/Adventure Game:
God of War: Ragnarök

Best Role Playing Game:
Elden Ring

Best Fighting Game:
MultiVersus

Best Family Game:
Kirby and the Forgotten Land

Best Sports/Racing Game:
Gran Turismo 7

Best Sim/Strategy Game:
Mario + Rabbids Sparks of Hope

Best Multiplayer Game:
Splatoon 3

Best Debut Indie Game:
Stray

Most Anticipated Game:
The Legend of Zelda: Tears of the Kingdom

Best Adaptation:
Arcane

Players' Voice:
Genshin Impact

Best eSports Game:
Valorant

Best eSports Athlete:
yay (Jaccob Whiteaker)

Best eSports Team:
LOUD

Best eSports Coach:
bzkA (Matheus Tarasconi)

Best eSports Event:
2022 League of Legends World Championship

Content Creator of the Year:
Ludwig Ahgren

Best Ongoing Game
Final Fantasy XIV

A decade after release, everyone continues to love Square Enix's vast MMO. It landed on PS5 in 2021, and has been bolstered over the years by four expansions: *Heavensward, Stormblood, Shadowbringers* and *Endwalker. Apex Legends, Fortnite, Genshin Impact* and *Fortnite* were the other contenders in this category.

Best Mobile Game
Marvel Snap

Card collecting games are all the rage right now. And Marvel has never been cooler. Put the two together and what do you get? *Marvel Snap!* You build a deck of twelve cards and then unleash them in combat against either humans or the AI. With over 170 characters to find, it's hard to put your phone away once you get hooked!

Best Independent Game
Stray

This indie cat sim was one of four games to claim multiple awards. The others were *Elden Ring, God of War: Ragnarök* and *Final Fantasy XIV.* Pretty decent company! You steer a kitty through a cyberpunk underground city. Seven nominations went its way in total, more than juggernauts like *Call of Duty: Modern Warfare 2.*

THE INSIDER TAKE

Developers Share Highlights from a Memorable Year

Swann Martin-Raget
Producer of Stray

What's the best thing you played in the last year?
I finally completed *Half-Life: Alyx* in VR and got a solid lesson in how to make a good video game. It had such a deep understanding of a new way to play and interact.

What element of *Stray* are you most proud of?
Something we didn't really anticipate is to see how cats in the real world were responding to the cat in the game. We tried really hard to make ours as realistic as possible, so seeing actual cats being interested in the sounds and animations was great.

What game are you most looking forward to?
We are always very interested in whatever Playdead Studios is working on.

Kantcho Doskov
Game Design Director on EA Sports FC

What's the best thing you played in the last year?
Elden Ring is the best game I've played over the last year. Incredible gameplay, endless build variety and an open world unlike anything I've ever seen.

What element of *FIFA 23* are you most proud of?
HyperMotion Technology, our cutting-edge machine learning algorithm – that learned from over nine million frames of motion capture by professional footballers – allowed us to create true next-gen gameplay in *FIFA 23*.

What game are you most looking forward to?
Looking forward to playing *FC 24* with my friends. Gameplay will use real match data from the world's best players, competing at the highest level, resulting in the most true-to-life football experience yet.

Jared Gerritzen
Chief Creative Officer of Ghostbusters: Spirits Unleashed

What's the best thing you played in the last year?
I've been loving *Shredders*, the snowboarding game. I love games that I can play over and over, especially in a sport I don't have the time to do as much as when I was a kid.

What element of *Ghostbusters: Spirits Unleashed* are you most proud of?
Eight-year-old me is so proud that I made a *Ghostbusters* game. Heck, adult me is proud! I'm proud we made a game that has brought the fans of this IP together.

What game are you most looking forward to and why?
Street Fighter 6. A lifelong favourite. I've put in so many hours by myself, with friends and family. The summertime is nostalgic for me with this game.

Alain Jarniou
Creative Director of WRC Generations

What's the best thing you played in the last year?
I spent hundreds of hours with *Horizon* and *Gran Turismo 7*. The one that surprised me was *Stray* – being able to play as a cat, with a smart story around it. Unexpected and super satisfying.

What element of *WRC Generations* are you most proud of?
The new League system is the master addition. It provides unlimited competitive content, along with a true interest for dedicated drivers. It uses the huge content of stages and cars we have been able to put in the game, after seven iterations.

What game are you most looking forward to?
Hollow Knight: Silksong is a long-awaited sequel to a gameplay masterpiece. I spent so many hours playing *Hollow Knight*, and restarting it from the beginning!

Supersonic Sales

No surprises here. *Sonic the Hedgehog* is Sega's biggest selling game ever. The blue blur has sold more than 44 million copies.

THE SONIC BOOM

Sega

■ Sega has been one of the biggest developers in the world for over fifty years. The Tokyo giant started out with arcade machines. Among its first creations was a submarine sim called *Periscope*! These days, the game developer is way too big for just one studio. The team behind Mega Drive classics *Golden Axe* and *Altered Beast* was called Sega R&D1 and the Sonic Team handles the company's sneaker-sporting mascot. In 2021 it opened a new Sapporo studio, but most of its projects are top secret.

Biggest Series:
Out Run

Sonic was the obvious choice here, but there's plenty of the speedster to come. Instead, we're celebrating a 1980s icon that reinvented racing. You zoom around sunny tracks against the clock, while dodging oncoming traffic. It's simple yet so very moreish, even over thirty years after it was first released.

Have You Played?

Sonic the Hedgehog   **Streets of Rage**   **Crazy Taxi**   **Virtua Fighter 4**

Biggest Series:
Resident Evil

This PEGI 18 game is definitely one for older fans and it has a different name in its home country. Japanese gamers know the survival horror franchise as *Biohazard*! There have been more than thirty *Resi* games, with over 131 million copies sold.

Iconic Moment

It's hard to put into words just how huge *Street Fighter II* was from 1991 to 1994. Its pixelated brawling made multiplayer a trend long before online gaming was everywhere!

RYU READY?

Capcom

■ The name Capcom is short for Capsule Computers, as a tribute to the arcade machines it was famous for in the 1980s. Like Sega, Capcom's selection of games is split across three teams. Division 1 created *Resident Evil*, *Devil May Cry* and *Mega Man*. Division 2 looks after *Monster Hunter*, while *Street Fighter*, the classic retro beat-'em-up, is handled by Division 3. Its main headquarters is in Osaka, where the various studios were originally called Planning Rooms.

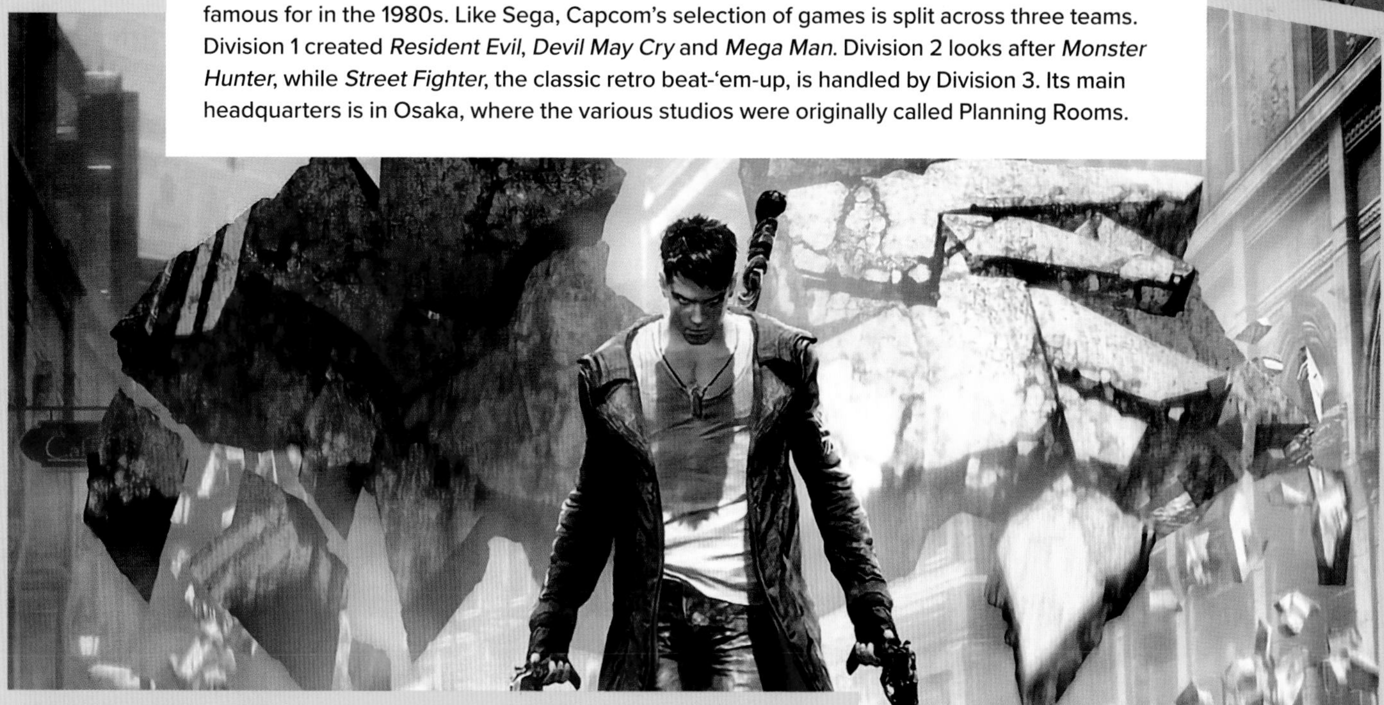

Have You Played?

Street Fighter IV

Monster Hunter: World

The Great Ace Attorney Chronicles

Mega Man 11

STATE OF PLAY
Console Catch Up
What's New With PlayStation?

MAKING ROOM
> *The PS5 is Sony's biggest console, and not just in terms of sales numbers! Measuring H390 x W260mm x D92mm, the console is taller than most microwaves.*

■ PS5 is the must-own console in the eyes of many gamers. It's also the hardest to get your hands on. Sony sold more than 25 million PS5s in its first two years on sale. But massive numbers of fans aren't able to get hold of a console, with many left disappointed again for the second year in a row!

Beautiful Stranger
There's a reason everyone wants a PS5. It's phenomenal! The machine is humungous – far bigger than any past PlayStation. But it looks beautiful in any TV or bedroom set-up. Buttons are minimal, giving it the appearance of an alien communications unit. Its DualSense controllers are a dream to handle, and have both haptic feedback and adaptive triggers. You really feel the tension in a bow when playing *Horizon Forbidden West*, or a tough tackle in *FIFA 23*.

And the games! *Marvel's Spider-Man: Miles Morales* came packaged with early machines and remains huge. Swing around a snowy Manhattan, unleashing bio-electric blasts! *Sackboy: A Big Adventure* is a classic platformer, with ace co-op options, so you can play with your friends and family! *Astro's Playroom* is the perfect introduction to everything those clever controllers can do: feel the crunch of your footsteps, zip your spacesuit up with your fingers and blow (yes, blow!) into the mic to turn a fan on.

The Big Plus

The biggest change in the world of PlayStation is Sony's relaunch of PS Plus. It's a gaming subscription service that now comes in three options, one for whatever kind of player you are! PS Plus Essential is the basic package, giving subscribers two downloadable games each month plus online play. The mid-tier option is PlayStation Extra. This opens up a catalogue of more than 400 PS4 and PS5 games to download. The most committed option is PS Plus Premium. It gives you access to all the above, plus another 340 games! PS3 titles are available through cloud streaming, and you can also download a selection of PS1 and PS2 classics. Definitely check out the *Jak & Daxter* games for some blast-tastic platform capers!

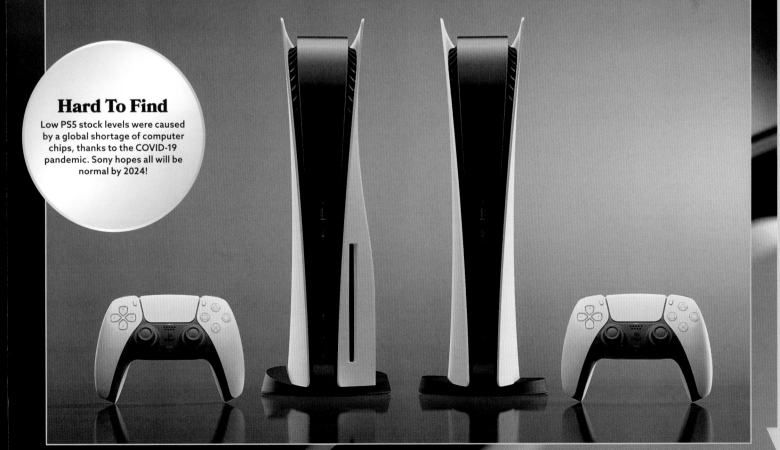

Hard To Find

Low PS5 stock levels were caused by a global shortage of computer chips, thanks to the COVID-19 pandemic. Sony hopes all will be normal by 2024!

Top 5 PS5 Exclusives

Uncharted: Legacy of Thieves Collection

Two of PS4's best games come together in one collection. *Uncharted 4: A Thief's End* is a fitting farewell to the iconic treasure-hunter Nathan Drake, while no-nonsense Chloe Frazer fronts another can't-miss adventure in *Uncharted: The Lost Legacy.*

Did You Know?

PS5 architect Mark Cerny has helped design every Sony console since PS2. But his breakthrough moment was 1980s arcade classic *Marble Madness!*

Horizon Forbidden West

Flame-haired machine-smasher Aloy is cooler than ever in this spectacular sequel. Cinematic moments leave a lasting impression, but taking your time to explore the breathtaking world is super-satisfying. Seriously well-written characters and ace combat will have you coming back again and again.

Sackboy: A Big Adventure

The star of *LittleBigPlanet* returns for masses of fun! It's a co-op platformer where our hero can slap, roll and nosedive his way to Dreamer Orbs. Plasma Pumps are the coolest bit. They let you hover in the air and unleash enemy blasts!

Ratchet & Clank: Rift Apart

The loose-lipped lombax and his robot mate return in an essential PS5 platformer. It's packed with joyous levels, engaging puzzles and classic funny one-liners. Bionic-armed female buddy Rivet is incredibly loveable, too.

Gran Turismo 7

The drive of your PS5 life. This is as serious as racing gets, with over 400 cars to collect. All the vehicles have realistic physics and look sensational – especially once the dynamic weather system kicks in. You'll want it to rain just because it looks so great.

PS5's Predecessors

PS2

PS1's turn-of-the-century successor went even more massive. Released in 2000, it eventually sold 155 million. If you were into *Grand Theft Auto*, this was the machine to play it on. *Gran Turismo* and *Metal Gear Solid* were also big games for PlayStation 2.

PS1

Released in 1994, the first PlayStation was originally created as a Super Nintendo add-on. It would have been called SNES-CD! Instead, Sony launched its own machine and created a pop culture icon. More than 102 million PS1s have been sold.

PS4

The console that restored Sony's reputation. Its controller was a huge improvement, with a slick touchpad and tactile triggers. Ten years since its November 2013 release, it still has a huge install base. 106 million consoles have been sold in total!

PS3

The 2006 machine introduced the ability to play Blu-rays, but found tough competition in Microsoft's Xbox 360. That meant it sold less than PS1 and PS2. 87 million is still a huge number though! Its last ever game came out in 2020.

BUILDING WORLDS

Minecraft

Developer Mojang **Publisher** Mojang
Platform NS, PC, PS4, XBO, XBX/S **Rating** PEGI 7+

■ Mojang's big block party shows no sign of fading away. It was named the best title of the year by gamers aged thirteen to twenty-five – despite being released back in 2011! Each year it drops twelve months of must-own DLC, memorable builds and near-infinite fun.

Build, Build, Build

Minecraft gives players unlimited creativity in a 3D sandbox world. You can build a simple home or elaborate castles, piers, suspension bridges ... anything in your imagination. Creative mode gives you limitless resources, while in Survival mode, you craft weapons to fend off mobs like creepers, skeletons and zombies.

Minecraft's monster year delivered the Trails and Tales update, loads of can't-miss additions, and an entirely new spin-off game too!

Each biome in Minecraft contains a huge range of blocks to be mined and then crafted into new creations.

Your imagination is the limit in this sandbox-style game. Build castles, rockets, real-world skyscrapers or even your own house.

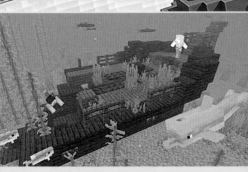

Alex and Steve are the default skins, but you can update these to something more personal.

Pandas are one of the most popular mobs of the game, wait till you see one sneeze!

Best New DLC

Camp Enderwood

A new summer camp with masses of stuff to try! Characters include Glamper, Craft Lady and Moth Creature. You can go horseback riding, toast marshmallows or join a scavenger hunt. As always, watch out for spooky surprises though …

Mega Man X

As well as introducing Capcom's blue bomber, this add-on also gave us some exciting new baddies. You get four classic villains: Chill Penguin, Storm Eagle, Armored Armadillo and Sting Chameleon! If you manage to beat them all, you can take on Sigma in a four-stage fortress.

Holiday Resort

Ten mini-games and more than 160 custom models make for the perfect vacation. You don't even need to pack a rucksack! With over 1,000 rooms, the five-star resort takes hours to explore. Ride jet skis, go dancing or just enjoy a hot dog by the beach!

Ten Top Tips

It's never too late to get involved in Minecraft! Fast-track your way to block brilliance with these essential hints …

01 Chop down any trees near your initial base – it gives skeletons and zombies less to hide behind!

02 Build a second base with a chest, bed and crop farm. You can escape here if your main base gets besieged!

03 Don't use wood for any base buildings. It can be set on fire by hostile mobs or lightning strikes!

04 Also build a greenhouse as early as you can to protect your crops from animals and mobs.

05 Apples are the best way of easing hunger, but hard to find. Animals are the best choice in the early stages.

06 Baby animals take twenty minutes to grow up. Don't kill them for food in this time, as you get less meat.

07 Always carry both a short- and long-range weapon. A sword and bow-and-arrow is a good combo.

08 When working near lava, fill a pool of water then stand in it to protect you from the heat.

09 Working underground? Build a clock from redstone and four gold ingots. You'll always know the time of day.

10 You're 40% more likely to catch a fish if you try while it's raining.

Watch out! Pillagers, unlike the neutral villager mob, will attack in raids, shooting players with their crossbows.

Grrrrrrr! Groaning zombies are another hostile mob. They attack players when the sun goes down.

With the recent Village & Pillage update, villagers spawn at a higher rate than they did before. Making it much easier to fill newly-built villages.

BUILDING WORLDS

Minecraft Legends arrives!

Minecraft Legends is a whole new game. It's still set in a block-based world though. Phew! Lush biomes are threatened by dastardly piglins. These oinking enemies want to corrupt the Overworld, and it's your job to build alliances then snuff out their threat.

The mix of action and strategy includes some neat twists on *Minecraft* staples. You have a sword – but it doesn't work on piglin structures or portals. But you can use the hero's lute to create mobs and golems, which aid you in battle. Allies can also be summoned by the bewitching Flames of Creation. And instead of changing the landscape, you need to explore it for tactical advantages!

Say You'll Be Mine

Just how big is Minecraft? More than 176 million gamers played it in February 2023 alone!

Grunters, bruisers and runts are just some of the piglins that you'll face in Minecraft Legends.

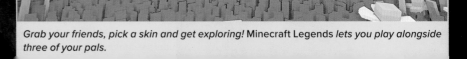

The First of Stone is one of four new "first of" mobs that you can recruit to help in battles.

Grab your friends, pick a skin and get exploring! Minecraft Legends *lets you play alongside three of your pals.*

Trails and Tales is here!

Minecraft evolved yet again with the exciting 1.20 Update – AKA Trails and Tales. Its best addition was seven new default skins. Players don't have to choose between either Steve or Alex. Creators of the game Mojang are keen for *Minecraft* to be a space for everyone. You can see all seven new skins over on the right!

Another cool inclusion is camels! This new animal mob can be ridden by either one or two players. They have an ace dash ability. Also, most hostile mobs can't get you while you're on the back of one. Sniffers are also new. They won the Minecraft Live 2022 Mob Community Vote. They can sniff out seeds to find new plants – but you need to revive one first by finding its eggs underwater!

Other fresh content from Trails and Tales includes hanging signs, chiselled bookshelves, and a beautiful cherry blossom biome. Even if you've been playing *Minecraft* for years, it's like uncovering a whole new game!

Use your banner of courage to rally the troops in the fight against the piglins.

Collect coins in game and spend them on special abilities or items with merchants.

When hostile mobs are attacking, make sure to call on your own army for backup.

Skin and Bear It

Say hello to your seven new Minecraft skins ...

Ari

Efe

Makena

Noor

Kai

Sunny

Zuri

Hogwarts Legacy

Developer Avalanche Software   **Publisher** Warner Bros.   **Platform** NS, PC, PS4, PS5, XBO, XBX/S   **Rating** PEGI 12+

■ **Harry Potter and the amazing action-RPG? Kind of! While this open-world tale is set in the famous school, there's no Harry, Hermione or Ron. Instead, you create your own character, selecting their appearance, house and even how they speak!**

History Lesson

There's a good reason why Harry is missing. This particular adventure through Hogwarts is set in the 1890s.

Your character is starting school in the fifth year. They are able to cast a mysterious type of magic, which impresses some classmates, but has others wild with envy!

Some familiar faces do pop up. Avid book readers will love interacting with Peeves, the Fat Lady and Nearly Headless Nick. Newcomers include your mentor Professor Fig, and baddies Ranrok and Victor Rookwood. You'll grow to despise them just as much as Draco Malfoy or Voldemort!

A Kind of Magic

Magic is the focus of *Hogwarts Legacy*. Character progression is all about brewing potions, mastering spells and harvesting plants. You then unleash your learnings on a host of witches, wizards and goblins! There's lots of player choice to contend with too. The way you act with certain characters affects the ending – meaning every single quest can shape your tale in a unique way!

Ogres are just one of the creatures you can battle.

Calling all witches & wizards – what will you create?

Quests include helping to free a dragon. You can't catch or ride them unfortunately!

Did You Know?

PS5 and PS4 players get an exclusive mission. It's called the Haunted Hogsmeade Shop quest, and unlocks your own store in Hogsmeade when completed!

Fans can visit all their favourite Wizarding World locations including the Forbidden Forest.

Broom Service

Despite the lack of Harry, there are loads of series staples to enjoy. Hogwarts Castle is fully explorable and packed with dungeons, puzzles and secret passageways. There are magical beasts to tame, mount and ride. You can fly around on a broom – and even enter broom races. Sadly, there's no playable version of Quidditch though.

Stand in awe at the foot of the legendary Hogwarts staircase. So much history unravels before you!

Expelliarmus! Work on your spells in the Hogwarts classroom with your very own wand.

Have You Played?

HARRY POTTER AND THE PHILOSOPHER'S STONE

The first Potter game saw you collecting beans, and witch and wizard cards. Despite its simplicity, it sold 8 million copies on PS1!

HARRY POTTER: QUIDDITCH WORLD CUP

A Potter sports game, by the brains behind Madden and FIFA! You could play as the house of your choice, or countries, like Japan, Spain and Bulgaria.

HARRY POTTER AND THE PRISONER OF AZKABAN

Fantastic action-adventure for PS2 and Xbox. Puzzles were fun yet taxing, and you chose to control either Harry, Ron or Hermione.

LEGO HARRY POTTER COLLECTION

Wonderful compendium of LEGO brilliance, packed with memorable levels and unlockable characters. Brick or treat? Both!

Top Tips
Prioritise finding Titan Pokémon, using the Path of Legends storyline. These unlock new ways to move, like dashing, climbing and swimming!

Pokémon
Scarlet & Violet

Developer Game Freak   **Publisher** Nintendo   **Platform** NS   **Rating** PEGI 7+

■ This Pokémon pairing follows a familiar formula. *Scarlet* and *Violet* are identical to play, but each one includes unique creatures for you to collect on your open-world journey. Larvitar, Stonjourner and Great Tusk are exclusive to *Scarlet*. If you get *Violet*, you have the chance to catch Eiscue, Shelgon or Salamence.

Profess Yourself

There are now different professors for the first time in series history! *Violet* players get cool Turo, and *Scarlet* adventurers get sassy Sada. Whichever you pick, Pokémon-hunting takes you across the Iberian-themed world of Paldea.

There are unique stories to enjoy. Victory Road follows the tradition of taking down eight rival gym leaders, and Starfall Street sets you against a gang of rebellious students. Your Pokémon are cleverer than ever, too. You can send one out to automatically battle wild Pokémon and pick up items using the new Let's Go! mechanic. Nice!

Discover new Pokémon, like adorable Sprigatito.

Watch out for Team Star and their Starmobiles!

Raids brought Pokémon like Charizard to the game.

Red and Blue Army

These games mark the ninth generation in the series. It started out as *Pokémon Red* and *Blue* for the handheld Game Boy back in 1996.

Genshin Impact

Developer miHoYo **Publisher** miHoYo **Platform** PC, PS4, PS5 **Rating** PEGI 12+

■ Collectible characters, a mystery to solve and an expanding world to explore. *Genshin Impact* has all these and more! This free-to-play adventure comes highly recommended for anyone into open-world RPGs.

Teyvat Traveler

Seven nations make up the fantasy setting of Teyvat. As the Traveler, you get to spend time exploring them to find your twin. You can choose to be male or female, and pick up three companions as you go. Switching between this awesome foursome in battle is a huge part of the tactical challenge.

There are more than fifty allies to unlock, all with a special attack and elemental affinity. Some are free – like Amber, who's deadly with arrows of flame! But many require you to spend Primogems, a premium currency which can be bought with real-life cash. Thankfully, there's still loads of fun to be had with the free characters.

Missed Impact

Switch gamers spent all of 2022 waiting on their version of this beloved anime RPG, without any joy. The Nintendo Switch version was confirmed in January 2021 – then followed up by two years of silence!

With the update, Genshin introduced new characters like Arataki Itto.

The Primo Geovishap will change into different elements as you fight.

Roblox

Developer Roblox Corporation **Publisher** Roblox Corporation
Platform PC, XBO **Rating** PEGI 7+

■ *Roblox* **is so massive, more than half of America's children have played it at least once! If you've never tried it, it's a huge platform of games. You can enjoy other people's, or spend hours making your own! It's mostly free-to-play, but there are extras that cost a currency called Robux.**

The system launched all the way back in 2006. Back then it was PC-only. Two events later made it go massive! In 2014, it landed on Xbox One. Then the COVID pandemic happened in 2020. With everyone stuck at home, *Roblox* became a great way for kids to stay in touch. Its makers added a *Party Place*, and gamers were able to celebrate birthdays together without leaving the house!

Here to Stay

This year brought rumours that Roblox might shut down. Gamers across social media panicked ... but it was all nonsense! With 217 million active monthly players, there's no chance of it going anywhere. So keep playing, keep creating and remember to stop for a snack once in a while!

Always Changing

One of the most amazing things about Roblox is that it evolves so quickly. What you do this month will almost certainly be entirely different to what you're up to next month!

Take March 2023 as an example. If you loved *Stranger Things*, you could jump into an event and earn special items ahead of Season 5. More junior gamers could collect *My Little Pony* treats by visiting Maritime Bay in *Roblox*. Music artist 24Goldn hosted an in-game concert experience, while George Ezra dropped clothes based on the Gold Rush Kid album. Gucci, Walmart and the NFL also had special items to kit out your avatar!

H&M Looops into Roblox

Major brands are always battling for some *Roblox* love. Fashion store H&M were granted one of this year's main tie-ins. It unleashed an immersive experience called *Loooptopia*. Players could use digital versions of H&M clothes and accessories to outfit their avatar. It's based around a city square. From here, you can drop into Rainbooow Fields, Neon Studiooo and Fabric Fooorest to play mini-games and find new threads! Unused clothes can even be recycled for super-rare new garments. Nice!

Dyna-mite!
Roblox took two years to be turned into a proper product before its release in 2006. During those days it was known as *DynaBlocks*!

Roblox Deathrun *is a mega fun mini-game, where players race through an obstacle course, avoiding deadly traps.*

Host a virtual birthday bash in Party Place, *a new online server for players to throw parties.*

BUILDING WORLDS

Real-time Players

As you read this, there are 1.7 million people playing *Roblox* on either PC, Mac, Xbox or their phone. Cool!

Paris Visit

Actress and influencer Paris Hilton surprised the world with a truly unique *Roblox* experience. It was the first-ever fragrance signing in the metaverse! Players had six days to track down Paris' in-game avatar after a Tunnel of Love scavenger hunt. When they did, they'd receive a bottle of Gold Rush perfume featuring her digital signature. There was even a photo booth so players could capture proof for social media! 515,000 *Roblox* players snapped up the gift before it disappeared forever.

The beauty of the game is you can do anything. Even open your own bakery!

New items can be traded or bought with in-game currency.

Take on the role of either the cops or the robbers in Jailbreak, another top Roblox game. Players choose to either plan a robbery or catch the criminals.

Big Winners

After eight editions, the famous Bloxys were replaced by the Roblox Innovation Awards. Tricky RPG *Deepwoken* won the prize for Best New Experience, while *Bedwars* claimed the People's Choice category. It wasn't just about the awards though. Players also received items for getting involved. Those who visited the Voter's Hub scored the Innovator's Gold Tuxedo. And finding four missing pieces of the iconic Tilt earned a Fragmented Top Hat!

Dave & Busters, *the American arcade venue, launched an official* Roblox *experience.*

A game as adaptable as Roblox *obviously gives players the chance to change or create avatars.*

Must-play Roblox Games

Adopt Me

Roblox's most popular RPG. Adopt cute critters, keep up with their daily needs, decorate their homes and hang out with your friends. Collectible pets keep you coming back!

Blox Fruits

Hunt new weapons and fruits that grant special powers in this ace fighter. Keep your eye out for online codes that grant freebies on a regular basis.

MeepCity

This town and city builder is all about socialising. Up to 200 players can be in your game at once to chat, or join you for *Mario Kart*-style racing.

Sonic Speed Simulator

Yep, that speedster really does get everywhere! Zoom around 3D levels using favourites like Tails and Amy, hunting down Chaos Orbs to upgrade your XP.

All Star Tower Defense

Tower defence games are one of the most popular *Roblox* genres. This one is huge. You use a range of memorable characters to fend off enemy waves.

Doors

A survival horror game where you explore a world through spooky doors. You need to try to reach Door 100 without getting killed. Up to three friends can help!

BedWars

One of the best PvP games around. Leap between islands and destroy opponents' beds – but remember to defend your own. It's sure to make you laugh, yell and play again!

Warrior Cats: Ultimate Edition

First you customise your cat, then decide how to play. Do you want to fight other clans, or gently heal friendly faces? It's up to you!

Gotham Knights

Developer WB Games Montréal
Publisher Warner Bros. Games
Platform PC, PS5, XBX/S **Rating** PEGI 16+

■ Batman is dead. Commissioner Gordon is gone too. There's no time to mourn though. Instead, this co-op open-world game gives you the chance to continue their legacy as one of four upcoming superheroes. Nightwing, Batgirl, Robin and Red Hood all have unique powers and personalities.

Quinn and Bear It

Your chief enemy as you protect the city of Gotham is the mysterious Court of Owls. You also go fist-to-face with more familiar foes. Harley Quinn gets her own nefarious sub-plot, as do Clayface and Mr. Freeze. You can go it alone or team up with a friend to tackle the story together – with them dropping in or out at any time. Handy!

If you've played Batman's *Arkham* games, the punchy battles will trigger happy memories. The city of Gotham is the real star, though. It truly feels like an edgy, crime-ridden metropolis, with intriguing side quests and a cool new base called the Belfry.

Did You Know?

A six-issue comic book series was released alongside *Gotham Knights*. It's called *Gilded City*. Each issue comes with a code for an in-game item!

Among all the comic villains you get to battle in Gotham Knights *is the terrifying Clayface.*

Check Out

Want to play as the Caped Crusader instead? Grab *Batman: Arkham City* on PS4 or Xbox for a captivating battle of wits with the Joker.

Kick and flip your way through enemies. But watch out for Harley Quinn's sledgehammer!

Red Hood mainly fights with his dual pistols.

Robin can teleport to quickly tackle enemies.

The Fab Four

Robin

Batman's long-time sidekick is now a badass on his own. He's the stealthiest of the *Gotham Knights* quartet. Powers include attacking enemies in a cloud of smoke, and using a temporary portal to teleport away!

Nightwing

Dick Grayson grew up in a circus family, so is all about acrobatics. He also wields two Escrima sticks. Be sure to unlock the Flying Trapeze skill as soon as you can. Nightwing can then cruise around Gotham at speed on a super-cool glider!

Batgirl

Kickboxing, capoeira and jiu-jitsu come naturally to this feisty foe. And she's got brains to match her brawn. Batgirl hacks computers and other systems, both to advance the story and take out enemies – like electrocuting them with their own weapons.

Red Hood

Jason Todd is a notorious hothead. But he's at least trying to keep his temper in check. Anyone with dodgy intentions best steer clear when that plan fails. Skills include shooting unlimited rounds for a short time and attaching mines to an enemy, then throwing them.

BUILDING WORLDS

Tool or Nothing

Tools never break – and clothing and furniture don't take up inventory space in *Disney Dreamlight Valley*. Phew!

Step into a world where dreams come true.

What's happened here? Donald Duck sure looks confused.

Disney Dreamlight Valley

Developer Gameloft Montréal **Publisher** Gameloft **Platform** NS, PC, PS4, PS5, XBO, XBX/S **Rating** PEGI 3+

■ Mickey Mouse, Moana and Merlin do *Animal Crossing*? Yes please! Disney's world-builder lets you befriend loads of classic characters. Your customisable character wakes up in Dreamlight Valley, where Night Thorns have robbed villagers of their memories. You need to eliminate the Night Thorns and restore happily ever after!

It's a cool plot, but everything is non-linear. You can do whatever you want, whenever you like! Chatting to villagers and giving them gifts builds up your friendship level. As well as completing quests assigned by your new friends, you can harvest, mine and fish. Food is really important. If you want to get handy with a pickaxe or watering can, you need enough energy first.

Frozen Finds

Star coins are a crucial part of the game. Items you find around Dreamlight Valley can be sold to Goofy. Once you've done that, there are various ways to spend your cash! Kristoff from *Frozen* has a stall for crafting materials, while Scrooge McDuck is the man to visit for clothes and furniture. With cute friends to make and items to purchase, *Dreamlight Valley* just keeps pulling you back in for more Disney fun!

Clothing can be purchased from Scrooge McDuck if you save up your coins.

Things are getting spooky in Dreamlight Valley! Watch out for some Halloween-y twists.

There are plenty of opportunities to customise your items. Who wouldn't want a Stitch backpack?

Animal Magic

One of the quickest ways to earn rewards is by finding animals scattered around the valley – then feeding them their fave foods! There are eight different types to find: squirrels, rabbits, sunbirds, turtles, ravens, foxes, raccoons and crocodiles. Approach one and a button prompt appears. This opens your inventory, and you can choose which food to offer. Squirrels love peanuts, while raccoons adore blueberries. No, you can't feed Donald Duck to a crunchy croc! Those guys do love lobster, though ...

Listen Carefully

More than twenty Disney favourites live in the valley, and the list grows all the time. The best ones to befriend are those with real voices! Sadly, there's no Dwayne Johnson voice for Maui, and Anna and Elsa are both played by new voice actors. However, Tim Allen sounds great as Buzz Lightyear. Auli'i Cravalho is back as Moana, and Pat Carroll plays Ursula from *The Little Mermaid*. This is her final voice role, as Pat sadly passed away shortly before the game's release.

There are dozens of characters to assign you quests once you enter their realms.

You finally get the chance to speak your mind to baddies like Scar.

Back to Reality

Check Out Our Guide to Virtual Gaming

■ Virtual reality gaming is huge and, if you can afford it, there are tons of reasons to give it a go. Put on a headset to enter new worlds and experience games in a completely different way to using a controller. In *Ghostbusters: Rise of the Ghost Lord,* you and three friends can wear your own proton packs. *Hitman 3* grants huge freedom in how you take out enemies while *Marvel's Iron Man VR* turns you into Tony Stark!

Sony Shakes Things Up

VR had a quiet year, but Sony's PS VR2 was the big headline-grabber. It aims to take VR to the next level using PS5, like using vents to keep gamers cool while they play. A brand new *Horizon* game featured in the launch line-up, and *Star Wars: Tales from the Galaxy's Edge* and *Resident Evil Village* switched from other formats. The set-up definitely feels future-proof.

Top Headsets

HTC Vive Cosmos

Developer: HTC

A solid headset that works well with most modern PCs and laptops. It has six camera sensors and can even fit over your glasses! Intriguing experiences include *Creed: Rise to Glory,* a virtual boxing game and *Skyrim VR*, which gives you total freedom in the huge world of Tamriel.

Meta Quest 2

Developer: Meta Technologies

No VR headset is cheap, but the Meta Quest 2 is one of the more affordable. The 128GB version usually comes packaged with *Beat Saber* and can store up to forty additional games. Its clever touch-sensitive controllers feel like an extension of your own limbs too!

PS VR2

Developer: Sony

The newest headset on the list. This option is exclusively compatible with PS5. Like that machine's DualSense, the PS VR2's controllers have haptic feedback and adaptive triggers, meaning you can feel gaming experiences as well as see them. Other features include eye tracking and 3D audio.

Labo VR

Developer: Nintendo

VR for younger gamers with Nintendo Switch. It's a fun take on a very interactive VR headset. Players build cardboard creations then bring them to life in assorted games. It sold out long ago though, so you'll need to do some hunting online to track one down!

Best VR Games

Horizon Call of The Mountain

A spin-off to PlayStation's huge hit series. You play as ex-prisoner Ryas, who's seeking redemption, and Aloy makes an appearance! There's also a River Ride mode that introduces VR basics.

Jurassic World: Aftermath

Escape dinosaurs and solve puzzles in this survival adventure. As you'd imagine, it can get a little tense (and is rated 12 because of this), but anyone who loves the movies will enjoy running from raptors!

Beat Saber

A speedy block-matching game that has you working up a sweat. You swipe and slash coloured blocks in time to addictive beats. The song list has expanded and now features huge hits from Fall Out Boy, The Weeknd and Lizzo.

Spooks Like Fun!

The SCREAM Of The Crop For Halloween Frights

By Louise Blain

■ Looking for games that go bump in the night? Well, be scareful what you wish for when you enter Castle MacFrights in *Luigi's Mansion 3*. Mario's twin isn't very brave, but at least he's got the Poltergust G-00 to suck up all of the ghosts in his path. And don't worry if you feel as scared as Luigi. You can always get a friend to play with you as the gloopy green Gooigi in local co-op mode. Because sharing – or should it be scaring? – is caring!

The main characters in *Costume Quest 2* are super excited for the spooky joys of Halloween, but a nefarious dentist is trying to cancel it all. You could say he's the root canal of all evil. In a terrifyingly toothy situation, Wren, Reynold and their friends find themselves in a Halloween-free reality where brushing your pearly whites is the most important part of the day. Thankfully, this RPG is all about bringing back the sacred pumpkin-packed holiday by trying on new costumes, trick or treating and monster battling.

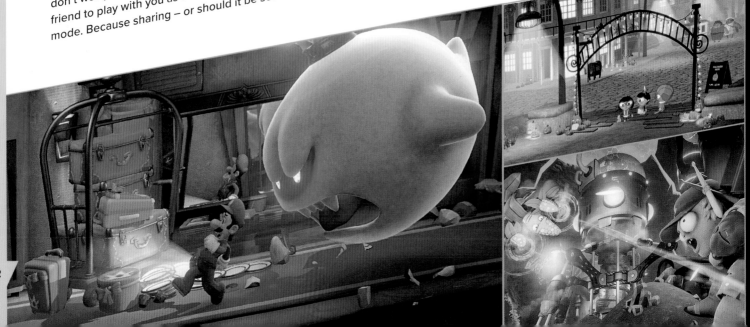

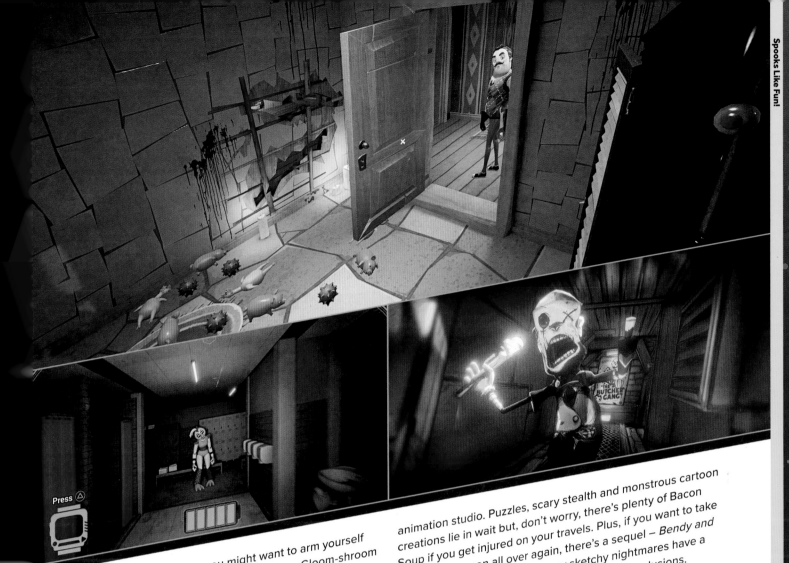

Press △

Speaking of monster battling, you might want to arm yourself with a Peashooter, a Cabbage-pult and maybe a Gloom-shroom or two, just to be safe. *Plants Vs. Zombies* hits you with shuffling graveyard groaners and you must protect your lawn from them. The original is still one of the very best tower defence games out there. Every level means new challenges as different kinds of zombies chow down on your plant-based weaponry, and even clamber into your pool. Just be ready for the theme song to get stuck in your head as you watch the undead lose theirs!

So far, these games have been more spooky than truly scary, so let's crank up the fear-o-meter a notch. *Hello Neighbor 2* follows the sneaky action of the first game by opening up the entire town. Here, you'll need to break into the houses of even more potentially villainous characters without being caught. And stealth and safety warning: remember not to hold your breath in real life the whole time. It makes it much harder to run away from the moustachioed Mr Peterson while shouting "goodbye, neighbour!".

Tick That was the sound of the fear-o-meter clicking even higher with *Five Nights At Freddy's: Security Breach*. Once again, you're stuck back inside one of Freddy Fazbear's famous pizza restaurants overnight. The only problem is the terrifying animatronics, who sadly don't just want to play hide-and-seek. Using security cameras is vital to keep a beady eye out and stay alive until dawn. Prepare for some jump scares and you'll be fine. Promise.

Still feeling brave? Good, because *Bendy and the Ink Machine* is a cartoon-style survival horror game set in a creaky old animation studio. Puzzles, scary stealth and monstrous cartoon creations lie in wait but, don't worry, there's plenty of Bacon Soup if you get injured on your travels. Plus, if you want to take on the Ink Demon all over again, there's a sequel – *Bendy and the Dark Revival*. Will these scary sketchy nightmares have a happy ending? You can, errr, draw your own conclusions.

And finally, it turns out that running away to an entirely different solar system isn't safe either. *Subnautica: Below Zero* is set on a freezing ocean planet and takes us deep below the waves. The catchily named Planet 4546B from the original Subnautica has even more horrors than we first thought. There's nothing quite like popping down to the ocean floor for some essential crafting bits and realising you aren't alone. These toothy terrors definitely think you're food and not friends. Mind the Squidsharks ...

SEARCHING...

Soulslike

Your Guide to the Gaming Genre

■ The Soulslike genre is relatively new. FromSoftware launched *Demon's Souls* as a Japanese PS3 exclusive in 2009. Its dark fantasy setting, brutal timing-based combat and severe difficulty made it a cult hit. Western gamers were so desperate to try it out that they had it imported. Luckily, it was localised for the USA later that year, and for Europe in summer 2010.

Fear We Go

That game's popularity inspired a sequel, *Dark Souls*, in 2011, and a new genre was born! The combat mechanics in the games mean players need strategy and tactics when fighting enemies. Vast worlds welcome exploration, and stories that come to life in your imagination. Failure, strangely, is welcomed. Your character dies a lot, which only makes completing an adventure sweeter.

Multiplayer fleshes out the genre in clever ways. Some games let you see what fellow players are up to, or leave messages to help (or confuse!) them during quests.

Did You Know?

Demon's Souls was widely dismissed after its Tokyo Game Show reveal in 2008. Most felt it was too difficult to ever catch on!

Top 5 Soulslike Games to Play Right Now

Elden Ring

FromSoftware's latest smash shares *Dark Souls* elements, like having one chance to retrieve souls and runes after you die. But the studio's earlier games were pretty linear. *Elden Ring*'s massive open-world takes the genre to new territory – in every sense!

Star Wars Jedi: Fallen Order

Looking for a gentle way into Soulslikes? This is your game. It's based around blocking and parrying, but won't hurt your brain with its difficulty. New hero Cal uses his lightsaber and force powers to down enemies, with XP upgrading his combat skills.

Dark Souls

2011's spiritual sequel to the original game that inspired a whole new genre. It's possibly even more hair-tearingly tough, and includes some fresh twists! Combat takes on a whole new level with improved armour and weapons systems.

Stranger of Paradise: Final Fantasy Origin

An action-packed retelling of the original NES RPG. It's intended as a grown-up take on the usually family-friendly series. You need to hunt down a bad guy called Chaos while collecting loot, and indulging in lots of screen-filling combat.

Salt and Sanctuary

A hand-drawn, 2D genre game that you can play on Xbox One, PS4 and Nintendo Switch. You start out on a brilliant boat level and the hardcore action never stops coming. There are 600 items to use, along with a branching skill tree that makes your character feel unique to your game.

CONSOLE HEAD TO HEAD

Mega Drive vs Super Nintendo

The first consoles of the 1990s are iconic now – and many retro addicts own both! Back then, their rivalry was as heated as Nicki Minaj vs Cardi B, or Loki vs Thor! Here's everything you need to know about the two machines from the era that also gave us *Jurassic Park*, *Pokémon* and *Friends* ...

Mega Drive

The Sega Mega Drive was beloved around the world for its sleek look, responsive three-button controller and incredible games. Sonic swiftly became its mascot, and the groundbreaking exclusives that came out were side-scrolling *Golden Axe* and the seafaring *Ecco the Dolphin*. Sports sims, like *Madden* and *FIFA* were also considered strongest on the Sega machine. The end result was a pop culture phenomenon.

Drive On
- The Mega Drive was known as the Genesis in America.
- Seventeen of its games were playable online, but only in Japan.
- Its final ever official game, *Show do Milhão Volume 2*, emerged in Brazil in 2002.

The entire ocean is yours to explore in Ecco.

The classic side-scroller game, Golden Axe.

Memorable Games

SONIC THE HEDGEHOG 2
An astonishing platformer that made an entire generation of kids happy in 1992. The split-screen mode, that pits Sonic against Tails, is still addictive now!

STREETS OF RAGE 2
Still considered the best beat-'em-up ever, three decades after release. Levels were packed with colour, action and OTT bosses. The electronic soundtrack remains a hit.

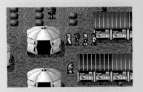

PHANTASY STAR IV
SNES was known for having the best RPGs, but Mega Drive won with this one! The combat system introduced combo attacks instead of solo ones, and characters looked and talked like real people.

By The Numbers

Original release date:
October 1988
UK release date:
September 1990
Publisher: Sega
Worldwide sales:
30.75 million
Number of games: 900+
Bestselling game:
Sonic the Hedgehog
(14.4 million)

By The Numbers

Original release date:
November 1990
UK release date:
April 1992
Publisher: Nintendo
Worldwide sales:
49.1 million
Number of games: 1757
Bestselling game:
Super Mario World
(20.6 million)

Super Facts

◉ The SNES went by different names. It was called Super Famicom in Japan and Super Comboy in Korea.

◉ Many original consoles have turned yellow, as the plastic is sensitive to UV light!

◉ It launched in Japan with just three games: *F-Zero*, *Pilotwings* and *Super Mario World*.

◉ An abandoned CD-Rom add-on became Sony's PlayStation.

Super Nintendo

Nintendo's 16-Bit console was released later than the Mega Drive, but it eventually outsold it. Nintendo was officially the winner of the console war! Along with essential *Mario* games, the SNES gave fans *Final Fantasy VI*, *Super Metroid* and the definitive version of *Street Fighter II*.

POW! Ryu hits his opponent in Street Fighter II.

Memorable Games

THE LEGEND OF ZELDA: A LINK TO THE PAST
A brilliantly realised world, with a loveable cast and a moreish mix of puzzles and combat, plus a smart item system combined for the best action-adventure that had ever been played.

SUPER MARIO KART
Mario's first crossover into the world of racing. Series staples like power sliding and red shells that make you want to throw the controller all started right here!

SUPER MARIO WORLD
Seventy-two levels of platforming wonder, spread across nine unforgettable worlds, like Chocolate Island. This game also gave us Yoshi and a lifetime of very happy memories.

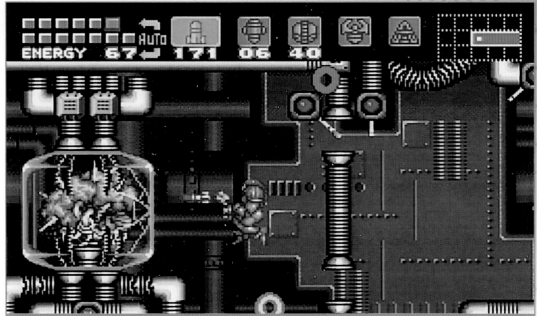

Join 2D Samus as she explores levels and unlocks new areas of the map in one of the original Metroid *games.*

STATE OF PLAY

Heroes of the Year

Gaming's Biggest Superstars

Sonic

Game Sonic Frontiers
First Appearance Sonic the Hedgehog
Occupation Freedom fighter
Height 100 cm **Age** 15 **Hair Colour** Blue
Eye Colour Green **Home** Christmas Island
Voiced by Roger Craig Smith

Sega's sensational speedster shows no signs of slowing down. In his home nation of Japan, open-world adventure game *Sonic Frontiers* was the fastest-selling in the series since *Sonic Adventure 2* way back in 2001! The movie spin-off *Sonic the Hedgehog 2*, with Jim Carrey as Dr. Robotnik, was a huge smash too.

Marvin the Martian

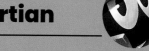

Game MultiVersus
First Appearance Haredevil Hare (cartoon)
Occupation Ruler of Mars **Height** 69 cm (approx)
Age 75 **Hair Colour** N/A **Eye Colour** Black
Home Outer Space **Voiced by** Eric Bauza

MultiVersus has a wild and wonderful cast, from Batman to Scooby Doo to Arya Stark. In season two, they were joined by a cartoon favourite from 1948! *Looney Tunes* character Marvin has popped up in *South Park*, *The Simpsons* and *Animaniacs*, and is now a gaming favourite, too.

Bayonetta

Game Bayonetta 3
First Appearance Bayonetta
Occupation Nun
Height Variable **Age** 600+
Hair Colour Black **Eye Colour** Grey
Home Vigrid **Voiced by** Jennifer Hale

This not-so-wicked witch has hair to die for. Literally! Bayonetta can use it to take down enemies, and also summon demons. An even cooler power is Bat Within. It turns her into a group of bats, stopping her from taking damage! Don't like bats? Turn her into a crow or panther instead.

Ryu

Game Street Fighter 6
First Appearance Street Fighter
Occupation Martial artist
Height 175 cm
Age 34
Hair Colour Black
Eye Colour Brown
Home Suzaku Castle
Voiced by Kyle Hebert

Ryu is the longest-running fight-game character, having appeared in *Street Fighter's* 1987 debut and every game since. He was based on a real-life karate master called Mas Oyama. New faces for *Street Fighter 6* include graffiti artist Kimberly, break dancer Jamie and muscular Marisa.

Lost in Translation

Ryu's most famous quote is, "You must defeat Sheng Long to stand a chance." Some *Street Fighter II* players figured this referred to a secret character. In fact, it was a translation mistake! He should have said, "If you cannot overcome the Shoryuken, you cannot win."

The Legend of Zelda: Tears of the Kingdom

Developer Nintendo **Publisher** Nintendo **Platform** NS
Rating PEGI 12+

■ It's heeeeeeere! The most anticipated Switch game in forever proved worthy of every last drop of hype. In *Tears of the Kingdom*, Link soars across and above Hyrule, on a mission to take down the forces threatening his world.

Link to the Skies

While *Breath of the Wild* mostly kept Link on the ground, this sequel is all about going up, up and away. Exploring the skies is a key element in taking down Bokoblins and seeking out returning big boss Ganon. Link can even fly a hot air balloon, giving players some of the most spectacular views the series has ever seen.

This isn't the first time Link has been able to soar over Hyrule. It's been a while though! 2011 favourite *The Legend of Zelda: Skyward Sword* gave you the chance to float over Skyloft and its surrounding airborne islands. That game is still considered an all-time classic – and *Tears of the Kingdom* is arguably even better. Not sure? Play it and decide for yourself!

One of the mighty new enemies is a Flux Construct, a collection of giant cubes held together by magic. They can take many forms.

Stop and Go

As well as his hot air balloon, Link can travel by makeshift car and nifty hovercraft. But don't spend all your time hurtling around the game world: it's always worth stopping to take in the scenery around you. It's a game so pretty that even the imposing Death Mountain looks gorgeous, in its own way. *Tears of the Kingdom* took six years to develop. Play it and you'll see that every single second was worth it!

Special Edition

Like the game itself, the *Tears of the Kingdom Collector's Edition* is a work of wonder. You get a steel poster, breathtaking artbook and pin set. Oh, and the game itself, obvs!

The hero of Hyrule is back! Link's look has been updated since the Breath of the Wild version and he's got plenty of new clothing options.

Check Out

Link and Zelda go to war with Ganon yet again in *Breath of the Wild* spin-off *Hyrule Warriors: Age of Calamity*. Pick it up for loads of hack-and-slash chaos!

Enemies that players know and love to fight are back, like the one-eyed Hinox.

The Zonai were an ancient magic-wielding race, whose mysterious ruins were in Breath of the Wild.

Too Much Breath

Tears of the Kingdom exists because Nintendo began brainstorming DLC ideas for *Breath of the Wild*. The team quickly realised they had too many! When those changes became bigger and bigger, the studio decided DLC wasn't enough and that they were really developing a sequel.

Loved climbing, gliding and riding in Breath of the Wild? *Get ready for even more locations to explore.*

Minecart travel from the previous game has evolved!

Try out new abilities, like Fuse, Recall and Ultrahand.

THE HISTORY OF THE LEGEND OF ZELDA

Changing Faces

Majora's Mask is probably the weirdest *Zelda* game ever – there was a creepy alien abduction side quest, and Zelda only appeared in a brief flashback!

Link to the Past, Present and Future

Without *Lord of the Rings* and *Peter Pan*, there would be no *Zelda*. Series mastermind Shigeru Miyamoto based the 1986 adventure on a mix of his childhood memories, and the legendary J. R. R. Tolkien book series. His designer Takashi Tezuka then took inspiration from the eternally-young Disney character, Peter Pan, to craft the main character, Link, and an iconic franchise was born.

Royal Flush

There have been dozens of main *The Legend of Zelda* games. They're famous for breathtaking scenery, vast landscapes, unforgettable characters and hack-slash action. The usual storyline follows pointy-eared Link and magical princess Zelda as they save the magical land of Hyrule from warlord Ganon.

The Legend of Zelda series usually falls into the RPG game genre. But creator Miyamoto doesn't agree with this! In *The Super Famicom* magazine, he describes *Zelda* as a "real-time adventure game". Through its history, the series has created new features that changed the world of gaming: it was the first ever video game that let you save your progress!

Play by the Hyrules

❷ In America, anyone who purchased the first *Zelda* became members of the Fun Club. They received regular newsletters in the post to say thanks!

❷ Although it was released in 2011, *Skyward Sword* is set earlier than any of the other games in *The Legend of Zelda* series.

Four Unforgettable Zeldas

The Legend of Zelda

As the first game in the series, it must be credited here! Console owners had never before enjoyed such a liberating mix of combat and exploration. Its memorable "secret found" jingle has made it into almost every game since.

The Legend of Zelda: A Link to the Past

Widely known as the greatest Super Nintendo game ever! It perfected the top-down viewpoint and introduced Dark and Light parallel worlds. Link also felt properly free to control. Players could move the hero diagonally, run using Pegasus Boots, and swipe his sword sideways!

The Legend of Zelda: Ocarina of Time

Few dreamed *Zelda* could get better than *A Link to the Past*, but N64 technology meant exactly that. In 1998, Nintendo created an ingenious targeting system and fresh third-person perspective. And, most jaw-dropping of all, a 3D world for Link to explore!

The Legend of Zelda: Breath of the Wild

Hyrule is even more explorable than ever. The open-world adventure was released in 2017 and is still the standard for Nintendo Switch games. It's a high benchmark to meet! Every new feature sings, from breakable weapons to item crafting to slo-mo attacks to ... ah, it's all incredible. You have to play it!

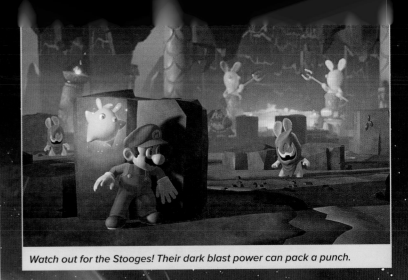

Watch out for the Stooges! Their dark blast power can pack a punch.

Mario + Rabbids
Sparks of Hope

Developer Ubisoft Milan / Paris **Publisher** Ubisoft
Platform NS **Rating** PEGI 7+

■ **Mamma mia! Mario has moved on from his classic karting and platforming in this new game.** *Mario + Rabbids Sparks of Hope* **is tactical and turn-based, featuring the unexpected sight of our plumber pal wielding a gun! You build a team of three and take down the space-menace Cursa together. There are cute Rabbids to pair up with, or traditional buddies like Luigi and Rosalina.**

It plays much more like *XCOM* or *Shin Megami Tensei* than a standard *Mario* game. But is still a great game for all ages. Level up your characters by collecting Skill Prisms, and then grab coins to spend on healing items and new weapon skins.

Fight Club

Sparks of Hope is the sequel to 2017's *Kingdom Battle*. The biggest difference is combat. In the last game, everything was grid-based. Now you can move your trio around freely, working out the best way to take down an enemy. This small tactical change, gives players the chance to explore *Sparks of Hope*'s colourful worlds, and keeps the adventure fresh.

DLC

Sparks of Hope released three DLC packs. One gives players the chance to play as the Rabbids' original rival, Rayman. Also included is a fresh adventure called The Tower of Doooom.

Skill Prisms can be used to level up characters.

Pose for a pic with your new Rabbids pals.

Mario's dual slingers are his favourite weapons.

Explore five different planets, like Palette Prime.

Unleash the Toxiquake

The Sparks are creatures that help out on your journey. Each has a unique power to be used in battle. You can equip one for each hero to start, and unlock another slot later on. Some are sensible, like Pulser, who can revive all allies within range. Others are pure fun. The favourite is Toxiquake. It's unlocked when you finish Beacon Beach, and blasts three shockwaves of ooze!

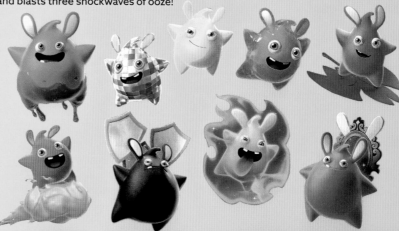

When it rains in Sparks of Hope, *it pours lava!*

Recognise the Voice?

Charles Martinet returns in the roles of Mario and Luigi. He's voiced both characters, plus Wario and Waluigi, since 1992!

Intergalactic, Planetary

Sparks of Hope has five different planets to explore. Jupiter, Mars ... hang on, nope, this isn't a science book! They're actually called Beacon Beach, Pristine Peaks, Palette Prime, Terra Flora and Barrendale Mesa. The scenery is different in each. Beacon Beach is a once-sunny isle overwhelmed with Cursa's moody Darkness. Terra Flora is more welcoming, with blue skies, green grass ... and pink trees.

THE HISTORY OF MARIO

King Kong in Dungarees

Mario's first appearance wasn't in a *Mario* game! He played the main character in 1981 platformer *Donkey Kong*. The protagonist was supposed to be Popeye, but designer Shigeru Miyamoto couldn't get the rights to the spinach-munching sailor. So he created the 'stached plumber instead.

His original name was Mr Video! In 1985, Luigi came together with his big bro for groundbreaking NES platformer *Mario Bros*. The pair leapt through levels on a mission to rescue Princess Peach from King Koopa, who'd later be renamed Bowser. An iconic duo was born.

Different Kind of Jumper

Mario is the bestselling video game franchise ever, ahead of *Tetris* and *Pokémon*. The *Super Mario* games are most popular, followed by *Mario Kart* and *Mario Party*. It's seen crazy spin-offs, too. In *Mario is Missing*, Luigi searches Beijing and San Francisco for his lost brother. Then there's possibly the most bizarre game in the series: *Mario Family*, where you colour in new jumpers for Mario and pals!

Hoopsy Daisy

A tie-in with EA saw *Mario* characters added to *NBA Street V3*. You could take on LeBron James and Shaquille O'Neal using Luigi and Princess Peach!

Here We Go!

❷ Yoshi was named the most popular *Mario* character in a recent poll. Mario was second. Toad finished third, Peach fourth and Bowser fifth. Poor Luigi!

❸ The main man was named after an estate agent called Mario Segale, who rented Nintendo their American HQ!

❸ In the arcade game *Donkey Kong Jr*, Mario was the baddie! He'd captured Donkey Kong and you had to use DK's son to rescue daddy.

Four Mega Marios

Super Mario World

Surely the best 2D platformer ever. Anyone who played back in 1992 still raves about levels like Donut Plains and Chocolate Island. Discovering Yoshi for the first time is pure joy, as is finding secret exits to open up new parts of the map.

Super Mario Galaxy

The Wii game that unleashed Mario across the universe. You visited various planets and worlds to collect 120 stars and save us all from Bowser (obvs!). Cunningly, you could use the motion controls to grab poles, catch objects and ice skate!

Super Mario Party

The Switch game every family should own. It's actually the eleventh game in the series, but if you buy it, then you don't need any of the others. Fighting for stars on the main game board will bring laughter and tears, while mini-games like Rumble Fishing never get old.

Mario Kart 8 Deluxe

The biggest *Mario Kart* ever. It's got five speed classes, forty-eight courses and up to twelve players online! But even in the single-player mode, this is exceptional. Experienced players will get all their favourite power-ups and characters, and newcomers will learn fast thanks to Smart Steering.

Top Tips
Switch characters as often as possible, as they level up individually. There are ten tiers in total, each with an extra hit point, life or special move.

Teenage Mutant Ninja Turtles: Shredder's Revenge

Developer Tribute Games **Publisher** Dotemu **Platform** NS, PC, PS4, PS5, XBO **Rating** PEGI 12+

■ *Teenage Mutant Ninja Turtles: Turtles in Time* is one of the greatest beat-'em-ups ever made. But it came out in 1991, so newer gamers have never played it. To solve that problem, the publisher of *Streets of Rage 4* unleashed *Shredder's Revenge*!

Raph vs Rocksteady

The name may be different, but it's brilliant for all the same reasons as *Turtles in Time*. Leonardo, Donatello, Michelangelo and Raphael feel fast yet powerful in crunchy combat.

Opponents include Shredder, Bebop and Rocksteady, all looking how they did in the early 1990s. The colourful levels stay true to the series' history, from stinky sewers to Krang's futuristic Dimension X.

There's both an arcade and story mode, and unlockables tempt you into multiple playthroughs. You don't have to control a turtle, either. Casey Jones, Splinter and the original April O'Neil are all playable, too!

The final boss Shredder will transform into Super Shredder.

Play as April O'Neil and use cameras as weapons!

Totally tubular! The turtles get to cruise the skies.

Split Personalities

❷ All four original voice actors from the 1987 TV show have come back to take on roles, and not just as goodies. Cam Clarke plays both Leonardo and Rocksteady!

Did You Know?

Kirby is usually pink – but in 2004's *Kirby & The Amazing Mirror*, you could use spray paint to make him grape, chocolate or chalk coloured. Fab!

Kirby's Return to Dream Land Deluxe

Developer Nintendo **Publisher** HAL Laboratory **Platform** NS
Rating PEGI 7+

■ There have been over thirty years of Kirby! Nintendo's famously hungry blob was first released on the original Game Boy in 1992. To wish him a happy birthday, the mega-publisher reinvented the 2011 Wii platformer for Switch. Kirby and pals go questing together after a suspicious spaceship crash-lands on Planet Popstar.

On the spacecraft is an alien called Magolor, and you need to help him get home. This isn't as simple as catching the next space-bus! Five key parts of his ship are scattered across the planet. After finding these, there are further twists to come. Oh, and a four-headed dragon!

Bandana Breakfast

Gamers who played the original will love the fresh new features! Original buddies King Dedede, Meta Knight and Bandana Waddle Dee can be controlled in a four-way co-op – or you can unleash four Kirbys! There are new mini-games, too. Coolest of all, Kirby can earn a fresh mech suit ability that arms him with rockets and lasers!

One of the bosses, Whispy Woods, requires a team to take down.

Watch out for Waddle Dee's classic weapon, a spear!

059

Finished the game? Try playing again as Knuckles!

Soldiers are one of the enemies in the game.

Sonic Frontiers

Developer Sonic Team **Publisher** Sega
Platform NS, PC, PS4, PS5, XBO, XBX/S **Rating** PEGI 7+

■ **Four words: Sonic. Goes. Open. World. What's that? You want more? Okay then. The spiky speedster's first sandbox adventure mixes old-school platforming, ring-collecting and rail-grinding with a ton of exciting new stuff.**

Happy Trails

The best addition is an ability called the Cyloop. It gives Sonic an energy trail as he speeds about, drawing shapes behind him. Complete a circle around a small enemy and it flips them into the air, opening it up to attacks. Or deploy it in empty areas to reveal hidden rings, or memory tokens that help free Sonic's pals.

As ever, the story finds Sega's blue blur hunting chaos emeralds and freeing furry friends. Amy, Tails and Knuckles must all be rescued as you speed and spin across Starfall Islands. Dr. Eggman and his artificial intelligence Sage also need to be eliminated forever. Or at least until the next *Sonic* game!

Isle of Hogs

The wonderful Starfall Islands were inspired by *The Legend of Zelda: Breath of the Wild*. There are five in total. Starter location Kronos Island is packed with lush forests and ancient ruins, and Chaos Island feels genuinely menacing. It's set in the sky, under grey clouds and the shadow of a volcano. The other islands are called Ares, Rhea and Ouranos. All of them are named after legends of Greek mythology.

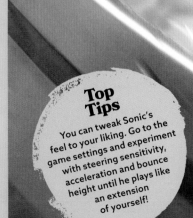

Top Tips
You can tweak Sonic's feel to your liking. Go to the game settings and experiment with steering sensitivity, acceleration and bounce height until he plays like an extension of yourself!

Cyber Intelligence

As if a collection of islands wasn't enough to explore, Sonic can head into Cyber Space! Defeat a big boss and you receive a gear. Place this in one of the portals found around the map and you jump into this mysterious dimension. There are thirty Cyber Space levels, with tasks that unlock the seven chaos emeralds. The tasks include time attacks, collecting five red rings and classic side-scrolling fun!

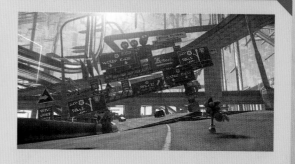

Race across the open worlds as the big blue blur!

Did You Know?
US writer Ian Flynn wrote the script for Frontiers after his Sonic the Hedgehog comics had a huge amount of positive feedback.

One of the Badniks that you'll face are the feisty Moto Bugs.

Enjoy the views from up high and collect as many rings as you can.

Floating platforms are a great place to find extra rings and some even better drops.

A Fishy Tail

Find purple coins scattered around the map and Sonic can go fishing! First you choose a spot to cast your line to, then hit the button when a fish bites to trigger a mini-game where you can reel it in. As well as earning fish tokens with a big catch, you can occasionally snag bigger prizes, such as Hermit Koco's Scroll, which unlocks fast travel!

THE HISTORY OF SONIC

Over Thirty Years of Sonic the Hedgehog

Nintendo had Mario, Namco had Pac-Man and Sega was on the hunt for its own mascot! The bright blue blur first landed on the Mega Drive console back in 1991. After years of searching for a Mario rival, Sega found their icon!

Chaos Unleashed

In the next two years, Sega released two more unmissable platformers, *Sonic 2* and *Sonic 3*. He even made friends with his former foe in later years, teaming up for *Mario & Sonic at the Olympic Games* in 2007! After these hits, Sonic's star faded as Sega moved away from console development. In one memorable misstep, 2008's *Sonic Unleashed* took the series to a darker place. Sonic would turn into a were-hog at night!

Thankfully, Sonic found a cure for that curse, in the form of newer, better games. If you want to give some of Sega's speedster's best games a go, the greatest hits collection *Sonic Origins*, allows new players the chance to enjoy the classic platformers on Playstation, Xbox, Switch and PC. So retro!

Super Sonic
➊ Sonic was the first ever gaming series promoted by McDonald's. It's sold fifty million Happy Meals over the years!

➋ Many believe Dr. Robotnik's name was changed in 1999, but he's always been known as Eggman in the series' homeland of Japan.

Did You Know?
Sega's mascot search came down to either Sonic or a red armadillo known as Mighty. He was added to the series in the *SegaSonic the Hedgehog* arcade game!

Four Super Sonics

Sonic the Hedgehog

In 1991, *Sonic the Hedgehog* was a game-changer! Stages were a dream to jump and spin through, collecting rings and bopping enemies. Mega fans know the 'level select' cheat code off by heart to this day. Up, down, left, right, A, B, C, start!

Sonic the Hedgehog 3

It's a tight call between this and *Sonic 2* for the series' best platformer. Everything great about the original was expanded even more: bigger stages, sneakier secrets, devilish bosses. It was so massive that some of it had to be split off into an entirely different game: *Sonic & Knuckles*.

Sonic Colours

Sonic's 3D adventures struggled to live up to his success in 2D. But this game was the exception. Released on DS and Wii, it took the series intergalactic, with Sonic destroying power sources on five power-up-packed planets. Helping him were Wisps, which gave him the ability to shoot lasers!

Sonic Mania

Thirteen levels of side-scrolling wonder, released in 2017 but giving players a throw back to the classics. Memorable stages like Green Hill Zone were cunningly remixed, and Tails and Knuckles were both playable. Time Attack mode brings a cool online element, with global leaderboards.

Star Wars Jedi: Survivor

Developer Respawn Entertainment **Publisher** EA
Platform PC, PS5, XBX/S **Rating** PEGI 12+

■ The sequel to *Star Wars Jedi: Fallen Order* is here – and this time, it's for next-gen consoles only. As a result, it's the most gorgeous Star Wars game you've ever played. And the fastest-loading too, meaning you'll be throwing around your lightsaber just seconds after turning on your machine!

Cal About You

You play as Cal Kestis. Once more, the Fallen Order frontman is back to battle the Galactic Empire. They're determined to wipe out the last few survivors of Order 66, which proclaims all Jedi to be traitors. Cal must survive using his trusty blade – and a couple of new abilities too.

The best of these abilities is inspired by Kylo Ren in *The Force Awakens*. It's a Force stasis move that allows you to freeze enemies and blaster bolts in mid-air! But it's a game about exploring as well as fighting, with loads of new planets to uncover. Familiar universe, fresh locations, feisty foes – what's not to love?!

Hear the infamous hum of the lightsabers as you go head-to-head with Jedi warriors.

Survivor's Foundations

Calling this an action-adventure is just the beginning. In fact, *Star Wars Jedi: Survivor* plays like the best bits of loads of other games – but with a Star Wars theme! The Respawn team admits combat was inspired by *Dark Souls* and *The Legend of Zelda: Wind Waker*. However, its progression mechanics feel very Metroidvania-like. And it has *Uncharted*-style cinematic scenes. Basically, there's something for fans of all genres.

Bode actor Noshir Dalal appears in TV series Star Wars: The Bad Batch.

Who is Cal Kestis?

Main man Cal is a latecomer to the Star Wars universe. That hasn't stopped him settling right in! A 2020 fan poll named him the 50th most popular character of all time. He was a Padawan during the Clone Wars, whose master was killed in the wake of Order 66. After this, he went into hiding on the planet Bracca. But an Imperial probe tracked him down, triggering the events of *Star Wars Jedi: Fallen Order*. If you've not played that game, be sure to do so before *Star Wars Jedi: Survivor*!

Cere Junda, a Jedi from the Stinger Mantis crew.

The Gen'Dai are a force to be reckoned with.

Check Out

Guardians of the Galaxy is the best sci-fi blaster of recent times. It's got loads of skills to unlock and laughs to enjoy as Star-Lord, Rocket and pals!

Everything You Need to Know About eSports

A look at the biggest games, teams, and players – and how you can get involved!

■ How to Get into eSports

The world of eSports is more competitive than ever. This means that anyone can get involved! Follow these seven steps to build your own legacy of online awesomeness ...

1. Pick a game you love and want to be amazing at, like *Fortnite* or *Overwatch*.

2. Practice makes perfect. Play as often as you can, but don't forget your schoolwork or job!

3. Brush up on secret tactics and specific techniques, using training modes or online guides.

4. Watch competitions on Twitch and YouTube. You'll pick up good habits from the pros.

5. Learn how to lose. Pro teams don't go for players who throw their controllers around!

6. Attend live events if there are any nearby, and study how teammates communicate.

7. Find a team at school or uni that competes in tournaments – or create your own with your friends!

COMMONWEALTH ESPORTS CHAMPIONSHIPS 2022 | ROCKET LEAGUE WOMEN | GRAND FINAL

ENGLAND 0 3:56 0 SCOTLAND

Teyvat Tournament

Genshin Impact isn't the most obvious eSport. That didn't stop UK universities launching their own tournament! It was called the Genshin Impact University Invitational, and saw viewers awarded Primogems (the in-game currency) for choosing their favourite teams.

eSports for Farmers

Hands up if you knew there was an official Farming Simulator League? Teams of three compete against the clock. They have to harvest crops, get them into bales and then transport them to a specific point on the map. Amazingly, loads of real-life farming brands like Trelleborg and Krone enter employees into tournaments!

eSports timeline

1972: The Intergalactic Spacewar Olympics in California becomes the first ever eSport event.

1980: Atari hosts the National Space Invaders Championships, with 10,000 competitors!

1990: A $10,000 prize goes on offer in the new Nintendo World Championships.

1997: The Cyberathlete Professional League is formed, focused on shooters like *Quake*.

1998: Sci-fi strategy game *StarCraft* strikes it big in South Korea, as players battle online.

2002: Pro eSports organiser LMG is formed, and gaming goes from hobby to career!

2005: The CPL World Tour lets gamers compete across an entire year for a $1 million prize pool.

2013: The US government recognises *League of Legends* as the first professional eSport.

2016: Fnatic, FaZe Clan and NATUS Vincere all join the new World eSports Association.

2020: *DOTA 2*'s The International 10 offers the first ever $40 million prize pool.

2023: Data experts Newzoo say more than 650 million people are watching eSports in one year!

Around the World: USA

The USA is one of very few countries where you can get a visa to play eSports as a career! No wonder it's home to heavyweights like Team Liquid, FaZe Clan and Evil Geniuses.

PUBG

PlayerUnknown's Battlegrounds is the bestselling PC game ever. That means you're competing with 42 million other players to get to the top – but there are loads of competitions if you do make it that far. Over the last three years there have been more than forty official tournaments, for $15 million in prize money!

Fortnite

Anyone can win big in *Fortnite*'s Arena mode by making their way up the Hype Leaderboard! It has a three-league progression system, where the top-tier Champions League often has cash prizes on offer. The best of the best compete in the Fortnite Champion Series (FNCS) for a prize pool of $10 million!

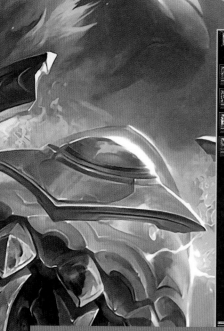

Team profile: Tundra eSports

Tundra was the top-earning team of 2022, to the tune of $18 million. Not bad given it only formed in 2021! It's hot on *DOTA 2*, and also plays *Rocket League* and *Fortnite*. Liverpool Football Club's Virgil van Dijk is one of its shareholders!

League of Legends

This battle arena favourite is the biggest eSport going. It's free-to-play, so anyone can compete – but making it to elite level is super-tough. Every winter, the best of the best compete at the World Championship. The winning team gets a 32kg trophy, $486,500 and global adoration. In 2018, the final was watched by 99.6 million!

Valorant

The fastest growing eSport keeps getting bigger. The shooter was only released in 2020, but the final of its Champions Tour was the ninth-most viewed event of the year! Its newness means great players can rise up the ranks quickly. Use the Shooting Range or Aim Lab trainer on Steam to hone your skills. Who knows how far you might climb?!

Around the World: South Korea

Loads of eSports megastars are from South Korea. *League of Legends* heroes Faker, Bang and Wolf are all South Korean. eSports has been on TV there for twenty years!

DOTA 2

Everything in *DOTA 2* is built around The International. Teams compete all year round on the DOTA Pro Circuit for invites to the most lucrative competition going! The event is crowdfunded, meaning masses of cash is up for grabs. In 2021, the prize pool hit $40 million! Reigning champs Tundra eSports scored $18 million for seeing off Team Secret in the final.

Around the World: China

China has a population of 1.4 billion — and nearly half of them are gamers. Mobile battle arena *Honor of Kings* is its most popular game. Hangzhou even has a dedicated eSports town!

Did You Know?

YouTube has an exclusive deal to broadcast the Overwatch League, Call of Duty League and *Hearthstone* tournaments. It paid $160 million for the honour!

Overwatch

Blizzard's blaster is so big it'll soon have its own dedicated stadium in Philadelphia! It's called the Fusion Arena and will hold 3,500 fans. The Overwatch League gathers teams from the USA, China, South Korea, Canada and London. San Francisco Shocks are its most successful squad. They won the league in 2019 and 2020, then finished runner-up in 2022!

Player Profile: Johan 'N0tail' Sundstein

The greatest eSports player of the last decade! The Dane has smashed all his rivals on *DOTA 2*. He won The International in 2018 and 2019, before taking a break from pro competition in 2021. In all, he's made over $7 million from being amazing at games!

Hearthstone

This card classic is different to most other eSports. It's all about individual glory! Sixteen *Hearthstone* masterminds fight to the finish in the big tournament. The reigning winner from December's World Championship is Team Liquid's BunnyHoppor. You'll need an incredible deck to climb to the top but there's lots of RNG. Chance can be a big factor so good luck!

Top Five Purpose-Built eSports Arenas

1. **Three Gorges Harbor eSports Stadium (China)**
   6,000 seats

2. **Hangzhou eSports Centre (China)**
   4,087 seats

3. **eSports Stadium Arlington (USA)**
   2,500 seats

4. **Gwangju eSports Arena (South Korea)**
   1,005 seats

5. **HyperX Arena (USA)**
   1,000 seats

Glossary

RNG stands for random number generator. All games have an element of this, with luck deciding the outcome of a shot in *FIFA 23*, or card effect in *Hearthstone*.

FIFA eWorld vs Real World

Argentina might have won the real World Cup, but they had to settle for second on the digital turf! Their representative, Nicolas Villalba, was beaten in the final of the FIFA eWorld Cup by Germany's Umut Gültekin. Umut is the second German winner in a row, following Mohammed Harkous.

Team Profile: FaZe Clan

Tundra isn't the only team with a link to real sports. FaZe Clan have ties to NFL player Kyler Murray, NBA star Ben Simmons and Manchester City! They're a pop culture phenomenon, and great at gaming too. FaZe Clan won four massive *Counter-Strike: Global Offensive* tournaments last year.

Games with the Biggest Prize Pools

1. **$40 million**
   The International (DOTA 2)

2. **$30.4 million**
   Fortnite World Cup (Fortnite)

3. **$10 million**
   World Champion Cup (Honor of Kings)

4. **$7.1 million**
   PUBG Global Invitational (PUBG)

5. **$6.4 million**
   Worlds (League of Legends)

World of Warcraft

Most competitive *Warcraft* matches are three-on-three, so you need to be a good team member to rise up the ranks in Azeroth. There's one big exception. It's called the Mythic Dungeon Invitational (MDI). That one is five-vs-five, and anyone can enter the time trials. 2,048 teams earn qualification spots, but only eight make the global finals!

Player Profile: Jaccob 'Yay' Whiteaker

The Game Awards' player of the year is a twenty-five-year-old American and *Valorant* expert. He steered OpTic Gaming to victory at Masters Reykjavik, and top-three finishes at Copenhagen and Champions 2022. Yay then jumped to super team Cloud9 for the 2023 campaign!

Did You Know?

Toronto is planning the world's biggest gaming stadium. It will fit 7,200 fans. You'll even be able to stay overnight – it will be called the eSports Performance Venue and Hotel!

Rocket League

Psyonix's blend of football and driving gets bigger every year. The first championship in 2016 was for $55,000. These days, competitors battle for $2.1 million! There are three qualification splits across the year. The best teams qualify for the Rocket League Championship Series (RLCS). NRG eSports, Vitality and Cloud9 are all past victors – but no one's won it twice!

Apex Legends

Finding *PUBG* too hardcore? Try this chaotic battle royale instead! It's gone massive with the help of Twitch streamers like Ninja and TimTheTatman. Long-distance combat can be a real game-changer here. So if you want to get competitive, focus on getting to high ground and picking off enemies from above!

Around the World: UK

eSports-wise, the UK isn't as advanced as other nations. But it's on the up! It's produced elite *FIFA* and *Rocket League* players, with 12,500 fans attending events at the SSE Arena.

THE
INSIDER TAKE

Developers Share Highlights from a Memorable Year

Erick Boenisch
VP of Development on NBA 2K23

What's the best thing you played in the last year?
Elden Ring really captured my attention and focus in a way that no game has in quite some time. Hats off to the development team and all involved for creating this masterpiece.

What element of *NBA 2K23* are you most proud of?
I'm extremely proud of how this team continues to innovate and push sports game boundaries through gameplay, atmosphere, emotion and presentation.

What game are you most looking forward to?
I have so many games I am looking forward to hopefully be playing in 2024, and beyond. Currently, my thoughts are centred around *Fable 4, Elder Scrolls VI, GTA 6* and *Dragon Quest XII*.

Catarina Macedo
Project Lead on Destiny 2

What's the best thing you played in the last year?
Besides *Destiny 2: The Witch Queen*, which was so incredibly inspiring, I loved spending dozens of hours losing myself in *God of War: Ragnarök*.

What element of *Destiny 2: Lightfall* are you most proud of?
I'm incredibly proud of the work all our teams did. The new Strand subclass, which includes grapple, is going to shake up our sandbox and the new enemy combatant – the Tormentor – will challenge your gameplay style in novel ways.

What game are you most looking forward to?
Besides our own, *The Final Shape* in 2024, I cannot wait to get my hands on *Hades 2*. The first game sits at the top of my five favourites. I am also really excited for *Final Fantasy XVI, Diablo IV* and *Starfield*!

Lee Mather
Senior Creative Director on F1 22

What's the best thing you played in the last year?
Maybe a little predictable, but it's *God of War* on PS5. A great story, driven by strong characters with real personality. Visuals, audio and gameplay were all beautifully polished and contributed to it being the complete package.

What element of *F1 22* are you most proud of?
The representation of a key moment in the history of the sport, where such a significant change in the rules, the racing and the way the cars look really contributed to a major change within F1.

What game are you most looking forward to?
The Legend of Zelda: Tears of the Kingdom. I'm a huge fan and loved *Breath of the Wild. Ocarina of Time* is still my favourite game of all time.

Christian Cortez
Head of production on TMNT: Shredder's Revenge

What's the best thing you played in the last year?
Tunic for the hidden complexity of the design, which pairs well with such simple mechanics. I also loved its artistic direction.

What element of *Shredder's Revenge* are you most proud of?
Undoubtedly the respect of the licence, and all the references worked in for the TMNT fans. The team deeply loves the TMNT universe, and I believe we managed to share that passion.

What game are you most looking forward to?
I really loved *Star Wars Jedi: Fallen Order*'s approachable take on Dark Souls style combat without the darker, gothic-esque ambience. It's the perfect challenge and atmosphere! So I'm eager to play *Star Wars Jedi: Survivor*.

What in the Weird?

Wild and Weird Gaming Stories From Across the World

Anthem For a Cent

Everyone loves a bargain! US gamers who popped into GameStop last July were greeted by an incredible surprise. The world's biggest gaming retailer reduced the price of online shooter *Anthem* to $0.01. Yes, one cent! One Reddit user, Spider-Man_Fan, was so excited that he bought thirty-seven copies. BioWare's blaster was released in 2019 to mixed reviews. The studio had hoped to build upon the success of its *Mass Effect* series, but instead cancelled all future development of *Anthem* in February 2021.

Gaming is Good for You

Guess what! A new study reckons gaming can be good for you! Georgia State University compared how quickly gamers and non-gamers reacted to a screen of moving dots. The study took place in an MRI machine, so researchers could track everyone's brain activity. And the gamers were found to be quicker with their responses! "These results indicate that video game playing potentially enhances several of the subprocesses for sensation, perception, and decision-making skills," the authors wrote in their report.

Kermit Becomes Spider-Man

Spider-Man: No Way Home rewrote the webbed wonder's rulebook. As well as current-era Spidey Tom Holland, we also got appearances from former suit-wearers Andrew Garfield and Tobey Maguire. The world of video games soon went even further. *Marvel's Spider-Man Remastered* landed on PC in August, and was immediately modded to feature an entirely new lead character. Step forward, Kermit the Frog. Thanks to the work of talented modder TangoTeds you could play the entire game as the Muppet's great green talisman. What next? Miss Piggy taking down machines in *Horizon Forbidden West*?

Tiny Tina's Biggest Prize

Still enjoying *Tiny Tina's Wonderlands*? The kooky shooter was one of 2022's most addictive time-sinks. However much you're loving it, Twitch streamer Moxsy is probably enjoying it even more. Last summer he unearthed what's believed to be the rarest item in the game. It's called Ascended Warlock's Amalgam of Glorious Purpose, and grants the owner crazy boosts, like a 29.7% bonus to all damage, and 59.3% chance of landing a critical hit. Developer Gearbox says that the likelihood of anyone finding this item was one in 85 billion. Moxsy clearly needs to start buying lottery tickets!

Bestseller
No, it's not Mario! Nintendo's top-selling game ever is *Wii Sports*, to the very high tune of 82.9 million copies.

KINGS OF KONG

Nintendo

■ The creators of *Mario* have an incredibly rich history. The company started out in 1889 – yes, eighteen-eighty-nine – making playing cards! It wasn't until 1977 that Nintendo ventured into gaming. 1981's *Donkey Kong* wowed arcade addicts, and debuted a famous overall-wearing plumber. Future icons included Bowser, Link and Tom Nook. Its modern teams are spread across Kyoto, Tokyo, Paris and Redmond in Washington. From 1992 to 2016 it even owned the nearby Seattle Mariners baseball team!

Biggest Series:
Super Mario Bros

Mario and Luigi have enough history to fill this book. Their NES platformers drove console sales across the world, and made Game Boy the first must-own handheld. Many still think *Super Mario World* on SNES is the best game ever made. Then there's *Mario Kart*, *Mario Party*, *Mario Galaxy* ... not bad for a pair of super plucky plumbers.

Have You Played?

The Legend of Zelda: Breath of the Wild

Super Mario World

Mario Kart 8 Deluxe

Animal Crossing: New Horizons

GRIDIRON GIANTS
EA Tiburon

■ EA's Canadian team in Vancouver is famous for being the brain behind *FIFA* and the Florida studio is a big deal too. Tiburon had just three employees when it was formed in 1994. EA purchased it in 1998. It's grown massively since. Along with the *Madden* and *NBA Live* games, it's created non-sporting spin-offs. PS2 open-world game *Superman Returns* is among the most memorable – but not necessarily for positive reasons!

Iconic Moment
To celebrate twenty-five years of the series, EA Tiburon named the 2013 edition *Madden NFL 25*. Pretty cool. Although it makes you wonder what they'll call the sequel to *Madden NFL 24*!

Biggest Series:
Madden NFL

Tiburon began development on the official American Football series in 1996. Two years later it was owned by EA, and since then, it's beaten any possible rival games. Legendary coach and commentator John Madden advised the studio on gameplay in the early days. Spin-offs include *NFL Head Coach* and *NFL Street*.

Have You Played?

EA Sports MMA

Tiger Woods PGA Tour 14

NBA Live 19

Madden NFL 23

Take the Honda RA300 for a spin.

Forza Motorsport

Developer Turn 10 Studios **Publisher** Xbox Game Studios
w**Platform** PC, XBX/S **Rating** PEGI 3+

■ **It's another first place for this race ace! The eighth entry in the series reboots the 2005 original. *Forza Motorsport* is stunning to look at, packed with cool cars, and an absolute dream to drive, too.**

The game was created to work perfectly on Xbox Series X, and it shows off the capabilities of the console like no other racer. It handles dreamily at 120 FPS, even with a detailed dynamic weather system. You've never had a gaming experience like circling Maple Valley on a rainy night, admiring the reflections of other cars in the shimmering tarmac. Just remember not to get too distracted by the scenery!

Tyre-less Potential

Incredibly, *Forza Motorsport* was a day-one game on Xbox Game Pass. That means subscribers got to play it as soon as it came out for no extra cost! It's Microsoft's biggest success story of the year. And, with countless options when it comes to tyre management and fuel strategies, it's a drive you'll be kicking into gear for years to come!

Belgian Beauty

Having the Circuit de Spa-Francorchamps in the game is a big deal. It first appeared in *Forza Motorsport 5*. But its history goes a little further back than that! The circuit was designed in 1920, and has hosted an annual 24-hour endurance race since 1924! It's famed for its fast, hilly route through the gorgeous Ardennes Forest. Another *Forza* favourite is the Raceway Laguna Seca. It's got a steep downhill curve that drops five and a half stories in 450 feet!

Cadillac is one of the real-life car manufacturers.

There's a wide selection of tracks for you to try out.

Glossary

FPS: No, not first-person shooter! If you're talking about gaming tech, FPS means frames per second. It's the number of consecutive images displayed in one second. Most movies are 24 FPS. Forza Motorsport runs at 120!

As well as the newest in manufacturers' models, you can also try out classic cars.

New drive mechanics give the cars a realistic feel.

Find tons of recognisable logos across the game.

Take the wheel! You'll see your opponents go flying by as you take to the tracks.

Forza added 100 new models this year.

The Car's the Star

The world's biggest car manufacturers queue up to appear in the *Forza* series! And the latest game is just as packed. Classic cars include the 1958 Aston Martin DBR1, 1967 Ferrari Spa 300 and 1969 Chevrolet Camaro. Modern speedsters are included too! 2021 models from Porsche, Audi and Cadillac will put a smile on your face – and attract the envy of your family members!

Check Out

Grabbing an Xbox Series X to try *Forza Motorsport*? Grand Prix sim *F1 22* and off-road monster *Dirt 5* are also worth a spot in your racing collection!

THE HISTORY OF FORZA

Looking Back at the Drives of Your Life

Forza Motorsport changed all we knew about driving games when it landed in 2005. It was a sim racer that also had an arcade mode for casual players. That meant you got hooked, whatever your level of petrolhead fandom! 231 cars purred around a faultless blend of real and fictional tracks.

Podium Perfection

The first game was exclusive to the original Xbox, and as each new console came out, the new *Forza* game was a must-play! *Forza Motorsport 2* was the bestselling racer on Xbox 360. While *Forza Motorsport 5* is the seventh biggest-selling game of any genre on Xbox One!

Given all that success, Microsoft keeps evolving the series with each new console release, and even with current-gen. *Forza Motorsport 6* featured 450 cars, twenty-seven tracks and a brilliant, fan-fave narrative mode called Stories of Motorsport.

With the rebooted *Forza Motorsport*, Xbox Series X/S finally has the flagship drive that players have been waiting for.

Pause for Forza

❷ Playground Games filmed the real Australian sky for months using a 12K HDR camera to make it look authentic in *Forza Horizon 3*.

❷ *Halo 4*'s Warthog vehicle appeared as an unlockable easter egg in *Forza Motorsport 4*! It looked very cool, but sadly you couldn't actually drive it.

❷ The first *Forza Motorsport* was invented to challenge PlayStation exclusive *Gran Turismo*. It took the studio more than two and a half years to create.

Forza Motorsport 4 added the BBC's *Top Gear* track. And not just for racing. A bowling mini-game gave players the chance to knock down pins as they circuited!

Four Super Forzas

Forza Motorsport 2

Xbox 360's first *Forza* built on the original in every possible way. Online play was superb whether you used Xbox Live or split-screen. Its livery editor let you personalise cars. Plus, the vehicles suffered realistic damage. There were 349 cars in total – as well as real drivers like Johnny Herbert!

Forza Horizon

Seven years after *Forza Motorsport*, Microsoft switched its focus to street racing. A new series packed with races, stunts and chaos was born! The open-world map was set in Colorado, with your popularity boosted by drifting, jumping or driving on two wheels!

Forza Motorsport 7

The pinnacle of sim driving on Xbox One. By now, more than 700 cars were playable – including favourites from the *Forza Horizon* games! At long last, the drivers were finally customisable and there was a dynamic weather system, adding to the game's element of reality. It came out in 2017, but still plays exceptionally now.

Forza Horizon 5

Ten million players tried this in its first week, making it the biggest Xbox launch of all time! They weren't disappointed. The map is astonishingly huge and packed with landmarks like Mayan temples and an active volcano. Mini-games like Piñata Pop made this the most wild *Forza* ever!

Top Tips

This year F1 2022 includes some handy features to make driving simpler. But they do tend to slow you down, so if you're feeling the need for speed, turn off ABS and traction control.

F1 22 *gives gamers the chance to race with world-class drivers, like Sebastian Vettel.*

Be Kind, Rewind

Had a bad crash? F1 22 lets you go back in time! Select Instant Replay, rewind to before the error happened, then hit square (PlayStation) or X (Xbox).

F1 22

Developer Codemasters **Publisher** EA
Platform PC, PS4, PS5, XBO, XBX/S **Rating** 3+

■ The official Formula One game gives you the chance to try every car, driver and track from the most recent season. Long-time fans are used to that, but there are fresh elements to enjoy too. Three circuits have revamped layouts: Melbourne, Barcelona and Abu Dhabi. Two more, Miami and Shanghai, are completely new.

Sadly *F1 2021*'s Braking Point story mode has been axed. Instead, there's a feature called F1 Life. You customise your driver a bit like in *The Sims*, with officially branded shirts and headwear. Your crib is completely personalised too. Switch up your sofa, choose what art goes on your walls and show off supercars.

The Incredible Hülkenberg

An old fave remains the best feature. MyTeam puts players in the manager's seat, as well as the driving seat! You negotiate with sponsors, develop young drivers and can even sign up legends. There are nine legends in total, and Jacques Villeneuve, Mark Webber and Nico Hülkenberg are new to this game. Thankfully, you can set races to three or five laps, in case you don't have two hours to commit to every drive!

Did You Know?

There are twelve different assists in the game that can be toggled on or off, such as braking, steering and traction control.

Take part in live race lobbies through online Social Play mode, or just watch the matches from the crowd.

Mercedes-AMG Petronas added the W13 model.

Speed your way to the leaderboards in these cars.

Ferrari with a Difference

F1 developer Codemasters also make *Grid Legends*. That's inspired a brilliant crossover: the chance to drive supercars around F1 tracks! Eight are available, in a mode called Pirelli Hot Laps. It features forty challenges. You can purr around real circuits in a Ferrari Roma, McLaren 720S or Aston Martin DB11. Just don't play it in front of your dad. With those classic models available, there's no way he'll be able to resist 'borrowing' the controller …

Check out over twenty tracks from the cockpit.

Play as real-life racers like Norris, Perez or Alonso.

Top Eight

Max Verstappen won the real-life title – and he's the best driver in the game too.

95

MAX VERSTAPPEN

93

LEWIS HAMILTON

90

FERNANDO ALONSO

90

GEORGE RUSSELL

89

LANDO NORRIS

88

SERGIO PÉREZ

87

CARLOS SAINZ JR

85

SEBASTIAN VETTEL

WRC Generations

Developer Kylotonn **Publisher** Nacon
Platform NS, PC, PS4, PS5, XBO, XBX/S **Rating** PEGI 3+

Background | *World Rally Championship* has found a new home! It started out as a PlayStation exclusive back in 2022, made by Sony's Evolution Studios. This is the seventh game in the series from French studio Kylotonn. And the last. Sports giant EA has bought the license from 2023 onwards.

Features | Kylotonn says goodbye with one of the most comprehensive rally games ever. All thirteen locations from the 2022 championship are here, plus eight bonus ones. New Ford Puma, Hyundai and Toyota GR Yaris models are also faithfully installed. You can build a team or embark on a solo career, working your way up from the WRC 2 feeder circuit.

Gameplay | *WRC Generations* is about the scenery as much as the driving. Cruising through snowy Sweden almost feels like a holiday! Until you get distracted and plummet into the white stuff. PS5's haptic triggers are also used cleverly. Brake hard and you truly feel it in your fingertips.

Such realistic powder spray, you'd think you were skiing!

Speed through thirteen real-world rallies, like Rally Sweden.

My Generation
❷ Previous game *WRC 10* celebrated fifty years of the sport with a neat retro mode. That's been cut, but thirty-seven iconic old-school cars remain. You can test drive a 1972 Lancia Fulvia HF or 1985 Peugeot 205 without worrying about taking a theory test!

Noob Tip
Spend some time in the Livery Editor. You can fiddle with parts and change your paint job to make your early rides feel that touch more personal.

Check Out

Fancy something completely different from the same studio? Take on the daily life of a US cop in *Police Simulator: Patrol Duty*.

Dakar Desert Rally

Developer Saber Porto **Publisher** Saber Interactive
Platform PC, PS4, PS5, XBO, XBX/S **Rating** PEGI 3+

Background | This is the follow-up to the niche PS4/XBO racer *Dakar 18*. The first game didn't hit the mainstream, but its realistic mechanics got the Portuguese studio Bigmoon noticed. It was purchased by Saber Interactive, and they renamed it Saber Porto. Bigger budgets mean much bigger ambitions for this sequel.

Features | *WRC Generations* focuses on one year of the official competition, but its mud-churning rival pulls together three years. You get to tackle the 2020, 2021 and 2022 seasons with licensed bikes, trucks and cars. All in an open-world take on Saudi Arabia, including some really dynamic weather. How will you handle storming through the desert or a sudden sandstorm hitting your car?

Gameplay | The scale here is staggering. It's so huge, as a gamer, you can't measure it – but Saber Porto says it's 20,000 square kilometres. Handling is more hardcore than *WRC*, and switching between vehicles requires adjustment time. Trucks are great fun for newcomers, but you need experience to master quad bikes.

It's Rally True

❷ Bigmoon actually collaborated on the *World Rally Championship* series before it switched to Kylotonn! Working with previous developer Milestone, the studio provided 3D art for *WRC*, *WRC Shakedown* and *WRC 5*.

Admire the sand tracks your car makes as you storm across deserts.

The weather system is shockingly good. Feel the wind hit your speed.

DLC FTW

Four essential add-ons for your favourite games

■ These days, buying a game is just the beginning. Developers use patches to fix bugs and tweak gameplay. Modders build creative add-ons for their favourite games. But there are even more exciting expansions. DLC stands for downloadable content. Check out these four chunks of must-play extras from some of the biggest names in gaming!

Forza Horizon 5:
Hot Wheels

Just when you thought you'd seen it all in *Forza*, toy cars enter the game! The *Hot Wheels* DLC adds your favourite micro vehicles to Xbox's flagship racer. There are forty-two events and 156 missions. Ten new cars include a Chevrolet Camaro, Hennessey Venom and Brabham BT62. You can race these around over 200km of fresh track – full of loops and upside-down sections. Still not enough? Look out for the three dragons who've been added, too!

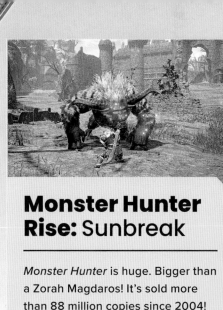

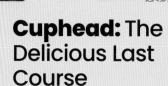

Monster Hunter Rise: Sunbreak

Monster Hunter is huge. Bigger than a Zorah Magdaros! It's sold more than 88 million copies since 2004! *The Sunbreak* DLC adds thirteen classic monsters from the past, along with four new ones. Fans got most excited about capturing the elder dragon Malzeno. It was inspired by legendary vampire Dracula. Defeating him can take up to an hour as you try out different tactics — but that only makes winning more special!

World of Warcraft: Dragonflight

Extra content for *World of Warcraft* just keeps on coming. *Dragonflight* was its ninth expansion pack! It's freshened up the amazing MMORPG yet again with a new level cap of seventy, and a feature called Dragonriding. You can raise and customise a dragon, then take it into battle! There are also five new zones to explore and fight in. These are Waking Shores, Ohn'ahran Plains, Azure Span, Thaldraszus and the Hidden Reach.

Cuphead: The Delicious Last Course

Cuphead and Mugman finally get a new partner! She's called Ms. Chalice and is an expert at charming people. In *The Delicious Last Course*, the trio travel across the Inkwell Isle. They need five ingredients to make a Wondertart! Ms. Chalice's skills include driving, tap dancing and turning into a ghost. Bosses are more bonkers than ever. Ice master Mortimer Freeze tries to finish you with icicles that come alive, and a giant orange whale!

More DLC

These weren't the only big hitters with must-play DLC. *FIFA 23* gave us both the women's and men's World Cups as their own unique game modes. And *Elden Ring* became even more massive. The free Colosseum update added three new arenas for player-vs-player combat!

Inside the Life of a Video Game Writer

Go Behind the Screens with a Top Industry Expert
By Will Porter

■ Will Porter has written for everything and everyone – providing words for interstellar journeys, bickering olden-time gangsters, terrifying zombie plagues and real world Hollywood A-list actors! So how does his job work?

I have been writing video games professionally for over a decade, and you may have played my stuff if you've journeyed to the stars in *No Man's Sky*, or fought for survival in *Project*

Zomboid. My name can also be found on *Mafia: Definitive Edition*, while Chief Porter is another of my characters who can be found cowering beneath the desks of the Sevastopol space station in *Alien: Isolation*.

Once upon a time I was a video games journalist, writing for a long-lost magazine called *PC Zone*. When print magazines became less popular, I decided to make the jump over to making

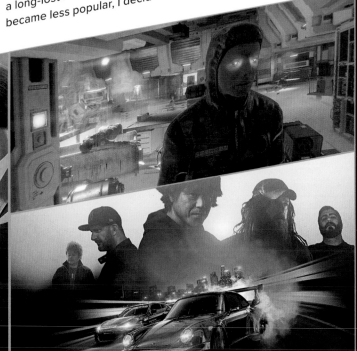

A huge part of the development process for any game is chatting to artists, making sure you are following the vision they have for this world or the creatures within it – and that they know your creative writerly thoughts too. My absolute favourite thing to do is work with mission designers. Games and levels go through countless different versions as they are developed, and checking in with the designer each time to work out what the game heroes should be saying while they duck, dock and shoot is always a treat.

It's often a satisfying puzzle to solve too. Just why is that door locked? What happened in this place to mess it up so bad? Why are a million enemies about to show up and give you a hard time? If I've done my job properly then it means players won't have to ask these questions.

It's not always sunshine making games. You get a lot of criticism, from both inside and out. Towards the end of a game's development, even the free fizzy drinks lose some appeal. It's easy to burn out, and lose some of the love. But if the game you make turns out good, it's worth it. Seeing people online enjoy themselves, laughing at your jokes, and engaging with your story, is an amazing feeling.

games. I had spent so many years interviewing developers, that the idea of sitting in their seat and creating mind-blowing experiences was hugely exciting.

It took ages to get in though! There aren't many writing jobs in games development, and studios (and gamers) have very high standards. I got my start on the *Need for Speed* franchise and my own game, *Project Zomboid*. Once I had those to show I wasn't completely clueless, then it was a little easier to persuade other game studios to give me access to their franchises and fridges.

On a big project, a writer (that's me!) works alongside the creative directors and game leads to create a story and characters that fit their vision. It's not just that though! We're creating a world (sometimes a universe!) for the player's story to happen within. Writers create a 'story bible' and a 'world bible' that explain what happened throughout the world of the game before the player showed up. For *No Man's Sky*, for example, I developed the entire history and evolutions of alien races, such as the Korvax, Vy'keen and Gek Dominion.

There's no set way that people become games writers. Some are discovered from the small projects they put online, some get noticed when they've been working on a game's QA (quality assurance). Increasingly, talent is discovered through someone's presence online and on social media. The biggest factor, however, is probably luck. I have one hundred percent lucked out to be able to do what I do, and if you want to join me then I've got my fingers crossed for you too!

Fun Fact

If you work in a big video games studio then you get FREE fizzy drinks, and crisps also sometimes too. They only start giving you funny looks when you start cramming them into your bag every day.

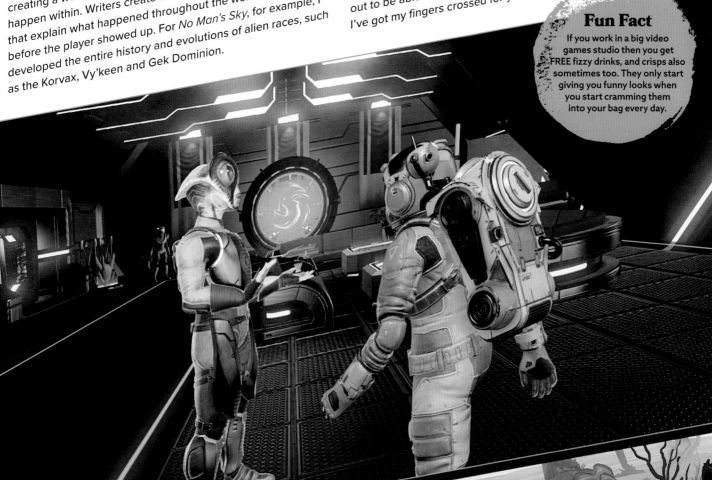

Metroidvania
Your Guide to the Gaming Genre

■ The term Metroidvania is a not-exactly-subtle combo of two dusty classics, released one month apart. In August 1986, 2D space-exploration game *Metroid* landed on the NES. Dracula-hunting platformer *Castlevania* hit the same console seven weeks later. A genre devoted to jumping around side-scrolling levels and unearthing secrets was born.

These games usually feature interconnected stages where parts of the world are inaccessible until you've collected the right items. Devoted players believe a true Metroidvania game needs to remain in 2D, and that the storyline shouldn't be linear. If you don't have to retrace your steps at some point, the developer is doing it wrong!

Perfect Symphony
Two giants of the genre are considered its benchmark. 1994 Super Nintendo adventure *Super Metroid*'s colossal world and range of items made every moment a joy. And in 1997, *Castlevania: Symphony of the Night* on PS1 integrated *Zelda*-like RPG elements to create one of the most immersive adventures of all time.

Forgotten Forbear
Metroid wasn't the first game of this type. Side-scrolling actioner *Brain Breaker* landed on the Sharp X1 computer in 1985. Brainbreakvania isn't anywhere near as catchy!

Top 5 Metroidvania Games to Play Right Now

Islets

Short-but-strong Switch tale set across a string of floating islands. Airship travel adds a new spin on Metroidvania tradition, and mouse-warrior Iko is both charming and sincere. It was created alone by a developer called Kyle Thompson. Well played, sir!

Metroid Dread

The first 2D *Metroid* in nineteen years has added some new stealthy skills for Samus. She can use camouflage to evade robots, but it slows her down. It feels modern and gorgeous, and retains all the classic elements that spawned a genre.

Hollow Knight

The modern Metroidvania that went mainstream, with three million copies sold. You wield a sword and explore a captivating underground world. It's an intricate mishmash of loads of series you love, with elements of *Mega Man* and *Zelda* skilfully reimagined.

Blast Brigade vs the Evil Legion of Dr. Cread

A rowdy take on the genre that goes heavy on humour. The lead character is called Jeff Jefferson! He's full of *Deadpool*-like wisecracks, but there's serious skill required too. You can aim your weapon in any direction, and so can your enemies. So, stay alert!

Castlevania Anniversary Collection

An incredible compendium of nine *Castlevania* games, one of which – *Kid Dracula* – has never been released in the West before. The very first NES effort is a beautiful intro to the genre, and *Castlevania III: Dracula's Curse* will keep you hooked too.

1994

What Games Were Big Thirty Years Ago?

■ Bright colourful pixels were all the rage in 1994. Kids raced down to Woolworths and Toys R Us to grab *Sonic 3* on its release day. That wasn't the only memorable platformer to land on the Sega Mega Drive. And it was a spectacular year for Super Nintendo, too!

Sonic the Hedgehog 3

One of the most hyped Mega Drive games that lived up to its pre-release frenzy. Buddy character Tails from *Sonic 2* returned, as players explored six new zones. Levels were three times bigger than the earlier games. Bonus stages were reworked too. Knuckles the Echidna also made his debut. This inspired cool spin-off *Sonic & Knuckles*, which had an adapter along the top of the cartridge. You could use this to attach *Sonic 3*, then replay it as Knuckles!

Earthworm Jim

A *Sonic*-inspired platformer with a couple of key differences. Jim could use his worm body to whip enemies. When that didn't work, he also had a gun at his disposal! It was very kid-friendly, though. Boss characters all had tongue-in-cheek names that got teenagers chuckling, such as Queen Slug-for-a-Butt, Evil the Cat and Bob the Killer Goldfish. Between the main platforming levels there was a racing mini-game called *Andy Asteroids* to enjoy too.

Scorpion Bites

1994 sparked a rivalry between two classic brawlers. **Street Fighter II** was the second-bestselling game, despite coming out two years earlier. But its dominance was challenged by **Mortal Kombat II**.

Donkey Kong Country

In the 1990s, the best platform games on Nintendo machines usually contained two words: Super Mario. *Donkey Kong Country* smashed that rule to smithereens. Its 3D graphics were groundbreaking, with detailed characters and beautiful backgrounds. Donkey Kong and nephew Diddy Kong were both easy to handle as you rode mine carts and evaded obstacles. Imaginative levels also served up tons of humour and sneaky secrets. It's still one of the best games ever made.

NBA Jam

Slam dunk! The *2K* series dominates modern-era basketball, but that wasn't the case three decades ago, when this arcade favourite ruled all. Teams of two went head-to-head in matches packed with power-ups and crazy dunks. Score three baskets in a row and you triggered the catchphrase, "he's on fire!" This gave you unlimited turbo and even better shooting accuracy. The game used real-life NBA player line-ups – but also featured hidden players, like US president Bill Clinton!

PlayStation Arrives

Sony's first **PlayStation** landed in Japan. They sold **100,000 consoles on day one.** The launch line-up featured eight games, including *Ridge Racer*, *Crime Crackers* and the catchy *Mahjong Goku Sky: Atsushi*.

Whether you pick two wheels or four, the new update has given players a lot of fun ways to get around in style.

Famous Fortniters

Reigning Super Bowl champ Patrick Mahomes openly admits to loving *Fortnite*! Other celeb fans include rapper Drake, *Stranger Things* star Finn Wolfhard and footballer Dele Alli.

Fortnite

Developer Epic Games **Publisher** Epic Games **Platform** NS, PC, PS4, PS5, XBO, XBX/S **Rating** PEGI 7+

■ **For many gamers, the past year can be summarised by three words: *Fortnite* Chapter 4! A new island formed after the climax of Chapter 3. This meant fresh territory to claim, weapons to unleash, and vehicles to go hurtling around on!**

Dirt bikes were an especially popular addition. They weren't just great for getting from the Brutal Bastion to the Shattered Slabs. You could pull off cool tricks, and use weapons without the need for a separate driver! The only catch was being more exposed to enemy attacks. Putting your foot down and racing away was a crucial tactic!

Banana Bonuses

Reality augments are another Chapter 4 highlight. The longer you remain in a match, the more of these perks you collect. They're random, but almost always very cool! You might be able to drive without using up any fuel, or be given glider redeploy for the rest of your current match. It means that, even in shootouts that seem doomed, there's always hope of a victorious comeback!

Know your Fortnite

Just starting out on your *Fortnite* journey? Then you need to know the differences between the three versions!

Fortnite: Save The World

When most people say *Fortnite*, they mean *Fortnite: Battle Royale*. But this version actually came first. It's a mix of tower defence, looting and shooting where up to four players team up for battle. You need to build fortifications, set traps and protect survivors from a variety of zombie-like creatures. It's set on Earth, but with a twist. A worldwide storm has caused 98% of the world's population to disappear!

Fortnite Battle Royale

The version of *Fortnite* most people refer to in the playground, or on social media. It's all-out battle royale mayhem! 100 players skydive onto an island, then scavenge for gear and fight to stay alive. The island gets smaller as a match progresses, as the storm surrounding it moves closer and closer. Last player or team alive wins! The game operates in chapters, which are then split into seasons. Every new seasons brings exciting new weapons, gear, and outfits!

Fortnite: Creative

The most chilled out way to enjoy *Fortnite*. If you love *Minecraft*, this is a great introduction. You make structures on a private island, then share them with up to 100 people for mini-game fun. Rules are totally customisable. And, of course, there are loads of ready-made maps awaiting you. Among the best is Prison Breakout, where you can side with the inmates as they look to escape – or the guards who want to hunt them down!

Fortnite Year by Year

2011 — Epic Games begins brainstorming a game that merges construction and shooting.

2014 — Alpha sign-ups get underway, meaning hand-picked gamers can try before release!

2016 — The company prepares to unleash *Fortnite: Save The World* at some point in the next year.

2017 — Epic swiftly adds *Fortnite: Battle Royale* after the huge success of *PUBG Battlegrounds*.

2018 — The sandbox of *Fortnite: Creative* gives players three different ways to enjoy the game.

2019 — *Fortnite* grabs the precious BAFTA prize for Best Evolving Game.

2020 — Five different seasons of Chapter 2 keep gamers hooked throughout the year.

2021 — Multiple sources reckon that Epic is beginning to plan a *Fortnite* movie!

2022 — Chapter 3's island explode into tiny pieces in the hour-long Fracture event.

2023 — Gamers rave over Chapter 4, and can't wait for news of the next one!

Go flying, try out a wheelie or a 360! The sky's literally the limit.

Big Numbers

Fortnite has more than 400 million registered players, with 83 million of these jumping back in at least once per month!

Doom was just one of the new crossovers that Fortnite delivered to gamers. Who's your new favourite skin?

Fortnite goes Mega!

All these changes happened in Chapter 4 Season 1. There was even more fun to come in Season 2! The update was called Mega, for good reason: a new biome called Mega City appeared on the southeast of the map. It's neon, futuristic and packed with grind rails!

Two-wheel vehicles were again a theme, but this time it wasn't dirt bikes. They were vaulted – booooo! – in favour of the Victory Crown Rogue. It's a two-person machine with nifty acceleration, sharp turning and a boost for extra speed. Another new additions was the Nitro Drifter: a four-seater car that can be slid using its handbrake. Ace!

Mega City has dark corners that provide shelter, tall buildings for vantage points and So. Much. Colour!

The aimbot gun was a big fan-fave out of the new weapons drops. Gamers love the lock-on feature.

Unleash The Dragon Ball

Fortnite x Dragon Ball was another super-special crossover. Son Goku, Vegeta, Bulma and Beerus all arrived in-game, and you could watch episodes of the show on a cruise ship!

Our Fave Fortnite Outfits

CAPTAIN AMERICA

GERALT OF RIVIA

AXION SENTINEL

CLAIRE REDFIELD

BRITESTAR

DARTH MAUL

FOLLY

ADONIS CREED

GUFF GRINGLE

RIFT KNIGHT KIERAN

Fortnitemares Returns

Halloween brought its usual round of spook-tacular *Fortnite* treats! The latest round of Fortnitemares saw DJ Lyka waiting for you at the Reality Tree. He had the power to turn you into a wolf-like monster, with wolf-themed abilities! Howler claws let you perform a slash-tastic four-combo melee attack. They also let you activate wolfscent. This gave you tracking vision, putting a mark on enemies nearby! Throw in the return of survival mode horde rush and it was another Halloween to remember.

Destiny x Fortnite x Fall Guys

Three of the biggest games teamed up for a crazy collaboration! Three new *Fortnite* themed ornaments dropped into *Destiny 2*. Some loved the Black Knight-themed Knightly Noire Titan. Others wanted the Drift-themed Painted Kitsune Warlock. If you didn't love those, you could go for the Oblivion-themed Eternal Vengeance Hunter.

Those treats felt minor when *Destiny 2* invaded *Fortnite*! Fans got an entire *Fortnite Creative* island to explore, inspired by the Crucible map Javelin-4. The crossover included skins of Ikora Rey, Zavala and Exo Stranger. Plus *Destiny*-themed cosmetics like the Crown-Splitter Pickaxe, Targe Back Bling and an awesome ridable Sparrow Glider!

And, finally, *Fall Guys* joined the party! Titan, Hunter and Warlock themes from *Destiny 2* all dropped into the bonkers battle royale. Fans loved the limited Major Mancake outfit in *Fortnite* that could be won by completing the Crown Clash challenge in *Fall Guys*. You had to play 100 rounds in any show. Let's hope for more crossover carnage next year!

Reality Augments, like Mechanical Archer were a new feature added this year.

One of the new locations to be added was Frenzy Fields, such a charming spot for a fight!

Watch out for new enemies and bosses, you can unlock enemies like the Cube Queen in Chapter 4.

As well as new skins and weapons, Fortnite also featured a new movement mechanic called hurdling.

The Reality Augments have added an extra layer of offence to the game, but can also be used to defend.

Check Out

Alternatives to *Fortnite* include *Darwin Project*, where you endure wintry elements while hunting opponents. There's also *Population: One*. It's a VR-based battle royale game! You can grab it on both Oculus and HTC Vive.

Drop points are just as chaotic as always, with players getting the chance to brawl in castles.

Ace New Weapons!

EX-CALIBER RIFLE
An un-scoped Marksman Rifle. It shoots blades that explode after a short time!

THUNDER SHOTGUN
Short-range high-damage blaster. It's slow to fire, but can unleash two shots at once!

TWIN MAG SMG
Submachine gun with two magazines attached to one, meaning every second reload is faster than the first.

RED-EYE ASSAULT RIFLE
Fully automatic rifle that deals great damage. Just remember that it needs to be un-scoped to reload!

HAVOC PUMP SHOTGUN
Madly aggressive shotgun. The mythic version can down an enemy with one hit!

KINETIC BLADE
A dazzling katana that can send foes flying with its knockback slash.

COBRA DMR
This cool semi-automatic had been vaulted – but returned in Chapter 4 Season 2!

Wild Hearts

Developer Omega Force **Publisher** EA
Platform PC, PS5, XBX/S **Rating** PEGI 12+

■ **Open world games are all the rage. But what if you want to go monster-hunting without worrying about getting lost, distracted or missing out on key story developments? You give *Wild Hearts* a go, that's what!**

In this linear adventure, players slay brazen beasts known as Kemono. It's set in the world of Azuma, which is based on feudal Japan. There are eight weapon types to master, like the wagasa – which is basically a massive umbrella with blades all around its edges! Definitely not one to take on your next rainy walk …

Karakuri Queen

Best bit of all is a mechanic called karakuri. To begin with, players use it to craft crates to access high ground, or to build springs to leap onto enemies. As you progress and upgrade, you can fuse items into weapons, shields, shrines and even a gigantic training bear! It means every resource you pick up early in the game can shape its later stages, keeping you hooked for all thirty hours of beast-hunting.

Explore the lush landscapes of Azuma as you uncover the mysteries it holds.

Watch out for the Deathstalker, a huge wolf-like Kemono creature.

Scars Above

Developer Mad Head Games
Publisher Prime Matter
Platform PC, PS5, XBX/S **Rating** PEGI 12+

■ Having a rough day? Dr Kate Ward is deffo doing worse! She's been transported across the galaxy to a creepy alien planet. Kate is investigating a strange artefact known as the metahedron – and looking for her missing teammates from a squad called SCAR. It stands for Sentient Contact Rescue and Response. You won't be surprised to learn that they're not stood around sharing cake and tea!

Appliance of Science

Gameplay is a mix of puzzling and action, with some clever uses of the alien environment. You need to set stuff on fire to stop Kate catching hypothermia. Plus, given her scientific background, she's able to engineer alien tech into new weapons – like a gravity grenade that temporarily slows down everything around you.

All these skills come into play when taking down alien bosses. For example, you can fire your ice launcher to freeze them, then attack them with acid or fire! It's not the most original game you've ever played, but at around seven hours long *Scars Above* never gets dull either.

Check Out

Returnal is the ultimate next-gen sci-fi blaster. You play as Selene Vassos, an astronaut trapped in a time loop on the planet Atropos.

Use your adapted tech to take out grotesque and dangerous aliens as you travel across strange, new planets.

From ice to fire to acid, you'll discover exciting locations in your journey, using items to keep yourself alive.

Dr Kate Ward starts her story on a spaceship called the Hermes, named after the Greek god of messages.

Fighting with fire! The thermic charger and fire ray are two weapons you can use to defeat enemies with heat.

Check Out
Love this and own a Switch? Then revisit the series that invented this genre: *Super Smash Bros. Ultimate.*

MultiVersus

Developer Player First Games **Publisher** Warner Bros. Games
Platform NS, PS4, PS5, XBO, XBX/S **Rating** PEGI 12+

■ Ever wondered who'd win a fight between Arya Stark, LeBron James and Batman? *MultiVersus* brings the answer in the most chaotic fashion imaginable. Cartoony characters dash, leap and punch their way through two-on-two combat, trying to knock their enemies off the TV screen. It's larger than life but authentic too. Maisie Williams voices Arya, and Matthew Lillard brings Shaggy from *Scooby Doo* to life.

Batcave Battles

There are only two attack buttons, but you can create combo moves by pointing the analogue stick in a particular direction at the same time. These fight moves are enhanced by perks, which are unlocked as you progress. Batman detonates smoke bombs, Shaggy munches a sandwich to become hangry and Arya can copy an enemy's face by knocking them out! Locations are a bit more hit and miss, but you never tire of doing battle in Scooby's Haunted Mansion or the Batcave.

Steven Universe and Superman are just some of the fan favourites.

Take your pick of a wide range of fighters. Tom and Jerry count as one!

Batman vs Harley Quinn vs Arya Stark? The madness of MultiVersus!

Find Your Friends

❸ An early patch removed Velma's ability to phone the police and arrest an enemy. Instead, she calls the Mystery Inc gang to take them away. Curious!

Bayonetta 3

Developer PlatinumGames **Publisher** Nintendo **Platform** NS
Rating PEGI 16+

■ The witching hour is at hand on Switch. In her third slash-tastic adventure, uber-cool Bayonetta gets a playable buddy. Viola wears a spiked leather jacket and wields a samurai sword. Together, they use demonic abilities to stop man-made bioweapons called Homunculi. It sounds otherworldly, but the settings are familiar: New York, Cairo, Paris and more. Combat is utterly wild, and all the more satisfying for it!

Did You Know?

The first *Bayonetta* came out in 2009. Creator Hideki Kamiya was keen to create a *Devil May Cry*-style game with a female protagonist!

Horizon
Forbidden West

Developer Guerrilla Games **Publisher** Sony
Platform PS4, PS5 **Rating** PEGI 16+

■ Aloy's machine-hunting sequel remains one of PS5's must-own adventures. It ended 2022 with a Golden Joystick for Best Storytelling, and an incredible seven Game Awards nominations! If you fancy exploring a massive post-apocalyptic world, forming alliances and unleashing legendary archery skills, this is the time to get involved.

Easter Egg

❷ There's a rack inside Latopolis with guns that look like the LSR44 Spoor. This was the main weapon used in Guerrilla shooter *Killzone: Shadow Fall*!

Marvel's Spider-Man 2

Developer Insomniac Games **Publisher** Sony
Platform PC, PS4, PS5 **Rating** PEGI 16+

■ Spidey's new web-slinger is the most secretive game of the decade so far! It was announced at Sony's official PlayStation Showcase in the summer of 2021. The watching masses immediately fell in love with the trailer. Then everything went quiet for two years!

That tease-tastic video did at least confirm the return of both Spider-Man and Miles Morales, following on from the two most recent games in the series. Even cooler was the arrival of Venom. The scary-toothed alien has been Spidey's main rival in the comics since 1984, and now you get to hunt him down in video-game form.

Made in Manhattan

With the game deliberately made to showcase PS5, everything looks phenomenal. Steam billows from manhole covers. Fights sizzle with electrical special powers. And New York comes to life thanks to authentic traffic lights, road signs and other details. Even the water in the puddles looks super real! It's the webbed wonder, flying around the hustling, busting city. You have to play it.

Spider-Men, Spider-Men. Miles Morales and Peter Parker team up in this new addition to the series.

Watch out for those jaws! Classic comic book enemy Venom makes a toothy appearance.

History Lesson:
Marvel's Spider-Man

You need to know the first couple of games to truly get *Spider-Man 2*. Spoilers ahead, obviously. New York is in chaos in the first game after an outbreak of the toxic Devils' Breath. Spidey gradually takes back the city by downing legendary villains like Electro, Vulture, Rhino and Scorpion. Eventually, he battles the dastardly Octavius for the antidote. That part is successful, but there's a traumatic twist that we'd best not mention here!

DLC

Another essential play is *Spider-Man: The City That Never Sleeps*. In this add-on to the original game, Spidey fends off a new crime wave headed by mob boss Hammerhead.

History Lesson: Spider-Man:
Miles Morales

This stunning spin-off introduces a second Spidey! Miles Morales is catapulted into the role when his Harlem home is threatened by the war between an energy company and a criminal army. Its setting is especially memorable: still Manhattan, but covered in snow! Miles has spent a year training under Peter Parker when he accidentally releases Rhino. Chaos unfolds! Among it all, Miles learns his friend Phin wants to avenge the death of her brother. Both these key storylines merge for one of the best action adventures you can play on PS5.

Diablo IV

Developer Blizzard Albany / Blizzard Team 3
Publisher Blizzard Entertainment
Platform PC, PS4, PS5, XBO, XBX/S **Rating** PEGI 18

■ *Diablo* is back – and this dungeon-crawler is basically a greatest hits package! You can be the speedy Rogue from game one, magical Sorceress from *Diablo II* or naughty Necromancer from *Diablo III*. One big difference from the other games in the series: it's the first *Diablo* to be rated 18.

Never played the series before? It's about exploring a dark fantasy world, slaying monsters and demons! Diablo is the name of the main bad guy. In the earlier games, you would fend off his hordes while upgrading your character with snazzy equipment and badass skills. Awesome.

Fallen Angels

This time around, the main villain is the demonic Lilith. The plot follows *Diablo III: Reaper of Souls.* Ongoing conflicts have left the world of Sanctuary short of angels and demons. That power vacuum gave Lilith the chance to inspire worshippers in the mortal realm. Your job is to restore good and banish her from Sanctuary forever!

Snow Business

Dungeon layouts in *Diablo IV* are generated randomly, so every playthrough is unique. There is some consistency though. Sanctuary is the main open-world setting, broken up into five regions. Fractured Peaks is a highlight, packed with snowy mountains and deep cave systems. The others are called Scosglen, Dry Steppes, Hawezar and Kehjistan. Prepare to get extra devious when you hack and slash through Hell!

Explore Fractured Peaks, one of the starting zones.

PvP gives you the chance to win Shards of Hatred.

Although there's the chance to play the game solo, some of the enemies are tough enough to require a team.

Check Out

Warhammer: Chaosbane serves up masses of speedy combat, with the brilliant bonus of four-player co-op!

There are five different regions in the game, each with their own unique landscapes.

Out of the four classes you can play as, the rogue is the most agile.

Feel the Power

Diablo is all about player stats – a little bit like *FIFA*! Attack and critical chance dictate your offensive abilities. Fending off enemies is all about defence and elemental resistance. These are bolstered by a new mechanic called Power. Angelic Power increases the duration of beneficial effects like healing. Demonic Power boosts the length of negative effects like de-buffs. Ancestral Power is the most exciting. The more you have, the better your chances of landing a critical hit!

Avarice is one of the world bosses. Watch out for his hefty step!

Future Temptation
Creator Hidetaka Miyazaki says his next project is in its final stages – could it be Elden Ring 2?!

Haligtree is a bright spot in the bleak setting of the Lands Between.

Elden Ring

Developer FromSoftware **Publisher** Bandai Namco
Platform PS4, PS5, XBO, XBX/S **Rating** PEGI 16+

■ Four Golden Joysticks, including Ultimate Game of the Year. Seven Game Awards nominations. 17.5 million copies sold by September 2022. *Elden Ring* is one of current-gen's greatest successes. So, is the open-world game that's co-written by George R.R. Martin deserving of all those awards? In short: yes. In more detail: yes, oh yes, oh yes.

Go Your Own Way

There's so much to enjoy in the spiritual successor to *Dark Souls*. Like that massive open world: The Lands Between are packed with caves, castles, churches, forests and ruins to explore. That's when you're not engrossed in the main story, or engaging in moreish side quests. Combat offers three classes with tons of pros and cons. Customisation feels endless. And the bosses ... so, so tough, but so, so glorious to overcome.

It's packed with so many shady characters that you might not meet them all in a 100-hour playthrough. Astel is a boss alien made up of star debris who some gamers remember fondly, and others have never encountered! That's the level of variety we're talking here. With hints at future DLC, this will stay essential all the way through to PS6 and Xbox Series YZ!

Players have a huge choice of weapons: incantations, bows or swords taller than you are.

Use Lone Wolf Ashes to summon a pack of canine companions to help you out in battle.

Did You Know?

Work on *Elden Ring* began in 2017, and it was developed alongside the hardcore *Sekiro: Shadows Die Twice*.

Try to track down the weirdest possible enemy.

Ride your magic steed through battles.

Trolls are a tough enemy to beat, but using incantations can help lower their HP.

Easter Eggs

Have you spotted all these references to other series?

GAME OF THRONES

Defeat Leonine Misbegotten in Castle Morne on the Weeping Peninsula and you receive a powerful blade made up of smaller swords all welded together. It's exactly like the throne from the iconic George R.R. Martin book and TV show!

FROZEN

No, this isn't April Fool's Day – there's an Anna and Elsa reference in *Elden Ring*! Obtain Blaidd's Armor, then read the item description. It says: "The pelt serves as a cape, to protect from the cold / Blaidd was the blade of Ranni, but the cold never bothered him anyway."

DEMON'S SOULS

It was inevitable that FromSoftware would reference its earlier games, and Patches is the most prominent example. The treacherous bald dude gets his own quest in *Elden Ring*. As well as *Demon's Souls*, he appeared in *Armored Core: For Answer*, *Dark Souls*, *Dark Souls 3* and *Bloodborne*.

BERSERK

This famous manga series began in 1989. It was a heavy influence on *Elden Ring*, which includes loads of Easter eggs to the comic. The Colossal Sword in the FromSoftware mega-hit is based on a blade wielded by dragon slayer Guts. And Malenia's helmet is uncannily similar to badass *Berserk* character Farnese.

Games on Film

Check Out these Movie and TV Spin-Offs

Minecraft at the Movies

Also on the way is *Minecraft: The Movie*, from *Nick & Norah's Infinite Playlist* director Peter Sollett. Its original March 2022 release date was delayed due to the pandemic.

Uncharted

Tom Holland loses the Spidey suit and steps into Nathan Drake's relic-hunting boots. The origin story in the movie is new, but there are action sequences faithful to the classic PS3 games. The incredible airplane scene from *Uncharted 3: Drake's Deception* is especially popcorn-worthy on the big screen.

Blasts from the Past Old-timers that are worth checking out

Street Fighter (1994)

Street Fighter is a so-bad-you-have-to-see-it tale based on Guile hunting down M Bison, with Ryu and Ken's help. Can you guess who plays Cammy? Kylie Minogue!

Prince of Persia: The Sands of Time (2010)

Jake Gyllenhaal and Gemma Arterton front an all-star cast in a three-star movie. Opposing them as the dastardly Nizam is acting legend Ben Kingsley.

Castlevania (2017)

This animated Netflix series was originally planned as a movie, but it was turned into an ongoing TV show. The first two seasons do a top job of adapting the 1989 game *Dracula's Curse*.

Tomb Raider (2018)

The best film in an up-and-down franchise. Alicia Vikander plays Lara Croft, with Dominic West (Prince Charles from *The Crown*!) playing her father. Croft takes on classic action, including exploring tombs!

Sonic the Hedgehog 2

Jim Carrey is back as Dr. Robotnik in a much-improved *Sonic* sequel. This time around he has a new ally: Sonic's long-time rival Knuckles, voiced by Idris Elba. There's plenty of action and humour, and a couple of genuinely emotional moments too. A super spike-tastic surprise!

Halo

The UNSC vs Covenant war switches from Microsoft console to dedicated TV show. It still features Master Chief, but fits into a different canon from the games. Voice actor Jen Taylor, who plays Cortana, should sound familiar. She played Princess Peach and Toad in the early-2000s *Mario* games!

Sword of Destiny

Netflix series *The Witcher* is the ultimate gaming spin-off show. Geralt of Rivia's tales span three seasons, with Liam Hemsworth taking over the main role from series four.

Arcane

Take *League of Legends*, add a dash of an angsty Hailee Steinfeld, mix in stunning cartoon visuals, and what do you get? *Arcane*! Steinfeld stars as Vi in this Netflix spin-off of the huge gaming series, which scored a second season in 2023.

What in the Weird?

Wild and Weird Gaming Stories From Across the World

FIFA or Real Life?

The Qatar World Cup triggered joyous scenes across Argentina as Lionel Messi won sport's biggest prize. It was a sad game for the losing finalists, France – and not just on the pitch. Due to some sneakily-named videos, 40,000 French football fans discovered that the real-life matches they thought they were watching were actually taking place in *FIFA 23*! Trickster streaming websites launched YouTube videos with titles like 'Live Germany-Japan Group E', at the same time as the real matches. Thousands tuned in to see the action, complete with Vietnamese commentary. But a closer look revealed that these were *FIFA* contests, rather than actual football!

Sonic's Lore Keeper

Sonic is officially old. How do we know this? Because Sega has hired a *Sonic the Hedgehog* 'lore master'! The new king of all things blue and spiky has to keep track of the characters and historical stories in the *Sonic* universe. They'll make sure that future games, books, movies and TV shows maintain accuracy and consistency. It's not just about the past, though. *Sonic*'s new gatekeeper also gets to brainstorm ideas for the series going forwards!

Teyvat Pizza Delivery

Genshin Impact wins the (unofficial) award for the year's craziest crossover. It teamed up with Pizza Hut for a range of cheesy content. Literally! Participating restaurants in China served fresh slices on plates featuring popular characters Eula and Amber. Meal deals also contained codes for pizza-themed furniture and other goodies within *Genshin Impact*. There was merch too, with the characters shown holding pizza on mouse pads and tote bags! It was the game's second collaboration with a real food company. In 2021, Diluc and Noelle appeared on chicken buckets at Chinese branches of KFC!

From Gamecube to Reality

It's not often that a pro sportsperson admits to learning their skills in games. NASCAR driver Ross Chastain did exactly that when he set the fastest lap record at Martinsville Speedway. He drove the whole lap clinging to the wall in fifth gear – a trick he learned on Nintendo! "I played a lot of *NASCAR 2005* on the Gamecube with [my brother] Chad growing up, and you can get away with it," he told NBC Sports. "I never knew if it would actually work." It did – as Chastain zoomed around in 18.845 seconds!

UNCHARTED TERRITORY

Naughty Dog

■ One of the best named studios is home to one of the all-time great games. Naughty Dog released *Uncharted* in 2007 but the studio's history goes back to 1984. Its first ever game was an education programme called *Maths Jam*! The California studio finally hit the big time in 1996 with PS1 classic *Crash Bandicoot*. As for that name? It was inspired by a sunglasses-wearing hound that founder Jason Gavin used to doodle when we wasn't working!

Iconic Moment

All-time-classic action-adventure *Uncharted 2: Among Thieves* made you fall in love with Drake, Sully, Ellie and Chloe for life.

Biggest Series:
Uncharted

PS3 exclusive *Uncharted: Drake's Fortune* astounded gamers upon release. Sequels *Among Thieves* and *Drake's Deception* were even more incredible. Set-pieces, storytelling, relic-hunting and character development all rivalled *Tomb Raider* in its heyday. All are worth revisiting on PS4 with *The Nathan Drake Collection*.

Have You Played?

Crash Bandicoot **Jak 3** **Uncharted 3: Drake's Deception** **The Last Of Us**

CALIFORNIA LOVE

CALIFORNIA LOVE
Insomniac Games

■ Insomniac and fellow Sony studio Naughty Dog work so closely together that the original *Ratchet & Clank* was built on the engine for Naughty Dog's *Jak & Daxter: The Precursor Legacy*! Insomniac also wowed the world with one of the earliest PlayStation mascots *Spyro the Dragon*. When the PS3 dropped, they changed their style with crazy shooter series *Resistance*. More recently, you'll know it best for essential PS5 open-world game *Spider-Man: Miles Morales*. Not a bad history!

Bestseller
For two decades *Spyro the Dragon* was Insomniac's biggest hit, selling 4.8 million copies. PS4 adventure *Spider-Man* smashed those numbers – eventually passing 20 million!

Biggest Series:
Ratchet & Clank

The live-wire lombax and his robot sidekick debuted on PS2 in 2002. Its blend of platforming, puzzle solving and funky gadgets were an instant hit. In the two decades since, it's constantly reinvented itself, and got better with every game. 2021's *Rift Apart* was even more fun, introducing new playable character Rivet, and mixing familiar planets with stunning new ones.

Have You Played?

Resistance 3

Sunset Overdrive

Spider-Man: Miles Morales

Ratchet & Clank: Rift Apart

Console Catch Up

What's New With Xbox?

THE BIG DAY > Xbox Series X launched on 10 November 2020. A whopping thirty-one games appeared in the Xbox Series X/S launch line-up, including *Forza Horizon 4, Sea of Thieves* and *Fortnite*.

■ Xbox Series X is the most powerful console ever made! It's capable of processing 12 trillion operations per second, making it eight times more powerful than the Xbox One. Microsoft's black box basically gives you all the goodness of a strong gaming PC, from the comfort of your sofa. And with Xbox Game Pass, you might never leave it again!

Rectangular Spectacular

While PS5 looks like a miniature spaceship, Xbox Series X keeps things simple. It's a sleek, tidy black cuboid. The only detail is a vent at one end, with a green interior. Despite the straightforward appearance, this is a beastly machine. Exclusives like *Halo Infinite* and *Forza Motorsport* look incredible, and show off that super-strong processing power. Xbox Game Pass offers up a rotating list of must-play games too.

The Xbox Series X controller is very different from PS5's DualSense. It feels traditional, that means there's no haptic feedback. However, the controller can be used across all Xbox consoles, as well as PCs – and Android phones! Xbox Series S is a genius invention, too. It's the perfect machine for those on a budget, and with a smaller living room shelf! Games are digital-only (so you don't have to find space for them), and it's less powerful than the X console – but it's around £200 cheaper, and those exclusives still play brilliantly!

Pass Master

There's no gaming subscription service quite like Xbox Game Pass. Loads of new games are available on it from the day they come out. Subscribers got to play recent favourites *Return to Monkey Island* and *Teenage Mutant Ninja Turtles: Shredder's Revenge* at launch, without spending an extra penny. And there are always at least 200 other games to try, too!

Some games do get rotated out of the catalogue, but even that isn't the end of the world. You can choose to buy the game while it's still on Xbox Game Pass for a 20% discount. Even if you don't, your progress is saved. That means if it comes back to Game Pass, or you decide to buy it later on, you can pick up right where you left off!

Did You Know?

Before being announced, the two machines were known together as Project Scarlett. Anaconda was the codename for XBX, while XBS was called Lockhart!

Top 5 Xbox Series X Exclusives

Forza Motorsport

A gorgeous reboot of the 2005 classic. It handles superbly, looks spectacular and offers an incredible roster of cars too. Jump in a brand-new Porsche 911 GT3, or zoom around in a 1958 Aston Martin DBR1!

Halo Infinite

The sixth game in Master Chief's shooter series. Campaign mode lets you roam Zeta Halo as the big guy, rescuing marines and smashing enemy towers. And, for the first time ever, online modes are free-to-play!

Sea of Thieves

Take to the high seas and plunder all rivals in this swashbuckling adventure! Going solo is fun, but building alliances is one of the best bits. Together you can go fishing, cook or even play musical instruments!

Grounded

It's 1990 and four teenagers have been shrunk to the size of ants. You need to pick one and survive in a backyard packed with bugs and insects! Spiders are the scariest enemy. But don't worry! There's a specific setting to help those with arachnophobia.

Ori and the Will of the Wisps

A Metroidvania platformer with masses of jumping, climbing and swimming. Guardian spirit Ori gets separated from sister Ku, and a sparkling – and heart-breaking! – tale unfolds. It's both emotional and unmissable!

Xbox Series X's Predecessors

Xbox

Microsoft's first console was released in 2001 in America, and 2002 everywhere else. It was unveiled to the world by Dwayne 'The Rock' Johnson! It transformed online gaming, especially shooters, with Xbox Live – which made games like *Halo 2* essential.

Xbox 360

The 2005 launch line-up for this one was phenomenal. *Call of Duty 2, Project Gotham Racing 3, Peter Jackson's King Kong, Tony Hawk's American Wasteland*: there was something for everyone. As well as those treats, it was the first console to give us in-game achievements.

Xbox One

This was intended as an all-in-one entertainment system. Hence the name! While some enjoyed its ability to sync with social media, most loved it for the games on offer. *Halo 5: Guardians, Forza Motorsport 5* and *Cuphead* were all must-owns on XBO.

FIFA 23

Developer EA Vancouver **Publisher** EA Sports
Platform NS, PC, PS4, PS5, XBO, XBX/S **Rating** PEGI 3+

■ EA's final ever *FIFA* game made history. Not just in ending a thirty-year partnership with the worldwide football association. There were huge on-field additions too! For the first time ever, *FIFA 23* includes women's clubs. You can use sides from the English Women's Super League and French Division 1 Féminine.

Slow and Steady

The action is less aggressive than in previous games. This is helped by a handy new movement system. Every one of the game's 19,000 pros is labelled with one of three acceleration types. Balanced players are your standard style of footballer. Explosive players burst into a sprint, but gradually slow down. Lengthy players take longer to get up to top speed, but can then maintain it. It's these guys who are most popular, given that they're generally tall and powerful – like Virgil van Dijk and Erling Haaland!

From the looks of it, *EA Sports FC* will be bringing a load of innovations to the footballing market. Most of them had roots in the highly playable FIFA series.

New Positions

Card-collecting mode Ultimate Team gets a welcome refresh in *FIFA 23*. The chemistry system, which rewards you for using players from the same team, nation, or league, is kinder. It's scored out of thirty-three rather than 100, and no longer forces you to line those players up next to each other. Position Modifier cards are brilliant, too. You can switch pros to their real-life positions, rather than shunt them up and down the pitch. So Joao Cancelo can easily move from RB to LB, or back again. Phew!

Back of the net! Unique camera angles give players a view from behind the goal.

89 RB
JOÃO CANCELO
86 PAC 86 DRI
75 SHO 82 DEF
86 PAS 75 PHY

Play as Real Madrid or any of the other 700 teams on the roster.

Use the mini-map to track your whole team during a match.

Gooooaaaaaaaaal! Celebrate your wins like Messi!

There are over 100 stadiums to play in, including the Lusail Stadium, where the World Cup final was held.

Iconic Inclusions

Three new icons join the *FIFA 23* roster, taking it to ninety-eight legends in total.

GERD MÜLLER

Germany's 1974 World Cup winner is one of the game's best strikers. He hammered 365 goals in 427 Bundesliga matches for Bayern Munich!

XABI ALONSO

The Spain legend returns, having last appeared in *FIFA 17*. A favourite at Liverpool, Real Madrid and Bayern Munich, his 87-rated base card purrs with quality.

JAIRZINHO

Many consider Pele the greatest player ever. Jairzinho was part of the same team that won the 1970 World Cup. He scored thirty-three goals in eighty-eight Brazil games.

Check Out

Prefer to focus on tactics and transfers than on-pitch skill moves? The timeless *Football Manager 2023* is as great as ever.

With FIFA 23's new mechanics, taking penalty kicks feels more dynamic.

Football is flying high, play as teams from Women's Super League and Division 1 Féminine.

Football is Life

Career mode options don't stop at your favourite real world teams! Fans of the hit Apple TV+ comedy *Ted Lasso* have the chance to play as AFC Richmond's most cheerful manager. As well as Lasso and Coach Beard, fan faves Roy Kent, Sam Obisanya and Jamie Tartt have all been carefully created for the game, plus all the other players that viewers have come to love and their home turf at Nelson Road.

THE HISTORY OF FIFA

Remembering Thirty Years of the Biggest Football Series Ever

FIFA very nearly wasn't called FIFA! Ahead of its launch in 1993, some EA bosses wanted it to have a different name in North America. It would have been *Team USA Soccer*. But the lead designer Bruce McMillan fought the change and the world's biggest sports series was born.

Skipper's Armband

These days the game is famous for Ultimate Team, but that mode wasn't introduced until *FIFA 09*. It was paid-for DLC. You still played with elite players, but only after creating yourself as captain of the team! Back then there were also exciting boost cards that increased player speed, or made refs more lenient.

Before FIFA Ultimate Team in the more recent games from the series, Career mode was the main focus. It was super creative, too. In *FIFA 97*, an indoor mode was added, this would go on to inspire *FIFA Street* and the modern Volta mode. *FIFA 99* featured a European Dream League, where the twenty best teams on the continent tussled for a fictional trophy!

Did You Know?
Spin-off games include PS1 effort *FA Premier League Stars*, which focused on the English top players, and sidelines sim *FIFA Manager*. That second one ran from 1997 to 2013!

Gooaaaaal

● *FIFA 23* icon Ronaldo didn't always have such a strong relationship with EA. In *FIFA 2000* his name was just No. 9!

● At 111 million copies, *FIFA* holds the Guinness World Record for the bestselling sports video game franchise.

● Chelsea and Australia striker Sam Kerr made history on *FIFA 23*, becoming the series' first female cover star.

Glossary

Isometric: A style of view that means something looks 3D, even when drawn in 2D!

Four Unforgettable FIFAs

FIFA International Soccer

EA's first football game dropped on the Mega Drive with sixteen days of 1993 to spare – but still managed to be the year's bestseller! Its isometric viewpoint astonished even veteran fans. Seventy-six national teams featured, with fictional names. Most of the England team were named after the developers!

FIFA 07

The PS2 game where *FIFA* began to win over fans who'd worshipped *Pro Evolution Soccer* for half a decade. Ball physics were completely reworked, to make it a separate game mechanic from players. Previously it felt stuck to their feet. It sold one million more copies than the previous *FIFA 06*.

FIFA 11

When the PS3 was huge, the series unleashed a Creation Centre. Using an online browser, you could create your own teams and import them into the game! From Liverpool 1979 to Sunday League United, the possibilities were endless. It's one of FIFA's most-missed features.

FIFA 23

The series' last game adds domestic women's teams for the first time (international ones arrived in 2015). Slowed-down gameplay speed and new changes to Ultimate Team, like revised chemistry, make for a spectacular last release in the series.

Top Tips

Pack your defence with 'Pick Artists' and 'Acrobats'. It'll make sure you get to have a ton of interceptions.

Madden NFL 23

Developer EA Tiburon **Publisher** EA Sports
Platform PC, PS4, PS5, XBO, XBX/S **Rating** PEGI 3+

■ *Madden 23* pays tribute to the man who gave the series its name. Legendary Raiders coach and commentator John Madden passed away in December 2021. EA put his likeness on the cover, and included a special one-off mode. The John Madden Legacy game pits two teams of his favourite players against one another. It takes place in California's Oakland Coliseum, where the great man forged his legacy. There's even a superb half-time tribute.

Field of Schemes

Elsewhere the American football sim looks to emulate reality with FieldSense. This new mechanic gives quarterbacks an aiming system, and runners can change direction much more naturally. The development team also made extensive improvements to gameplay elements, like run-blocking and line play. *Madden 23* Franchise mode, where you manage a team, gets welcome upgrades too. One of those is that you need to take a player's personality into account when trying to sign them. Some will only join if you play in a tax-free area of the USA, so choose wisely!

Touchdown! You'll be tackling opponents and cheering along in no time.

Add Tyreek Hill, Tom Brady and Zack Martin to your line, as well as many more pros.

NBA 2K23

Developer Visual Concepts **Publisher** 2K
Platform PC, NS, PS4, PS5, XBO, XBX/S **Rating** PEGI 3+

■ **The undisputed king of the court! This year, fans of NBA are stacked for options. In MyCareer, you take on a new pro, with a cunning twist: everyone hates him! So the storyline tasks you with upgrading his popularity along with his skills. If you don't fancy that, you can go back in time to sample MyNBA Eras. This new mode lets you pretend the past never happened. You can take over a team from either 1983, 1991, or 2002, and rewrite history with different signings and results.**

Hoop, There It Is

Character designs are a slam dunk in NBA 2K23. Tattoos, hairstyles and facial likenesses all look just like what you see on TV in this officially licensed b-baller. *NBA 2K23* also does women's sport better than any other game. You can play a full season as female pro teams. Or use The W Online mode to complete community goals specific to the women's game.

Nothing but net! Phoenix Sun's Devin Booker is just one of the real-life players.

Check Out

NHL 23 provides ice hockey with a twist, as female players get added to Ultimate Team for the first time!

Play WNBA's All-Star and Commissioner's Cup games.

Take on the Jordan Challenge and play through memorable moments.

Hole in One
⊕ EA's previous golf game was 2015's *Rory McIlroy PGA Tour*. The series started out in 1990! It had three real courses and a fourth fictional one called Sterling Shores. The computer version was so popular, it was ported to every console imaginable over the next four years!

EA Sports PGA Tour

Developer EA Tiburon **Publisher** EA
Platform PC, PS5, XBX/S **Rating** PEGI 3+

Background | After an eight-year break, EA golf games are back! This series is considered a 1990s classic, and gave us the amazing PS2- and PS3-era *Tiger Woods* games too. This is the first entry in the series not to be named after a real golfer since *PGA Tour 98*!

Features | *PGA Tour* is exclusive to current-gen. As a result, it's the prettiest golf game ever. It contains thirty courses, including all four Majors: The Masters, PGA Championship, U.S Open and The Open Championship. The women's Evian Championship is included too.

Gameplay | Every single shot in *PGA Tour* takes in three separate factors! They are backswing length, speed of follow through, and each player's individual attributes. It sounds complex but feels natural after a few rounds. Real pros include Jordan Spieth and Scottie Scheffler, and they all handle uniquely.

Take in some of the prettiest scenery around the courses as you swing!

Try out the range of pros, from Abraham Ancer to Xander Schauffele.

Check Out
Prefer your pitching and putting a bit more casual? Mario Golf: Super Rush lets you swing away with Luigi, Toad and Princess Peach!

PGA Tour 2K23 added a new course in their update. Top of the Rock is set on Table Rock Lake.

Another real-life location, Topgolf in Las Vegas gives players the chance to test their skills at the driving range.

PGA Tour 2K23

Developer HB Studios **Publisher** 2K
Platform PC, PS4, PS5, XBO, XBX/S **Rating** PEGI 3+

Background | *PGA Tour 2K21* offered a compelling round of golf, with one bizarre caveat. Elite players were included, but only as AI rivals! It'd be like buying *FIFA* but being banned from using Messi or Ronaldo [Ronal-doh!]. This follow-up unlocked real golfers for use across twenty courses.

Features | Tiger Woods once had his own gaming series, so his inclusion here is a big deal. MyCareer is all about creating a player with one of five archetypes, then steering them to golfing glory – while wearing gear from Air Jordan, Hugo Boss and Nike. There's an entire Online Society to compete against too.

Gameplay | Ball physics are incredibly lifelike, whether you're aiming a 300-yard drive or sinking a putt on a bumpy green. Swinging with the analogue stick feels authentic too. For old-school fans, there's a new three-click control system. This is tough to master – prepare to put a lot of balls in bunkers as you learn.

The Perfect Game

◉ Most 2K games are made by Californian developer Visual Concepts. This one, however, is the baby of Canadian team HB Studios – who scored club-swinging fame with predecessor *The Golf Club*. Prior to that they made EA Sports' much-missed *Rugby* and *Cricket* series!

Expert Tip

It's really hard to hit balls that dip before they reach you. To combat this, switch away from the default camera angle and instead try Strike Zone 2.

Back in the Day

The series began in August 1997 as a PS1 exclusive. Back then, Sony also made sports games centred on football (*NFL GameDay*), hockey (*NHL FaceOff*) and basketball (*NBA ShootOut 98*)!

MLB The Show 23

Developer San Diego Studio **Publisher** Sony / MLB Advanced Media **Platform** NS, PS4, PS5, XBO, XBX/S **Rating** PEGI 3+

■ *MLB The Show 21* made history two years ago. It was the first ever Sony game released on Xbox! The series evolved again twelve months later, landing on a Nintendo machine for the first time.

Whatever console you pick, there's masses of baseball to enjoy. You can control every match and trade over loads of seasons. Or just jump into a team's key moments in March to October mode! Diamond Dynasty is The Show's Ultimate Team equivalent – building a dream team using digital cards starring past and present greats.

Pitch Perfect

The Show 23 nails all the fundamentals of real baseball. Pitching is all about variety, mixing your speeds and direction. Fielding can be challenging, so try setting it to automatic! Batting is pure fun, especially when launching home runs deep into the crowd. It's wonderfully tactile, so you really feel those huge hits.

Play as your favourite team. Pick from thirty different MLB options, including the Yankees.

Using the overview mechanic, players can perfect their batting.

Undisputed

Developer Steel City Interactive **Publisher** Steel City Interactive
Platform PC **Rating** PEGI 16+

■ The eternal wait for a beastly boxing game is finally over! Following in the footsteps of classics likes *Fight Night*, *Undisputed* lets you battle fifty power-packing prize-fighters. All-time icon Muhammad Ali is in, and so are modern faves Jessica McCaskill and Tyson Fury!

Duck and Move

Undisputed is all about simulating the real boxing experience. There are more than sixty different punches, but footwork is also a big focus. That means feinting and moving around your opponent is just as important as learning how to launch a hefty haymaker.

Steel City Interactive deliberately launched the game on Steam first. The plan was to use fan feedback from the early access game to perfect the console versions, which would be released later. Loads of real boxing organisations jumped on board, like apparel brands Empire and Cleto Reyes. As a result, their gear can be used in the game, too!

And in this corner ... choose from over fifty fighters, including current boxers and timeless legends.

Undisputed *doesn't just feature real-world boxers, check out the real-world branded t-shirts and rings.*

The game features a women's boxing division, giving players the chance to take on their fave female boxers.

Noob Tip

While the game launched on PC, it doesn't support keyboard or mouse controls. So be sure to own a decent controller if you're planning a Saturday night slugfest!

1

STATE OF PLAY
Console Catch Up
What's New With Switch?

JOY TO THE WORLD
> *Animal Crossing, Fortnite* and *Dragon Quest* have all released limited edition Joy-Cons over the years. The rarest are themed on *Pokémon: Let's Go Pikachu & Eevee*. These sell for £150 on eBay!

■ Nintendo's portable player was a game changer! You can play it on a TV screen, or take it out of its holder to use on the move. It's packed with must-own games, most of them featuring a certain dungaree-wearing plumber! Yep, you can even sneak in a quick *Mario Kart 8* race while sitting on the loo. Just remember to wash your hands!

Making Exercise Fun
Switch really does have a game for everyone. *Splatoon 3, Mario Party Superstars* and *Just Dance 2023 Edition* are the recent additions to its family friendly line-up. *Pokémon Scarlet & Violet* and *Kirby and the Forgotten Land* also offer addictive co-op play. And it's better than

any other console for self-improvement. *Ring Fit Adventure* and *Big Brain Academy: Brain vs. Brain* will give both your body and your mind a fun workout!

Accessories are one of Switch's best features. Joy-Con controllers come in every colour of the rainbow – and you can pair them up however you like! The Switch Pro Controller is for those who want a more traditional experience on games, like *The Legend of Zelda: Breath of the Wild*. There's a Joy-Con leg strap, which is best enjoyed when playing football in *Switch Sports*. You can even get an official Pikachu headset, for when you want to keep the awesome soundtracks all to yourself!

UK's Number One

Nintendo Switch was the biggest-selling console in the UK in 2022! The total number of sales is top secret, but we know it was 60,000 more than Xbox Series X. (PS5 finished second.) Given the power of Microsoft and Sony's machines, it's a huge achievement for Mario and co. Well done, guys!

Switch's appeal to kids and adults alike was clearly a major reason for these huge sales. Three Pokémon games featured in the top twenty of the year: *Violet*, *Scarlet* and *Pokémon Legends: Arceus*! The Switch edition of *Minecraft* also made the big chart, alongside *Nintendo Switch Sports* and *Mario Kart 8 Deluxe*. With a line-up like that, it's going to have a storming future, too.

Did You Know?

The Switch was released in March 2017. As well as the normal console, you can get an OLED Switch with an even sharper screen – and the Switch Lite, which is a portable-only version. An option for everyone!

NINTENDO SWITCH™

Top 5 Nintendo Switch Exclusives

Mario Kart 8 Deluxe

Forty-eight tracks of red-shelling, banana-dropping fun. The racing is as great as it's ever been, and you get more characters than ever before. New characters King Boo, Dry Bones and Bowser Jr take the number of playable drivers to thirty-six!

The Legend of Zelda: Breath of the Wild

As Link, you'll lose hours and then days climbing, soaring and exploring the regions of Hyrule, as you battle enemies in the search for Princess Zelda. It's a colossal open-world adventure and one of the most gorgeous games ever.

Nintendo Switch Sports

Take down your family at one of seven sports, including football, bowling and golf! Each one uses the Joy-Con differently. You pretend it's a racquet for tennis and badminton, but wield it like a sword in chambara!

Super Mario Odyssey

Mario gets a new ally in this must-play platformer. It's a hat called Cappy! This clever headwear can be used to possess enemies and objects, helping to solve puzzles. With seventeen kingdoms to explore, it's as massive as it is magnificent!

Animal Crossing: New Horizons

The island getaway that's essential for all ages. It's a life sim you play in real-time, crafting, fishing and building a miniature community of characterful creatures. Seasonal items for events, like Toy Day (Christmas!), mean it's forever evolving, too.

Nintendo Switch's Predecessors

NES

Nintendo's first console launched in 1983. You know it as the Nintendo Entertainment System, but in Japan it was called the Family Computer (FC). This was soon shortened to Famicom. *Super Mario Bros*, *The Legend of Zelda* and *Metroid* all started out on NES.

N64

There's much more on the Super Nintendo elsewhere in this book, so we've skipped straight to its successor. The *Time* magazine named this Machine of the Year in 1996! Everyone remembers it for Bond game *Goldeneye* – one of the best shooters ever made.

Gamecube

The turn of the century saw Nintendo announce the Dolphin. Thankfully its name was changed to the Gamecube! There was no *Mario* at launch, but *Luigi's Mansion* and *Super Monkey Ball* still made day-one buyers happy. *Super Smash Bros. Melee* is the console's bestselling game.

Wii

The console that brought motion-control to the masses. And started Nintendo's love of clever accessories! The Wii Wheel and Nunchuck were both essential. Everyone had a chunky Wii Balance Board too – and to this day no-one has found the ideal place to store it!

Roguelike

Your Guide to the Gaming Genre

■ Before the rise of home computers in the 1980s, RPGs were limited to your living room floor or kitchen table. *Dungeons & Dragons* was king, creating a turn-based world where players evolved a character, unearthed items and slayed enemies. Technology eventually allowed these adventures to go digital, and the roguelike genre was born.

Crawl or Nothing

A key feature, as with *Dungeons & Dragons* and 1990s fave *Hero Quest*, is that your character can die. Forever. Fail to protect their health and you're forced to start again from scratch. As a rule, you start your dungeon crawl with basic weapons, upgrading your arsenal through play. Usually there are additional skills or spells to help you on your journey.

Roguelikes are especially popular among indie devs, with procedurally generated levels on-trend. 2D platformer *Spelunky* was a major influence. Derek Yu made it alone, but its tunnel-exploring, treasure-grabbing gameplay and severe difficulty earned worldwide acclaim — and copycats!

Glossary

Procedurally Generated: Using computer power and an element of randomness to create something unplanned! You won't replay the same levels again and again.

DIY Dungeons

An annual community competition invites fans to create a roguelike in one week. It's called The 7 Day Roguelike Challenge (7DRL Challenge), and had a massive 198 entries in 2022.

was inspired by a text-based *Star Trek* game from 1971!

Top 5 Roguelike Games to Play Right Now

Dicey Dungeons

A popular twist on the genre is combining traditional elements with deck-building. *Dicey Dungeons* is a cute example. You fight monsters and gather health to unlock characters and equipment – these help you fight bigger monsters and gather more health!

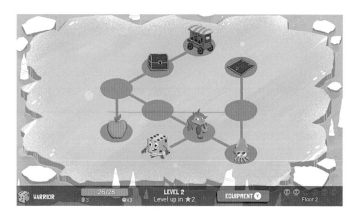

Spelunky 2

Derek Yu's super sequel contains all the best bits of the first adventure, like every play offering fresh challenges and paths. But it expands too. Four-way multiplayer is particularly riotous. Prepare your apologies now for when you accidentally KO your best mate!

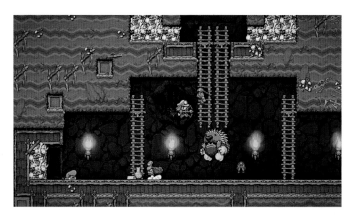

Enter The Gungeon

Still highly playable half a decade after release. As a Marine, Convict, Hunter or Pilot you need to find a magical gun that can 'kill the past'. Best weapons include a rocket launcher called the Stinger, and all-powerful Vulcan Cannon, which can decimate entire rooms!

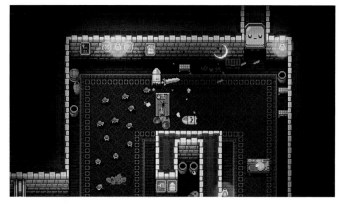

Hades

This tale of the Underworld is available on every format imaginable. As Zagreus, you need to escape one bad parent (Hades) to reach a kind one (Persephone). A neat feature for novice players is God Mode, where the game gets slightly easier every time you die.

Dreamscaper

A wonderful adventure of two halves. In the daytime you chat to people around town and upgrade your stats. After dark you enter your nightmares, dungeon crawling as a powerful dream warrior. Be warned that those bits can get super creepy!

REWIND TO ...

2004

What Games Were Big Twenty Years Ago?

■ 2004 gave us Green Day's *American Idiot* album, Megan Fox's film debut in *Confessions of a Drama Queen*, and ... *Peppa Pig*. You can be the judge over that last one! On the gaming front, it was all gold, with the PS2 at the peak of its powers, and Microsoft's first Xbox hot on its tails.

Half-Life 2

This Valve classic cost $40 million, as the studio looked to reinvent the shooter genre. It did so in style! Intelligent enemies forced gamers to play tactically rather than blast everything that moved. The tests for your grey matter didn't end there. Realistic physics meant you had to consider an item's shape and weight before completing puzzles. There were no cut-scenes: you controlled Gordon Freeman in his rebellion against an alien empire all the way through.

Halo 2

Sega, Nintendo and Sony dominated gaming during the 1990s. This shooter was the first (huge) sign that Microsoft was gatecrashing the big boys. It's the bestselling game ever on the original Xbox, having sold 8 million! *Halo 2* also set the standard for online elements we take for granted now, like matchmaking and lobbies. Oh, and it cemented Master Chief as a hero for the ages. Breathtaking, bombastic and brilliant.

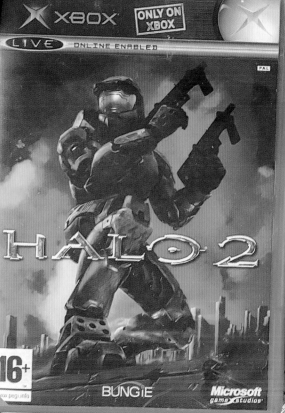

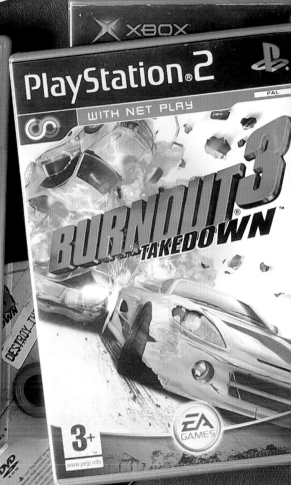

Gran Turismo 4

Seriously serious driving with all manner of top-drawer licences. It had 721 cars from eighty manufacturers, all with accurate dynamics under the hood. If you owned a decent steering wheel, it really felt like piloting an Audi R8 or BMW V12. A popular feature was Photo mode, where you could pose your car in cool locations – like the Grand Canyon! It's still the third bestselling PS2 game ever, only beaten by *GTA: San Andreas* and *Gran Turismo 3*.

BIGGEST-SELLING GAMES OF 2004

01. GTA: San Andreas
Publisher Rockstar

02. Pokémon FireRed & LeafGreen
Publisher The Pokémon Company

03. FIFA 2005
Publisher EA

04. Halo 2
Publisher Microsoft

05. Madden NFL 2005
Publisher EA

06. Dragon Quest VIII
Publisher Square Enix

07. ESPN NFL 2K5
Publisher 2K

08. PES 4
Publisher Konami

09. Need For Speed Underground 2
Publisher EA

10. Pokémon Emerald
Publisher The Pokémon Company

A Solid Year

2004 is considered one of the most important years in gaming history. As well as the hits highlighted here, there was also Metal Gear Solid 3: Snake Eater, Monster Hunter, SingStar, Far Cry and the launch of the Nintendo DS. Crazy!

Burnout 3: Takedown

Gran Turismo sound too hardcore? This would have been the driving game for you. *Burnout 3* was all about earning boost with crazy manoeuvres – then slamming into other vehicles to increase your chances of winning! It was a case of 'careful what you wish for' though. AI drivers upped their aggression each time you tried to nudge them into oblivion, adding a risk-reward mechanic.

Metroid

Metroid Prime 2: Echoes featured series classics, like a space-based story, alien enemies and devilish puzzles. It was also the first Metroid with multiplayer. To promote it, Nintendo created clever in-universe websites. Channel 51 was a conspiracy theory site with grainy videos!

139

The Best Gaming Merch

From funky trainers to Funko Pops, get these treats on your present list!

Playdate Console

This tiny console is a pocket rocket! It has a D-pad, two buttons, and a crank on the side. Games are released in seasons — and are free! — with two new ones automatically downloaded every week! In *Casual Birder* you take photos of winged wonders, using the crank to adjust focus.

Puma x Pokémon Trainers

Alright, that yellow is a little bit bold. You're not going to blend in wearing these. But style it out and you'll be the envy of all your mates! Puma's Pokémon shoes feature a sneaky lightning bolt, and Pikachu hanging off the side!

LEGO NES Set

The machine of the 1980s is now buildable in your own home! You build the TV, console, controller and game cartridge separately. Once that's done, you can plug the cart into the console! A lever on the side of the TV lets you move Mario across the screen. There are 2,646 pieces, with studs representing Goombas, Koopa shells and power-up mushrooms.

Paladone and Only

Paladone are one of the best merchants of merch! They offer something for everyone. You can get a heat-changing *Mario Kart* mug, PlayStation pen pot, Xbox playing cards and *Animal Crossing* logo light!

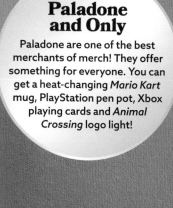

Stray X Travel Cat Backpack

Furry adventure *Stray* is the year's most creative game. Naturally, it's led to some creative merch – like an official backpack. This isn't for your gym kit or smelly football boots though. It's made to carry your cat! It comes in neon and charcoal, to reflect the visuals of the game, and can hold animals up to 11.3kg in weight.

Overwatch 2 Funko Pops

Loads of amazing games have been immortalised with Funko Pop vinyl figures. *Overwatch 2* is the latest! The first wave of characters includes Reaper and Cassidy. They're joined by two versions of Echo. Don't fancy her standard figure? Get the jumbo 25cm version instead! It looks fantastic, and glows in the dark too.

141

Ready to make a mess? Players can now take on tricolour turf war battles.

Check Out
Still own a Wii U? The first *Splatoon* is a great intro to squid life.

With tenta missiles and inkzookas, you're bound to have a ton of colourful fun!

Splatoon 3

Developer Nintendo **Publisher** Nintendo
Platform NS **Rating** PEGI 7+

■ This splat-tastic threequel is as messy as shooters get. There's no blood in sight, though. It's all about coating enemies in ink! You can do it in an offline story mode, or online against other goo-slingers. There's even a new card-collecting system called Tableturf Battle, which is basically *Splatoon* meets *FIFA* Ultimate Team.

Where It's Splat

There's loads to like for Inklings both new and old. The fresh setting of Splatsville provides a ton of alleys and warehouses to redecorate. And the story mode throws in sneaky puzzles for a change of pace. Fans of the first two games will enjoy a comforting sense of familiarity — both in the shootouts, and return of at least one very popular character (no spoilers!).

Co-op Salmon Runs are many fans' fave way to play. You and up to three teammates collect eggs and blast through waves of angry fish. It's intense but addictive, too. With none of the pain of having to mop up afterwards!

Give your friends a call and blast the ghasts as a team! Just watch out for whoever's playing as a ghost.

Play as a ghost and use their ghastly powers.

Squid flinging as a weapon? What next!

Ghostbusters:
Spirits Unleashed

Developer IllFonic **Publisher** IllFonic **Platform** PC, PS4, PS5, XBO, XBX/S **Rating** PEGI 12+

■ **Who ya gonna call? Your friends! A four-on-one multiplayer sounds like a mismatch. Until you discover that the 'one' gets to play as a ghost! You can fly, zoom through walls, and even possess NPCs as the four humans work together to hunt you down. It's a cool spin on a classic brand.**

spectral realm. All the old-school tools are at your fingertips when controlling a ghostbuster. You use a PKE meter to track ghosts, and a proton pack to capture them. You also need to consider distractions, such as keeping passing civilians calm, and teamwork. Five varied maps include a museum, prison and ship. It's slime time!

After Afterlife
Spirits Unleashed picks up following the events of the *Ghostbusters: Afterlife* film. Ray and Winston are back in business, after a force called the Nameless opens up a new rift into a

Shoot! Or be slimed! Winky's a little f-eye-sty.

Explore spooky locations like Firehouse HQ, Rock Island Prison or Whitestone Museum.

Haunted Hall of Fame
How many of these have you played?

GHOSTBUSTERS (1984)

GHOSTBUSTERS II (1989)

THE REAL GHOSTBUSTERS (1993)

GHOSTBUSTERS: THE VIDEO GAME (2009)

LEGO DIMENSIONS (2015)

Noob Tip
Every level has three rifts hidden in objects that allow the human-controlled ghost to respawn. Focus on destroying these before hunting the sneaky spook!

Overwatch 2

Developer Blizzard Entertainment **Publisher** Blizzard Entertainment
Platform NS, PC, PS4, PS5, XBO, XBX/S **Rating** PEGI 12+

Tracer's dual blasters pack a hefty punch.

■ It's all change in this super shooter sequel – and in the best way possible!
Teams of five strive to survive in online combat. That's one less than in the
original *Overwatch*. Smaller squads make the gameplay speedier than ever,
as players blast, bomb and slice their way to victory. Best of all, unlike the
original game, it's free-to-play!

All your favourite soldiers, scientists and cyborgs have been freshened up.
Doomfist switches from being a damage hero to a tank, with his rocket punch and
seismic slam causing massive damage. Orisa receives a big overhaul too. Her base
health and armour are boosted from 200 to 275, and her new secondary weapon is
the energy javelin. It's a spear that both stuns its target and deals sixty damage!

Team up with three other heroes when fighting tougher enemies, or hordes.

Basics of the 'Watch

If you've never played the *Overwatch* series, it's all about working as a unit to
balance out offence and defence. Teams are split into three classes. There are
two damage characters who focus on attacking enemies. Two support teammates
handle healing and buffing. And the lone tank aims to protect the rest of
the team. It's the perfect blend of strategy and anarchy!

Fast Starter

An astonishing 25 million gamers played *Overwatch 2* in its first ten days of release!

Explore the Esperança map with Lúcio.

Omnics are dangerous foes if you're caught.

Overwatch Overview

The four main modes explained...

Control

Classic *Overwatch*, basically! Two teams of five players work together to seize a single objective point. The first to win two out of three rounds wins.

Escort

Players need to guide a payload to its goal while opponents try to demolish it. It's a different item in every location. In New York, it's a fire truck, while for Monte Carlo, it's a Turbotron race car!

Hybrid

A mixture of Control and Escort. First you need to fight for control of an area. Then the attackers have to deliver their payload, while the defenders aim to take them down.

Push

The hot new mode for *Overwatch 2*! Two teams fight to guide a robot to their opponent's base. Whoever gets closest wins. Lisbon's Esperança map is fab for this!

Reinhardt's mighty rocket hammer is his primary weapon against enemies.

Popular character Lúcio returns as a support hero in Overwatch 2.

Titanic Beginnings

What you know as *Overwatch* started out as *Titan*! Blizzard wanted to make a class-based shooter. It spent six years on *Titan*, building a sci-fi blaster set on Earth. But it wasn't happy. So, in 2013, *Titan* was cancelled. Forty members of the team took the original assets, and started to build *Overwatch* instead. Finally, in May 2016, that game smashed onto PC, PS4 and Xbox One. A new shooter phenomenon was born!

Mei's endothermic blaster is ice cold!

Tracer's iconic orange shades can be bought!

Kiriko the support hero sends her kitsune spirit out to help.

Maps of Mayhem

Overwatch 2 is all about the maps. They're a brilliant hybrid of fiction and reality. In Rome, you can fight in and around the Colosseum, while F1 fans will love the race track running through Monte Carlo. New York is especially popular. It's got police cars, yellow taxis and a pizza parlour. Oh, and Grand Central Station! New ones are always arriving too. Season 2 added the atmospheric Shambali Monastery. Its Himalayan setting is breathtaking. That doesn't stop Escort battles turning it into carnage!

Noob Tip

Individual glory is pointless here, so don't just wade in! Use the new Ping system to chat with your teammates, swap instructions and tactics. There's no i in team – or *Overwatch 2!*

Actual rockets are what give the hammer its punch.

Head out into the city on missions and win battles.

Trash Talk

Love the banter in the first game? Then be very happy. *Overwatch 2* features 44,000 new lines of fresh chat!

The colossal ships are dramatic backdrops to your battles.

Ramattra's energy swarm is an impressive power.

Best new Heroes

Kiriko

The newest support hero grew up alongside Shimada brothers Hanzo and Genji. She can wall climb, teleport and rush opponents. Kiriko proved to be an instant hit. Fans unleashed her kitsune rush ability more than two million times in the game's first week!

Ramattra

Season 2's big newcomer. Ramattra is the first tank who can change form as part of his core kit. In omnic form, he uses the void accelerator to fire a stream of projectiles. Switch to nemesis form, and every punch creates a wave of deadly energy. It makes him super tough to defend against!

Sojourn

Sojourn rivals Genji for the best DPS (damage per second!) character going. Her charged overclock shots can take down opponents with brutal efficiency from any range. Handy given that mobility is one of her strongest features, with a truly badass power slide!

Junker Queen

Odessa 'Dez' Stone has ruled the Junker factions for more than a decade. Now the tank hero is taking on all rivals, and not just with weapons. Her commanding shout grants health and speed to allies! With her Aussie accent and champion attitude, she's *Overwatch*'s version of WWE star Rhea Ripley.

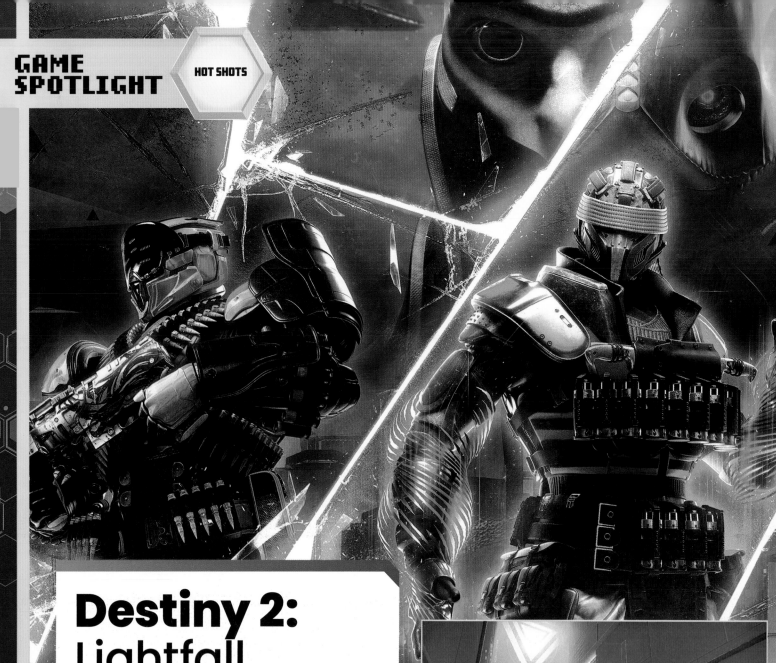

Destiny 2: Lightfall

Developer Bungie **Publisher** Bungie **Platform** PC, PS4, PS5, XBO, XBX/S **Rating** PEGI 16+

■ The seventh piece of *Destiny 2* DLC continues a storyline that began in 2017! In *Lightfall*, exiled emperor Calus storms the human city of Neomuna. He's after a mysterious device called the Veil. It's pretty important that the good-guy Cloud Striders protects it at all costs!

Lightfall, Calus, Action

Neomuna is based on the planet Neptune, and you can roam it at your leisure. Buddy character Nimbus helps steer you through the main campaign, dropping jokes and aiding you in battle. As ever, it's best played with two humans alongside you, working together to take down Calus' scythe-wielding Tormentors.

This is *Destiny*, though, so the fight doesn't end there! Even after finishing the campaign there's masses to do. *Lightfall* offers loads of new gear, fresh player vs player maps, and two new dungeons. Plus a new raid, called Root of Nightmares. Its bosses include Zo'Aurc, Explicator of Planets – and Nezarec, Final God of Pain!

Lightfall nails the futuristic locations. Explore beautifully-lit areas, like the Vex Network.

In the new Root of Nightmares raid, you'll infiltrate a pyramid ship that's almost been destroyed.

Check out the new gear in this DLC, players have extra fire power for the new enemies.

Strand Explained

Lightfall's most anticipated new feature was the new subclass. It's called strand, and is as great as everyone hoped! Strand is a new darkness power based on changing reality through manipulation. When Warlocks use it they can create minions who jump on enemies, then explode, while Hunters can unleash the arcane needle. This both tracks targets and unleashes vast damage when it connects! All classes also get a cool grapple hook to go leaping around Neomuna with, too.

What's Next?

The last piece of *Destiny 2* DLC, finishing off what Bungie calls 'The Light and Dark Saga', is coming in 2024. It's called *The Final Shape*!

Catching up with Destiny 2

If you've just started on *Destiny 2* then there's much to catch up on! Sadly, its early DLC packs have been shunted to the Destiny Content Vault. So there's no way to play *Curse of Osiris* or *Warmind*! But 2021's brilliant *Beyond Light* is still available. It's set on a moon of Jupiter and grants you awesome ice-based powers. 2022's *The Witch Queen* is much darker, and even better! This time, your Guardian needs to take down power-hungry hive god Savathûn. Most fans reckon it's the best bit of *Destiny* DLC ever!

Take on the Final God of Pain as you and your teammates tackle the additional raid, featuring a rotation of new challenges each week.

Try out aiming (and shooting!) in zero gravity.

Follow the very helpful Nimbus as he guides you around Neomuna's distinctly alien caverns, dungeons and ships.

STATE OF PLAY

The Bestselling Games of the Year

How Many Are In Your Collection?

Close Calls

Just missing out on the charts are *Red Dead Redemption 2*, *F1 22*, and *Assassin's Creed: Valhalla*. All three sold enough copies to make the European top twenty, but fell short of overtaking *Gran Turismo 7* in that precious final spot.

Japan

1. Pokémon Scarlet & Violet
2. Splatoon 3
3. Pokémon Legends: Arceus
4. Kirby and the Forgotten Land
5. Nintendo Switch Sports
6. Mario Kart 8 Deluxe
7. Minecraft
8. Mario Party Superstars
9. Super Smash Bros. Ultimate
10. Elden Ring

USA

1. Call of Duty: Modern Warfare 2
2. Elden Ring
3. Madden NFL 23
4. God of War: Ragnarök
5. LEGO Star Wars: The Skywalker Saga
6. Pokémon Scarlet & Violet
7. FIFA 23
8. Pokémon Legends: Arceus
9. Horizon Forbidden West
10. MLB The Show 22

Europe

1. FIFA 23
2. Call of Duty: Modern Warfare 2
3. Elden Ring
4. Grand Theft Auto 5
5. FIFA 22
6. Pokémon Legends: Arceus
7. God of War: Ragnarök
8. LEGO Star Wars: The Skywalker Saga
9. Horizon Forbidden West
10. Gran Turismo 7

Two games made the top ten in Japan, Europe and the USA. *Pokémon Legends: Arceus* and *Elden Ring* – and *Pokémon Scarlet & Violet* was very close! Unlike in Japan and the USA, Europe judged their sales separately, placing them 14th and 16th. Had they been combined they'd have taken 6th spot!

More games were sold in the UK than any other European nation. Just like in the Europe chart, *FIFA 23* finished top and *Call of Duty: Modern Warfare 2* second. But Brits love a block party – *LEGO Star Wars: The Skywalker Saga* was the UK's number three. Germany had the second most sales, then France.

America loves sports, with *Madden NFL 23*, *FIFA 23* and *MLB The Show 22* all making the top ten. Those numbers helped the *FIFA* series pass 260 million copies in its final ever year. *Madden*'s figures are massive too – it's sold 130 million since launching in 1990.

Splatoon 3 sold an incredible four million copies in Japan in its first two months on sale. Woah! That was enough for second spot on their chart. Last year, the entire Japanese top ten was made up of Switch games. The award-winning *Elden Ring* broke that record, slashing its way onto the elite list.

There was no new Nathan Drake game in 2022. That didn't stop the charming treasure hunter from smashing into the charts! The *Uncharted* movie finished tenth in the USA's sales rankings, just below *Encanto* and *Top Gun* – *Spider-Man: No Way Home* was number one. Not bad at all for a game spin-off!

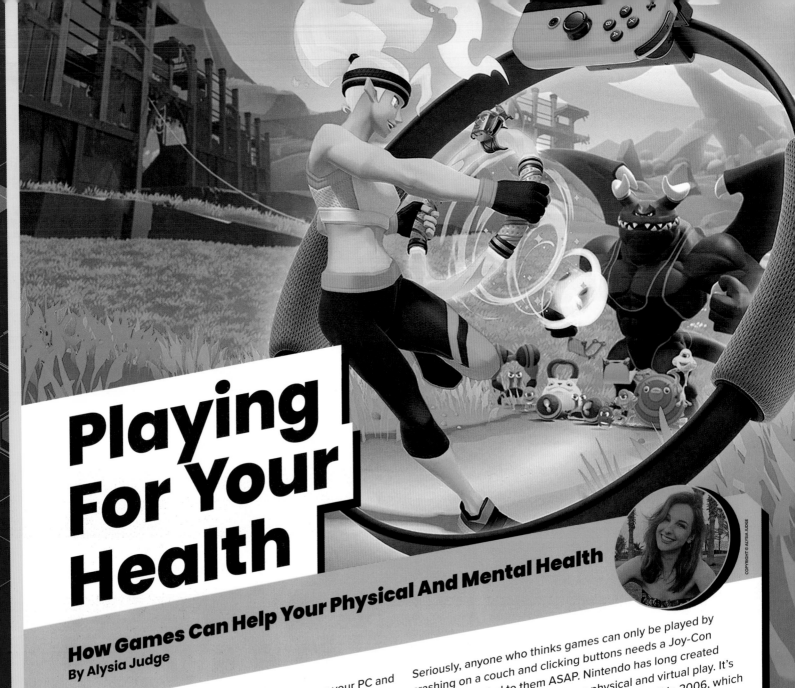

Playing For Your Health

How Games Can Help Your Physical And Mental Health
By Alysia Judge

■ At some point, someone has probably stood over your PC and asked in exasperation, "but why don't you go OUTSIDE?" Sadly, there are those who nurse the hard-baked belief that video games are a sedentary and solitary activity ... so imagine how rapidly their eyebrows shoot up to their hairlines when they find how good gaming can be for your physical and mental health.

Seriously, anyone who thinks games can only be played by crashing on a couch and clicking buttons needs a Joy-Con controller handed to them ASAP. Nintendo has long created games that blur the lines between physical and virtual play. It's developed accessories and consoles, like the Wii in 2006, which let us physically interact with our video games using motion controls – something that seems obvious now, but back then was a revolution!

Most recently, Nintendo created the *Ring Fit Adventure*. It's a game that comes with its own special controller that gets you moving and breaking a sweat! You strap a Joy-Con into

a steering wheel-shaped peripheral (the actual Ring Fit) and another to your leg, and you're ready to go. It challenges you to do squats, lunges and even bendy yoga poses ... but the best part? It's all disguised as a fun adventure where you battle monsters and collect treasure! *Ring Fit Adventure* is a tough workout, for sure, but it's a blast.

Of course, if you like to exercise with a punchy playlist, there are lots of physically challenging games that are packed with music. *Just Dance* has over forty hit songs to choose from that hone your coordination and timing. Or if you're lucky enough to have access to a VR console, *Beat Saber* puts you in the shoes of a futuristic warrior wielding two laser swords! But instead of fighting enemies, you slice through boxes to the beat of music.

Of course, video games can be good for our mental health as well as our physical well-being. They burst with opportunities for connection. This could be connection with friends through multiplayer or to a character or story that moves you deeply. In a video game, you don't just watch a character solving a problem like in a TV show, you solve their problems for them. That makes gaming an incredible source of rich, empathetic experiences that can hold a mirror up to your own life.

Take *Spiritfarer*. Here you play the caretaker of a boat that transports spirits to the afterlife. It's your job to help these spirits come to terms with their past and find peace. *Spiritfarer* is a beautiful, serene game that deals with heavy themes like grief in a gentle and heartfelt way.

Other games, like *Stardew Valley*, give space for reflection too. This cosy simulation invites you to run a farm away from city stress. While raising animals and tending crops, you have a list of achievable goals: milk the cows, explore the local caves for treasure, help a local find a missing item. When life can feel overwhelming and full of big decisions, games like *Stardew Valley* provide much-needed respite.

Of course, there are games that take the theme of mental health very literally. *Psychonauts* is all about exploring the inner workings of the mind. You play a psychic teenager who enters other people's heads to help them overcome their fears and anxieties. Talking about mental health can sometimes feel quite abstract, but *Psychonauts* gives a physical form to some of the darker thoughts in our heads and allows you to beat them – quite literally!

Whether you're looking to get fit or learn more about yourself or the world around you, there's a game out there for you. All you need is time, curiosity and a living room big enough to do lunges in!

What in the Weird?

Wild and Weird Gaming Stories From Across the World

Buy Every Console Ever

A French gamer may have unleashed the coolest eBay listing of all time. Kario30 decided to sell off a collection he'd built up over fifty years, containing every console ever! It included the basic versions, plus limited edition models, like all the variants of the Nintendo 64. There were 2,249 machines in total, including forty-five different types of Sega's Game Gear handheld! But there's a catch: two months after it went live, no one had met the asking price of 984,000 euros – which is one million dollars.

N64? Completed It, Mate

Continuing the retro theme, a Twitch streamer managed to complete every single N64 game ever released! The project took more than five years, and contained 296 games. Canadian streamer AceGamerSam started out with 2D side-scroller *Mischief Makers* in March 2017. The journey included *Goldeneye*, *Majora's Mask* and the notoriously terrible *Superman 64*. He saved *Super Mario 64* – a game that held a ton of good memories – for last.

A Precious Secret

Lord of the Rings: Return of the King is one of the few games to live up to the hype of the movies. So fans were stunned to learn, almost two decades after it came out, that it was built on a golf sim! Former EA employee Glen Schofield revealed that he and his colleagues decided to adapt the game *Tiger Woods* into Middle Earth because of the similarities between that game and the fantasy series. All those big stretches of open land, with fortresses to reach after a long walk. A hack-slash classic was born!

Elder Scrolls Gets Domino's

Feeling hungry during your next gaming sesh? You can now order pizza using *The Elder Scrolls IV: Oblivion*! The sandbox RPG arrived in 2006, but is still being modded by the PC community. One weirdough has made it possible to automatically order Domino's by talking to a character called Pizza Nickies Black! You get a 12-inch thin-crust pizza, eight garlic bread twists and a 20 oz bottle of Fuze Lemon Tea. The catch is that it only works in the USA. Still cool, though! The mod is called Nickies' Pizzabilivion, in case you want to check it out.

Hello. I assume you are here to order some pizza?

155

Pizza Nickies

Bestseller

The original still trumps all its successors. *Pokémon Red & Blue* sold 31.38 million copies, ahead of *Pokémon Sword & Shield* with 24.27 million.

PRINT TO THE UNKNOWN

Game Freak

■ The makers of Pokémon started out doing something completely different! Game Freak was a Japanese magazine that launched in 1983. Six years later it started trying to create games. NES puzzler *Mendel Palace* was its first game. Nintendo was impressed enough to trust the team with Game Boy favourite *Mario & Yoshi*. That was the start of a relationship which has spawned twenty Pokémon games so far!

Biggest Series:
Pokémon

The series you know and love began in 1996. *Pokémon Red & Blue* let you collect critters and then unleash them in battle. Those foundations remain strong twenty games later! *Pokémon Legends: Arceus* and *Pokémon Scarlet & Violet* were both developed by the Tokyo-based brainboxes.

Have You Played?

Pokémon Sun & Moon

Tembo The Badass Elephant

Little Town Hero

Pokémon Legends: Arceus

Biggest Series:
World of Warcraft

Any of Blizzard's big four could claim this spot! However, *Warcraft* is a mainstay of the studio's annual BlizzCon event. Since 2005, gamers have been able to enjoy new levels and expansions – and watch some of the world's biggest bands! Past headliners include The Offspring, Foo Fighters, Metallica and Muse.

OVERWATCH OVERLORDS

Blizzard Entertainment

■ Blizzard's list of big hitters is mind-blowing. It's the studio behind *Overwatch*, *World of Warcraft*, *StarCraft* and *Diablo*! Not bad for a company that started out in 1991 helping other studios port games to different formats. When a studio had a game created for one console, like the Sega Mega Drive, Blizzard (who were then called Silicon & Synapse, Inc.) would translate the game so that it could work on another platform, like a PC. That changed with beat-'em-up *The Death and Return of Superman*. In 1994, the team released *WarCraft: Orcs and Humans*, and its destiny was set. It now has nine studios and almost 5,000 employees!

Hearth of Gold

Another massive Blizzard hit is *Hearthstone*. The turn-based card game has been going strong since 2014, with 100 million players and a $100,000 annual World Championship.

Have You Played?

StarCraft II: Rings of Liberty

Diablo II: Resurrected

WarCraft III: Reforged

Overwatch 2

CONSOLE HEAD TO HEAD
PlayStation vs Nintendo 64

The new kid on the block vs the refreshed old-timer. That was the story in the 1990s, as Sony burst onto the console scene. Sega would eventually fall away following the release of the Dreamcast. Nintendo was going nowhere though, as the N64 picked up where the SNES left off. Here's the tale of two machines!

Nintendo 64

Every Nintendo machine makes a big deal out of that iconic plumber. Sure enough, *Super Mario 64* and *Mario Kart 64* appeared high on its must-own list. But it's most remembered for *Zelda* and *Bond*. 007-themed shooter *Goldeneye* saw evenings disappear in a flash as you and three mates took one another down in split-screen gunplay. In a neat feature, the machine also came in a variety of colours – including fire orange!

By The Numbers

UK release date:
March 1997
Publisher: Nintendo
Worldwide sales:
32.93 million
Number of games: 393
Bestselling game:
Super Mario 64
(11.91 million)

Memorable Games

SUPER MARIO 64
Mario's first 3D game unearthed some cynics, who didn't want to leave their side-scrolling days behind. But its star-collection mechanic and Bowser boss battles soon won everyone over!

GOLDENEYE 007
Incredible shooter that made multiplayer essential long before the *Call of Duty* era. Its stealthy single-player campaign nailed the feel of being Bond too.

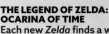

THE LEGEND OF ZELDA: OCARINA OF TIME
Each new *Zelda* finds a way to wow. This one did so with a 3D world that felt fully explorable, and fresh mechanics, like its lock-on camera and horseback riding!

Mario Kart's *popularity still isn't slowing down.*

Vertical Suplex! That's got to hurt.

PlayStation

PS1 launched in Japan just one week after the Sega Saturn. Fans formed long queues to snap up Sony's first machine. Its hype became so huge that it received 100,000 pre-orders in North America! Early hits included *Tekken* and *Ridge Racer*. Over the next-half decade, games like *Gran Turismo* and *Tomb Raider* cemented its status as a pop culture icon. It was also famed for its surreal adverts. In one, a man in a *Crash Bandicoot* suit was asked to leave Nintendo HQ after rocking up with a megaphone!

SlayStation

🔵 PS1 was the first ever console or computer to sell over 100 million worldwide!

🔵 It features twice in the TV show *Friends*, with the boys playing *Crash Team Racing* and *Twisted Metal 2: World Tour*.

🔵 Essential peripherals included a memory card for game saves, and multitap for four-player chaos!

By The Numbers

UK release date:
September 1995
Publisher: Sony
Worldwide sales:
102.49 million
Number of games: 3,061
Bestselling game:
Gran Turismo (10.85 million)

Gran Turismo was one of the most popular games and helped make PlayStation a successful console.

Memorable Games

WIPEOUT
Insta-classic racer set in 2052! You sped ships through futuristic levels, hitting boosts and unleashing rockets at rivals. Its electronic soundtrack was a huge influence on PS1 going mainstream.

TOMB RAIDER
A loveable hero, 3D visuals, taxing puzzles and combat-exploration combo made Lara Croft's debut unputdownable. It inspired more than twenty additional games, and three movies.

FINAL FANTASY VII
The classic series had always been viewed as a Nintendo fave. But PS1 saw it switch from cartridge to CD, with astonishing results! Its gameplay depth, graphics and story transformed RPGs forever.

Street Fighter 6

Developer Capcom **Publisher** Capcom **Platform** PC, PS4, PS5, XBX/S **Rating** PEGI 12+

■ **The greatest brawler in gaming history returns. As ever, one-on-one action is frantic and packed with all the specials you love. Ryu's dragon punch, Guile's sonic boom and Chun-Li's spinning bird kick remain as essential as ever. But this time, there's a story mode too.**

It's called World Tour, and you compete as a fully customisable character. Luke offers you training in a place called Buckler Security, before you set off for Italy, France and more. Masters provide you with secret techniques, and battles pop up organically as you roam the streets. It's an impressive new direction for this old fave.

Tidy Drive

Classic punch-ups also get refreshed. New players can be initiated swiftly via the dynamic control system. This lets you unleash a spectacular combo with one button press! Don't worry, old-school six-button controls are here too. Also new is the drive gauge. This gives you five unique techniques to master, adding variety beyond the eighteen-character launch list.

Showtime! The electric Blanka is back and ready for action in Street Fighter 6.

Back to fight her foes, Juri uses her classic Taekwondo moves.

This new instalment is set after Street Fighter III, after the 4th and 5th games jumped back in time.

Fights take place all across the world as players progress through different stages.

Did You Know?

The logo for Street Fighter 6 was changed drastically after being widely ridiculed following the game's announcement trailer!

Wham! Luke returns as the main protagonist. He'll go head-to-head against rival, Jamie.

You can choose from a whole host of characters to battle!

New Faces

Kimberly

This fan of 1980s pop culture is too cool to enjoy rom-coms! She's an African American college graduate and graffiti street artist who wants to be a ninja. Her mentor is Guy, who appeared in Final Fight before debuting in Street Fighter Alpha.

Marisa

An Italian jewellery designer who hates heights but loves a fistfight – and at 2.02 m and 122 kg she's pretty handy in that department. She's voiced by Allegra Clark, who also plays Bloodhound in Apex Legends and various characters in Horizon Forbidden West!

Manon

This elegant damsel is proud of her supermodel career. She's also a world champion judoka! Manon loves the colour gold and her family – and hates crowds and chatterboxes. Her voice actress, Cherami Leigh, played Ophelia Strange in The Addams Family 2.

JP

International investment boss with a wise head and deadly battle skills. He can dispatch clones across the screen, or even teleport! When not fighting, he apparently likes hanging out with his cat Cybele and playing chess.

THE HISTORY OF STREET FIGHTER

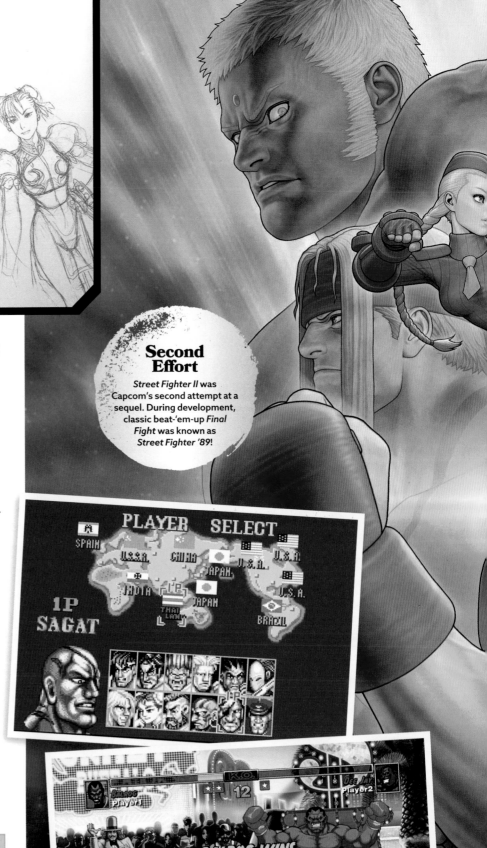

Ken You Feel The Love Tonight?

Ryu. Ken. Chun Li. Guile. M Bison. *Street Fighter* has spawned more iconic characters than perhaps any series in gaming history! It started out as an arcade-only brawler in 1987. Most people agree that the first game wasn't the best in the series, it didn't get great reviews! There were ten foes to fight against – but you could only play as Ryu.

Instant Smash

The players' reactions were very different five years later. *Street Fighter II* was an arcade hit from the outset, and converted to all of the big consoles. The Super Nintendo version is especially legendary among fans, thanks to its six-button controls! Four main games followed that one, as well as more than twenty other spin-offs.

The series has crossed over in every imaginable way. There have been comics, trading cards, anime shows, even movies and toys, too. The 2004 Sota range of figurines is now so rare that the Akuma and Zangief toys sell for over £100!

Second Effort

Street Fighter II was Capcom's second attempt at a sequel. During development, classic beat-'em-up *Final Fight* was known as *Street Fighter '89*!

Street Factor

❷ Boxer Balrog is known as M Bison in Japan. To avoid legal action from Mike Tyson, Capcom switched boss names around, with Vega becoming the main villain!

❷ *Street Fighter III* is the most controversial game in the series. It ditched every classic character other than Ryu and Ken!

❸ The series spawned an educational film called *Street Fighter II: Return to the Fujiwara Capital*. Ryu and pals travelled back in time to give Japanese kids a history lesson!

162

Four Super Street Fighters

Street Fighter II

The greatest fighter ever, and it's not even close. Never before had gamers been able to enjoy one-on-one combat using a selection of unique characters and special moves. Even the bonus levels, where you smashed up crates and a sports car, felt pixel-perfect.

Ultra Street Fighter II: The Final Challengers

The best way to enjoy the 1991 classic. A Switch exclusive, it includes all the original iconic characters, plus Evil Ryu! There's also a cool first-person mode called Way of the Hado. You fight off enemies by unleashing hadoukens and shoryukens with the Joy-Cons!

Street Fighter IV

Street Fighter IV reintroduced many of the characters ditched by *Street Fighter III*, and was the series' best game in two decades! Elimination mode was especially heated, where you could build a team of combatants for three-on-three fisticuffs.

Street Fighter V: Arcade Edition

Despite the title, this is actually a PS4 and PC game. And it's ace! You get twenty-eight characters, including Cody from *Final Fight* and newbs Kage and Luke. Arcade mode features more than 200 endings – enough for you to be playing this until *Street Fighter 7* hits!

FIGHT CLUB

DNF Duel

Developer Arc System Works **Publisher** Nexon **Platform** NS, PC, PS4, PS5 **Rating** PEGI 12+

■ *DNF Duel* features the craziest backstory of any fighter! It's set in a multiverse where the gates that allowed characters to move between dimensions shut down years ago. But now they're opening up again, renewing old rivalries and throwing together sixteen combatants with a variety of intentions!

Often a character's background is explained by their name. There's Enchantress, Dragon Knight, Ghostblade and Troubleshooter. More mysterious are female ninja Kunoichi, and Swift Master – who can harness the power of wind. Thankfully not in the same way as your kid brother!

Last-minute Awakening
Despite the complex backdrop, gameplay is a breeze. Attacks are classified as weak, medium, skill or magic. Many are unleashed with a single button, adding real pick-up-and-play value. But there's nuance too. Like the awakening mechanic, which gives you extra abilities when your health hits 30%. Can you turn a certain defeat into a shock comeback win?!

Did You Know?
DNF Duel is a spin-off from *Dungeon Fighter Online*, which launched on PC in 2005. It's even inspired an anime TV series called *Slap-up Party: Arad Senki!*

With a name like Striker, you'd guess she's good at getting the hits in! Pick from sixteen different characters to play.

Ninja Kunoichi has a move called Substitution Jutsu, which catches opponents off-guard by transforming her into ... a log!

Each character has unique strengths and weaknesses, as well as signature moves.

AEW Fight Forever

Developer Yuke's **Publisher** THQ Nordic **Platform** NS, PC, PS4, PS5, XBO, XBX/S **Rating** PEGI 16+

■ Always figured WWE is the only wrestling heavyweight in town? Not any more! AEW is the big new rival, and in recent times, it's seen massive names like Daniel Bryan and Dean Ambrose jump ship to join. Both feature in its debut grappler. They're now known as Bryan Danielson and Jon Moxley.

Feel the Sting

Other recognisable faces include CM Punk, Chris Jericho and Sting. There's a familiar feel, too. That's because developer Yuke's spent two decades working for *WWE*! It made both the *Smackdown* and *2K* games. Moves feel larger than life yet easy to pull off, with all your favourite's signatures and finishers included.

Unlike *WWE* games, it offers an especially cool feature: inter-gender matches. Always wanted to see how Britt Baker would fare against Dean Ambrose, or have Jade Cargill take down Jericho? Now you can! There are plenty of traditional options like tag-team bouts and ladder matches too. If you've had enough of *WWE* super villain Roman Reigns, there's finally a legitimate Plan B!

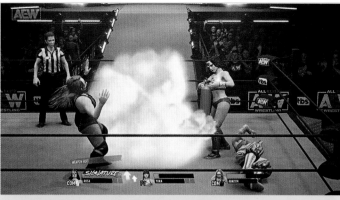

As well as giving gamers the chance to play with female wrestlers, AEW *also let's you play male vs female!*

Chaos is a ladder! Fight your way to the top and try not to come crashing down.

American Nightmare

AEW executive Cody Rhodes is featured in the game — despite going in the opposite direction to Daniel Bryan, and joining WWE last year!

It's in the Name

The game was originally announced as *Crystal Legacy*, before its name was changed. If both players choose the same character, then the second one has their name changed. For instance, Sho Kamui turns into Jin Sawamura!

Noob Tip

Fill the meter at the bottom of the screen to unlock your super. Do it three times for the most powerful move of all! Most of these are unleashed by doing a double quarter-circle, then pressing Attack!

Breakers Collection

Developer Qubyte Interactive **Publisher** Qubyte Interactive
Platform NS, PC, PS4, PS5, XBO, XBX/S **Rating** PEGI 12+

Background | Ever heard of the NeoGeo? It was a super expensive handheld console released in 1991. *Breakers* was its version of *Street Fighter*! This collection brings together both the original and *Breakers Revenge* for a modern console audience. If you love Ken and Ryu, it's easy to pick up and play!

Features | There are loads of ways to enjoy the original two games: ranked battles, arcade mode and the classic one-on-one versus mode – both online and offline! Brazilian fighter Rila plays like Blanka's sister, while main character Sho Kamui is a karate expert whose kicks can shoot flames!

Gameplay | Stop us if you've heard this one before. *Breakers* features bright 2D characters in one-on-one battles that are the best of three rounds. Told you it was like *Street Fighter*! One difference is using four buttons rather than six, which actually makes it easier for newcomers. There are ten characters for players to master.

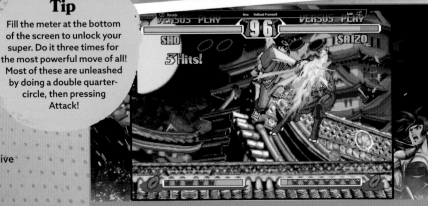

POW! Everyone knows feet kick harder when they're in 16-bit. Three hits to Sho Kamui!

Ever the classic back story, Tia the Thai kickboxer is fighting her way through the main characters in search of her missing brother.

Tap your feet or kick them? The combo of upbeat tunes and beat-'em-up gameplay is gaming gold.

Check Out

Kukoos: Lost Pets is a super-cute four-player adventure from the same studio. You roam a planet filled with water, rescuing fuzzy friends and trying to restore harmony!

A quiff that rivals the true King of Rock and Roll, God of Rock character King has a matching white jumpsuit.

God of Rock

Developer Modus Studios **Publisher** Modus Studios **Platform** NS, PC, PS4, PS5, XBO, XBX/S **Rating** PEGI 16+

Background | Just like *Breakers*, *God of Rock* was made in Brazil. But this is a very different kind of fighter! It's more like *Guitar Hero* or *Beat Saber*, with you hitting moves by nailing button prompts at the right time. You'll tap your feet even when your character is being booted into the air!

Features | As well as local or online multiplayer, story mode takes you in branching directions. There are twelve different characters, and eight eye-popping stages. Oh, and a track editor. Don't like one of *God of Rock*'s forty songs? Add or remove notes to mix them up!

Gameplay | *God of Rock* stays true to classic fighters despite its rhythm-action twist. You start off hitting normal moves, building towards EX and special moves. Stay ahead of your opponent and it's time to finish them off with a round-ending super attack. Familiar, but so much fun all the same.

God of Mock Stars

◉ The cast here has its roots in real-life rock and roll. Spaceman Ziggy is very obviously inspired by David Bowie alter-ego Ziggy Stardust. And King has a huge quiff and hip-swing move, just like Elvis Presley in his prime.

Play as wrestling legends, like Kurt Angle, Dave Bautista or Hulk Hogan.

With over 200 famous fighters to choose from, you'll have a hard time picking just one.

Did You Know?

The *WWE 2K23 Icon Edition* comes with exclusive John Cena cover art created by WWE artist-in-residence Rob Schamberger.

WWE 2K23

Developer Visual Concepts **Publisher** 2K **Platform** PC, PS4, PS5, XBO, XBX/S
Rating PEGI 16+

■ **2K's latest brawler is heavily focused on one bruising new match type. War Games! It throws two teams of four into a steel cage for complete carnage. It starts off one-on-one, with partners arriving at brief intervals. You can whack opponents with chairs and road signs, or soar off the top of the steel to inflict huge damage. Sound like mayhem? That's because it is!**

All your favourite modes also return, like MyRise. Players can build their own wrestler, then manage their rise to the top of WWE. Even better is Universe. You book every match, pretending to be the owner of WWE. This year you can choose which cut-scenes play before and after bouts, giving you total control of every twist and turn in the storylines!

Tired Legs

Gameplay is similar to *WWE 2K22*, and that's no bad thing. The series famously took two years off before that game, because *WWE 2K20* had been so awful! A cool new feature is breaking pins by flicking on the right stick. It really gives you the sense of 'kicking out'. And it gets really difficult late on in matches, when your wrestler is exhausted!

Make a powerful pounce on your opponents, just like Bad Bunny

Light heavyweight fighter The Miz has a selection of flashy attire.

DLC

Twenty-four extra wrestlers were added to WWE 2K23 across five DLC packs. Highlights included Bray Wyatt, Wade Barrett and NXT team Pretty Deadly.

Play as female wrestlers, like Rhea Ripley and Bianca Belair, in your virtual ring.

Drew McIntyre makes a dramatic entrance with his infamous sword.

You'll never give up with John Cena on your wrestling roster.

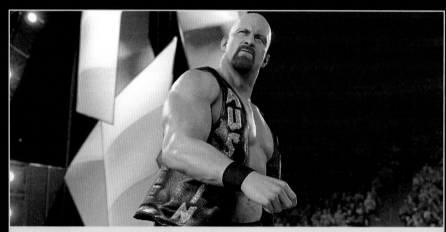

Dare to face the stare of Stone Cold Steve Austin?

Ludwig Kaiser and Gunther are an even match. Replay classic rivalries or try creating new ones!

Drew McIntyre versus Roman Reigns! Which heavyweight will win?

Four Must-play Wrestlers

Cody Rhodes

The American Nightmare returns to the series after a nine-year absence – and immediately gets one of the game's most realistic models!

Bron Breakker

This beardy beast was NXT Champion for over a year. Look familiar? He's the son of 1990s favourite Rick Steiner!

Cora Jade

Cool skater Cora will quickly remind you of former Divas Champion AJ Lee. Expect her to be in the series for years to come.

Bad Bunny

The swag-tastic rapper was this year's pre-order bonus. Sounds mad, but he was surprisingly great during a brief WWE stint in 2022!

THE HISTORY OF WWE 2K

This Famous Series Goes Back Further Than You Think

Call yourself a *WWE* expert? But did you know that *WWE 2K14* isn't the first game in the series? It goes way back! The popular punching series has had a few name changes over the last two decades – but so has *WWE*!

Laying the Smackdown

When Japanese studio Yuke's released *WWF Smackdown* on PS1 in 2000, it became an instant classic. Characters felt chunky and looked real. Finishers were easy to nail. And it was wonderfully fast and frantic. Sequels continued throughout the PS2- and PS3-era. A decade on, publisher THQ dropped the *Smackdown* name, and released *WWE 12*.

Tragically, THQ closed down. When it folded, another publisher named 2K picked up the reins – and gave the game a new name! Developer Yuke's stayed in charge of making the game and that's why the series' history goes back so far. With a small twist: Yuke's stopped working on it in 2019, and is now in charge of rival game *AEW Fight Forever*!

In the Ring

❷ The first five *Smackdown* games didn't have that name in Japan. Instead, the series was known as *Exciting Pro Wrestling*!

❷ The Rock, Triple H and Undertaker have appeared in every single game since the series began in 2000.

❸ There was no *WWE 2K21*. Instead, fans got *WWE Battlegrounds*, with larger-than-life models fighting in the Everglades and a military camp!

Undertaker's Speciality

Long-lost match types include Buried Alive from the PS2 years. You had to get your opponent into a coffin, then slam it shut!

Four WWE Wonders

WWE Smackdown vs Raw

PS2's first WWE game had fans raving about the leap in quality. It introduced online matches, and let you choose whether to fight clean or dirty – just like actual WWE! Cool mid-match mini-games like tests of strengths and stare-downs added even more fun.

WWE Smackdown vs Raw 2008

Short-lived third WWE show ECW snuck into this one. That meant the welcome inclusion of hardcore favourites Sabu, Terry Funk and Tommy Dreamer. ECW stood for Extreme Championship Wrestling – and the E inspired new weapons like guitars and baseball bats to set on fire!

WWE '13

The final game in the series published by THQ. That's not the only reason older fans remember it fondly. Its Attitude Era mode let you replay the best matches of the 1990s and 2000s. Accurate arenas, entrances and commentary were all recreated for the experience!

WWE 2K19

This was so good that when its sequel failed to match expectations, WWE 2K21 was cancelled! Matches perfectly mixed speed with realism, while dedicated fans shared lifelike creations of those who missed out on the roster. Plus there are eleven versions of Daniel Bryan. Yes!

CONSOLE HEAD TO HEAD

PlayStation 2 vs Xbox

Rivalries are a huge part of the gaming industry. The 1990s were all about Sega vs Nintendo and which console was better. The turn of the century triggered a whole new gaming rivalry: multimedia giants, Sony and Microsoft. Gamers loved PlayStation's additions to the PS2, but a new black box with exciting abilities was tempting too ...

Memorable Games

GUITAR HERO
This made plastic guitars cool to own – at least for a few years! You matched the coloured prompts to buttons on your pretend Gibson SG, rocking out to legends like Queen, David Bowie and Motörhead.

LEGO STAR WARS: THE VIDEO GAME
We'd never played anything like this in 2005. A deep story, levels packed with secrets and hilarious cut-scenes sparked a trend, which saw *Harry Potter* and *Jurassic Park* immortalised in brick form too.

PRO EVOLUTION SOCCER 6
Believable player behaviour, slick passing options and the immense Master League mode sent this supermassive – despite fake names, like Merseyside Red and Man Blue!

PlayStation 2

In the 1990s, PS1 made gaming cool. In the 2000s, PS2 made it essential for the whole family. It's the bestselling console ever made, and with good reason. *Grand Theft Auto* and *Metal Gear Solid* found their prime form on PS2, *Ratchet & Clank* and *Kingdom Hearts* wowed gamers young and old, and *FIFA* and *Pro Evolution Soccer* enjoyed their best years on the machine. Throw in accessory-based experiences, like *SingStar, Guitar Hero* and *Dance Dance Revolution*, and you have a console like no other.

By The Numbers

UK release date: November 2000
Publisher: Sony
Worldwide sales: 155 million
Number of games: 4,379
Bestselling game: Grand Theft Auto: San Andreas (17.33 million)

San Andreas swapped GTA's focus to gangs.

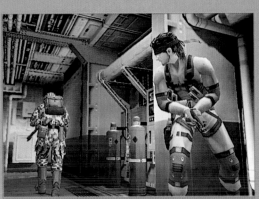

Sons of Liberty was the second 3D Metal Gear.

Xbox

Why did Microsoft decide to build its own games console? The PS2 was capable of playing DVDs, and this concerned the bosses at Microsoft. Xbox launched over a year after its rival, but still scored massive appeal. 1.5 million Americans bought one in the first six weeks on sale. It became beloved among shooter fans thanks to *Halo*, *Half-Life 2* and *Call of Duty*. Handily, Xbox was the first console to contain a hard disc drive for game saves – ensuring that we'd never have to worry about memory cards again.

By The Numbers

UK release date: March 2002
Publisher: Microsoft
Worldwide sales: 24 million
Number of games: 998
Bestselling game: Halo 2 (8.46 million)

Console Yourself

❷ Xbox was so high-tech, Microsoft lost over $125 every time a machine was sold!

❸ Microsoft boss Bill Gates sold the very first Xbox, at a glitzy launch in Times Square.

❷ Rejected names included WEP (Windows Entertainment Project) and MTG (Microsoft Total Gaming)!

Memorable Games

TOM CLANCY'S GHOST RECON
Tactical shooter that helped launched Xbox Live – and made us all quickly familiar with terms like gamertag and Xbox Achievements. Not only that, it was a really fun blaster!

HALO 2
The shooter that had us all joining clans and taking out strangers. Its Master Chief-focused campaign was incredible too – with one of the most controversial endings of all time!

PROJECT GOTHAM RACING
Gorgeous driver that was about more than speed – to progress you had to show off skills like power sliding too! San Fran and New York felt lifelike, and the cars were a dream to handle.

Halo was one of the console exclusives for Xbox.

Play as Freeman and shut down Combine.

THE
INSIDER TAKE
Developers Share Highlights from a Memorable Year

Yosuke Hayashi
Director of Wild Hearts

What's the best thing you played in the last year?

Elden Ring. It's truly an adventure into uncharted territory and I have been fascinated by its game design, which allowed me to have an experience that could not easily be had in any other entertainment medium.

What element of *Wild Hearts* are you most proud of?

Its a classical yet fresh hunting game experience. Players can experience a new kind of hunting experience where they confront and defeat kemono by making full use of things they craft called karakuri.

What game are you most looking forward to?

The Legend of Zelda: Tears of the Kingdom. I'm really looking forward to seeing how it will change from *Breath of the Wild,* which reimagined many conventions of the *Zelda* series.

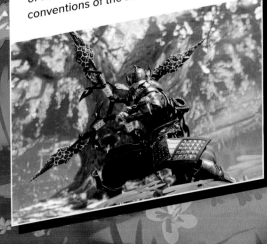

Andrew Shouldice
Designer of Tunic

What's the best thing you played in the last year?

I really enjoyed *Outer Wilds* – it's exactly my kind of game. I know I'm late to the party, but I was saving it until after *Tunic* was done.

What element of *Tunic* are you most proud of?

I'm really happy with how the instruction booklet turned out. It was so rough for so long that it was really gratifying when it all came together near the end of development.

What game are you most looking forward to?

I've heard great things about *Ghost Trick,* so I'm excited to try out the remaster on Switch. And *Tears of the Kingdom,* of course!

Simon Read
Founder of New Star Soccer

What's the best thing you played in the last year?
Nintendo Switch Sports! I've had great fun playing with my children – especially the sword fighting!

What element of *New Star Soccer* are you most proud of?
From a technical standpoint it's all the teams and competitions in the game, from lower leagues through to the World Cup. More important than that though is the world the player builds in his or her own head.

What game are you most looking forward to?
Right now it's *Undisputed*. I loved the old *Fight Night* games so I'm excited to see an up-to-date boxing simulation.

Dino Zucconi
Lead Designer VC of WWE 2K23

What's the best thing you played in the last year?
Elden Ring took seven months of my life and I loved it. I also greatly enjoyed Rollerdrome. Both deserve a mention, as different as they are.

What element of *WWE 2K23* are you most proud of?
The John Cena Showcase. Players get to step into the boots of several of Cena's greatest opponents, in some of the most important matches of his career, with the goal of beating the man who claims he'll "Never Give Up".

What game are you most looking forward to?
Two games in the *Like a Dragon* franchise. *Like a Dragon: Ishin* comes out first, and I'm incredibly excited to finally get to play. Then *Like a Dragon 8* gets my undivided attention.

SALT LAKE WIZARDS

Avalanche Software

■ This Utah studio spent the last six years creating *Hogwarts Legacy*. But it's done a little bit of everything since being formed in 1995! Its first games were the Mega Drive and SNES versions of fighter *Ultimate Mortal Kombat 3*. It made the official games for *Rugrats: The Movie*, *Bolt* and *Toy Story 3*. Previous owners Disney closed the studio down in 2016. Thankfully, Warner Bros. brought them back to life, and *Hogwarts Legacy* was born!

Dash in the Attic

Still got *Disney Infinity* figures gathering dust? It's worth checking their value. A boxed Black Suit Spider-Man will make you £40!

Have You Played?

Toy Story 3

Disney Infinity 3.0

Cars 3: Driven To Win

Hogwarts Legacy

Biggest Series:
Disney Infinity

There's every chance this toys-to-life series was your entry into gaming! First, you bought physical figures like Mr. Incredible, Black Widow and Luke Skywalker. Then, by placing them on a base, they came to life on screen. The sandbox world contained loads of secrets to unearth and unique special attacks. Sadly, the entire *Disney Infinity* universe was shut down in March 2017.

FANTASY FANATICS

Square Enix

■ No one does RPGs quite like this Japanese giant! *Final Fantasy*, *Dragon Quest* and *Kingdom Hearts* all call Square Enix home. It's actually two companies who merged together in 2003. Square began in 1983 as the gaming division of a power-line construction company! Enix is even older. It started in 1975, publishing newspapers with property adverts inside. Its first game was *Door Door* for the NES. In 1986, *Dragon Quest* was unleashed on the same console, transforming RPGs forever.

Biggest Series:
Final Fantasy

The biggest RPG series of all time. It launched in December 1987 with a last-minute name change. During development it was called *Fighting Fantasy*! Since then, its mix of magic, combat and exploration has wowed gamers across the globe. It's sold a humungous 173 million copies, inspired hundreds of copycats, and spawned movies and mountains of merch. Woah!

Picture Perfect

Enix kept its publishing empire going despite the successful move into gaming. In 1991 it started their *Gangan* line of Manga comics, which is still popular today!

Have You Played?

Legend of Mana

Kingdom Hearts III

Dragon Quest XI S

Final Fantasy XVI

17

STATE OF PLAY

The Year's Best Indie Games

Ghosts, stars and a fantastic fox! These are the top new titles you may have missed ...

Tunic

Developer Andrew Shouldice **Publisher** Andrew Shouldice
Format NS, PC, PS4, PS5, XBO, XBX/S **Rating** 7+

Imagine a game that blends *The Legend of Zelda* with *Dark Souls*. Then stop imagining it and play *Tunic*. It does exactly that! You play as a fox and can only open up new areas of the map when you've unlocked the necessary skill. That usually requires some seriously tough puzzling! You get very little dialogue and the game has its own language which you have to figure out as you play. One of the best parts is the manual. We're not joking! It's full of maps and illustrations. They're pretty and come in very handy during the adventure itself.

Cult of the Lamb

Developer Massive Monster **Publisher** Devolver Digital
Format NS, PC, PS4, PS5, XBO, XBX/S **Rating** 12+

This roguelike is all about a baby sheep who's been possessed!
Go out on crusades across five different regions, rescuing cute
creatures and animals, then convince them to join your cult!
Once back at your base, you need to provide followers with
shelter and cook food to help them survive. The crusades are
procedurally generated. That means every playthrough feels
different, even once you're familiar with the story!

Glossary

8-Bit/16-Bit: A 'Bit' is
a measure of computer
information. NES games
in the 1980s were 8-Bit,
while Sega Mega Drive
games ushered in the
16-Bit era!

Sea of Stars

Developer Sabotage Studio **Publisher** Sabotage
Studio **Format** NS, PC, PS4, PS5, XBO, XBX/S
Rating 12+ (TBC)

This RPG is properly gorgeous! It's about
Valerie and Zale, who use the power of the sun
and moon to battle a dodgy alchemist. Tackle
puzzles and fights with a party of six characters.
And, with a title like that, of course you can go
sailing too! It's a prequel to 2018 platformer *The
Messenger*. That game cleverly spanned two
passages of time. Levels set in the past looked
8-bit, while future levels were 16-bit! It's still well
worth a play on PS4 or Xbox One.

And the winner is ...

Feline-focused *Stray* (which
you can read all about later in
this book) beat *Tunic* and *Cult
of the Lamb* to win Best Indie
Game at this year's Game
Awards. All three games
feature creatures as playable
characters. Also nominated
were demon-slaying action
game *Neon White* and kung-
fu brawler *Sifu*.

Oxenfree II:
Lost Signals

Developer Night School Studios
Publisher Netflix / MWM Interactive
Format NS, PC, PS4, PS5 **Rating** (TBC)

Spooky thriller *Oxenfree* scored tons of awards after its release in 2016! Now there's finally a sequel. In the first game, main character Alex investigated ghostly events on a place called Edwards Islands. This time the theme is similar, but with a fresh cast. Environmental researcher Riley is our new hero. She's back in her small Oregon hometown to figure out strange radio signals. Riley soon discovers she can open tears through time. With *Lost Signals* set five years after the first game, that means plenty of easter eggs for those who played the original!

Slap City

Developer Ludosity **Publisher** Ludosity **Format** NS, PC **Rating** 7+

This hilarious four-player brawler is beyond insane on Switch! It brings together characters from other Ludosity games for *Super Smash Bros.*-style carnage. Leap around the screen, punching, grabbing and combo-ing your way to victory. The leading ladies from *Ittle Dew* and *Princess Remedy in a World of Hurt* are two of its most-loved characters. Bosses from those games, like *Ittle Dew*'s Ultra Fishbunjin 3000, are also available if you fancy engaging your mischievous side!

Dew You Really Like It?

It was another massive year for *Stardew Valley*. The country life RPG swept past sales of 20 million! Incredibly, 5 million of those sales have come since 2021. As well as raising animals and growing crops, there's so much else to do, like dating other characters, catching fish and crafting scarecrows. You can play it on console, phone – or even forgotten Sony handheld PS Vita!

Fueled Up

Developer Fireline Games **Publisher** Fireline Games **Format** PC, PS4, XBO **Rating** 3+

Fueled Up is an alien journey like no other. You work together with three other players to fix damaged spaceships. The threat here isn't gravity, or being lost in space. It's a giant purple octopus! Things get super intense as you race against the clock to extinguish fires and dodge asteroid showers. But hilarious too – characters include a grumpy banana, a spanner-wielding cat and a floating brain! If you've ever played and loved *Overcooked* then this is the intergalactic game of your dreams.

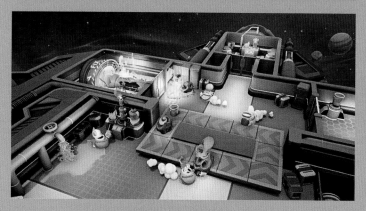

WEIRD & WONDERFUL

Fall Guys

Developer Mediatonic **Publisher** Epic Games
Platform NS, PC, PS4, PS5, XBO, XBX/S **Rating** PEGI 3+

■ *Fall Guys* is packed with jellybean-battling brilliance – and it's completely free-to-play! Compete in mini-game mayhem for up to sixty players. Win matches or complete challenges and you score kudos. This can be spent on nameplates, emotes and plenty of other treats to customise your character!

Rise of Fall

The game has actually been around since 2020, but two years later it was made free for everyone. Since then, it's gone supermassive. Each season lasts a few months and adds a new theme. Season two was called Satellite Scramble and was all about space. Season three switched to Sunken Secrets, offering five rounds set underwater!

Like *Mario Party*, some games require teamwork, while others are every Bean for himself! In Fall Ball, you work together to get the ball into the other team's goal. While Hit Parade is a bonkers obstacle course packed with turntables and balance beams. First to the end wins! With fresh content dropping all the time, it's never too late to get involved in this chaotic classic.

Check Out

Fancy a furry rumble instead? *Super Animal Royale* is mega cute and pits sixty-four players against each other. Fight to be the last critter standing!

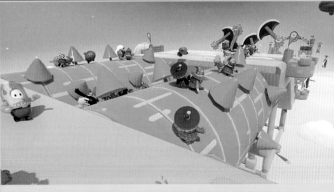

The obstacles are getting trickier in this race-to-the-finish frenzy.

Masters of the Fall-Guys-verse

Much like *Fortnite*, *Fall Guys* loves a crossover. Characters from *Sonic the Hedgehog*, *LittleBigPlanet* and *Ratchet & Clank* have all scored in-game costumes. It goes both ways too. Mattel recently released a four-pack of toys featuring He-Man, Skeletor, Teela and Battle Cat as Fall Guys Beans. To celebrate Godzilla arriving in the game, publisher Epic even unleashed a 28cm Godzilla plushie!

Go for gold! Build up your points by landing through the best hoop.

There are new themes to explore and new outfits to win.

'Tis the Season

The genius of *Fall Guys* is its seasonal structure. Even if you dip out for a few months, there's always something fresh to come back to. Those who play regularly are rewarded too. Satellite Scramble introduced eight new rounds, like Hex-a-Terrestrial, where you have to navigate floating platforms without making a mistake. Pixel Painters, where you hop on tiles to spell out patterns, is addictive too. New mini-games stay even after seasons end, meaning *Fall Guys* is always getting bigger and better!

Whoosh! Soar straight to the next round by beating others to the finish line.

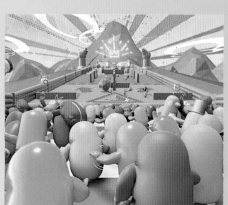

Avoid Total Knock Out! Players will have to time their jumps carefully.

WEIRD & WONDERFUL

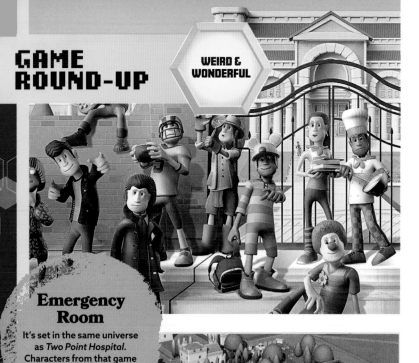

Emergency Room

It's set in the same universe as *Two Point Hospital*. Characters from that game pop up here too!

Two Point Campus

Developer Two Point Studios **Publisher** Sega **Platform** NS, PC, PS4, PS5, XBO, XBX/S **Rating** PEGI 3+

■ It's *Pitch Perfect* meets *The Sims*! Construct a university and choose its staff. Not just lecturers, either. There'll be no one to clean the loos if you don't appoint a janitor! Classrooms and libraries need building, and you must keep students happy. Each year lasts around twenty minutes, at which point a new bunch joins the uni. It's easy to lose hours and then days to your uni-running decisions!

It's a tough job to keep a campus of this size running smoothly. Time management skills will be put to the test to keep students happy.

Going to class is hungry work! It's a good job the campus chefs are on hand.

The Outbound Ghost

Developer Conradical Games **Publisher** Digerati **Platform** NS, PC, PS4, PS5, XBO, XBX/S **Rating** PEGI 7+

■ This one sounds scary. You have to guide moody ghosts into the afterlife! But its super cuteness takes away a lot of the fear factor. As well as the loveable main character, you build a party of four phantoms to quest with. Battles are based on you pressing a button at the correct time. The main enemy is red-faced grump Adrian, who pushes you off a cliff at the start of chapter two! If you fancy a spooky spin on *Paper Mario*, get ghosting!

Mansion of Delusions

Lv.14

Did You Know?

Lead designer Conrad Grindheim launched a Kickstarter for *The Outbound Ghost* in 2021. It needed 10,000 Euros, but got 25,000!

No Man's Sky

Developer Hello Games **Publisher** Hello Games **Platform** NS, PC, PS4, PS5, XBO, XBX/S **Rating** PEGI 7+

■ This epic journey through the universe is finally available on Switch. You travel across galaxies, hunting rare plants and trading with aliens! You need to focus on strengthening your suit for survival, and upgrading your ship so it can go further. Other than that, the journey is up to you! Even though the game's been out on other formats since 2016, you're guaranteed to spot creatures that no one else has found before. Amazing!

Explore exotic landscapes, marvel in the unusual horizons and befriend new and exciting creatures.

Did You Know

There are over 18 quintillion planets to find in *No Man's Sky*. That's your next Christmas holiday sorted!

There are a few ways to upgrade your exosuit in No Man's Sky, *one of the easiest is to hunt down space stations – there's an exosuit upgrade waiting for you on each one.*

The Divine Force introduced a whole new combat system to the game.

Star Ocean:
The Divine Force

Developer tri-Ace **Publisher** Square Enix **Platform** PC, PS4, PS5, XBO, XBX/S **Rating** PEGI 12+

■ If you want to learn everything about this sci-fi RPG, you need to finish it twice! You choose to explore the planet of Aster IV as either space merchant Ray or kickass princess Laeticia. But the pair split up at certain points in the story – and you only see cutscenes for that character! Even if you just play through once, there are forty hours of characters to meet, and combat to unleash.

Check Out

Fancy experiencing the original game, from 1996? Grab the remastered *Star Ocean First Departure R* for PS4 or Nintendo Switch!

Playing as Laeticia gives you more info on the world of Star Ocean.

Ray's science and tech knowledge can be a huge help when exploring.

Harvestella

Developer Live Wire Inc. **Publisher** Square Enix
Platform PC, NS **Rating** PEGI 12+

Pet and play with Totokaku, you can also keep them as a companion.

■ Looking for a Switch RPG with a *Final Fantasy* flavour, but set in a different world? Try *Harvestella*! There are loads of similarities. You can choose one of twelve classes to take into combat, like fighter and mage. Chatting to NPCs fleshes out the story, and you can fish, cook and craft when not taking on its fanciful tale. The game name relates to harvesting crops, in order to end a plague called Quietus.

Emo Music

You'll quickly get to know and love the fictional towns of Lethe, Nemea and Shatolla. But it's the characters who make this memorable. From siren princess Emo, to missionary Shrika, to spearman Asyl, building a party and taking it into quests is the best part of *Harvestella*. Boss fights get seriously tactical, and are a welcome change of pace from the calm of farming! It all adds up to a unique adventure that feels equal parts cute and wholesome.

Rune-ing Up That Hill

Want even more farming and dungeon-crawling? Try *Rune Factory 5*. You tend the land for local villagers, while also fending off giant monsters!

Shrika the missionary is one of the many colourful characters that you'll meet.

Strengthen your bond with your party and you can use special attacks.

Be careful of the Quietus, a season that causes all crops to wither.

Expert Tip

Pack food and drinks before venturing into a dungeon, to restore health. Oh, and a repair kit too. These can fix broken ladders and bridges!

Dragon Quest Treasures

Developer Tose **Publisher** Square Enix **Platform** NS
Rating PEGI 7+

■ The amazing *Dragon Quest* series can be overwhelming for new players. That's where this spin-off comes in! It's a more straightforward adventure that's still packed with charm and character. Blue-haired Erik and sister Mia live on a Viking ship. One night they bump into the mysterious Porcus and Purrsula, who tempt them to the floating land of Draconia. Here you can recruit monsters, bash baddies, and hunt treasure – hence the title! Junior role-players will adore its gentle story and colourful cast.

Did You Know?

The first *Dragon Quest* game landed in 1986. For the next twenty years it was known as *Dragon Warrior* in the USA!

The twins are joined by their cute companions, Porcus and Purrsula.

Pekotte, a tough enemy to face, can also be recruited to the party!

One of the first quests you'll get pits you against the Heartless Hunter.

Astra's Playroom

Three captains (Zax Ja'kar, Extilior and Astra) arrived with *Moonbreaker*'s release, and Krafton aims to release new ones every four months.

Moonbreaker

Developer Unknown Worlds Entertainment **Publisher** Krafton
Platform PC **Rating** PEGI 12+ (TBC)

■ Want a turn-based board game that never needs unboxing? Try *Moonbreaker*! Assemble a crew of ten and go into battle. Then it's about positioning your troops and using their skills to your advantage. Its creators say it has ten years' worth of storylines ready for future updates! It really is like *Warhammer*, too. There's an incredible range of options to customise individual figures. If you've ever fancied drybrushing, stippling or airbrushing, this is the game for you!

Stray

Developer BlueTwelve Studio **Publisher** AnnaPurna Interactive
Platform PC, PS4, PS5 **Rating** PEGI 12+

■ You have never, ever, ever played anything like *Stray*. Unless you're already a cat! In this cat sim, you get to roam an underground city – clambering, meowing, nuzzling, sleeping and doing most other stuff you expect from a furry feline.

This isn't all just pointless fun, however. Dotted around the city are robots who set you tasks, which advance the storyline. These bots are trapped underground, and need your aid to escape – before they, and you, are infected by mutated bacteria called Zurks.

Drone Alone

Helping on your quest is a drone companion called B-12. It provides light, acts as your translator, and can take down Zurks using a gadget called the Defluxor. Use it with care though – it overheats quickly and once that happens, you're in for a quick trip to kitty heaven …

As a cat, you can use inventive tactics to travel to new areas.

Here, kitty, kitty! Meet the game's protagonist.

This cat is on a mission! Complete the tasks to help the robots.

A Song or Eight

The main story in *Stray* only takes a few hours to complete. Don't be put off though, as side quests are solid too. There are six badges you can unlock to adorn kitty's coat. Homeless musician bot Morusque plays a new song each time you come to him with a piece of sheet music. There are eight spread across the slums. Once you've brought him all eight, you get one of those six badges to wear with kitty pride!

Mirror Image

Videos of cats watching *Stray* went viral after the game's release. By the end of 2022, Twitter account @CatsWatchStray had 36,000 followers!

Scratch Posts

Stray's genius isn't just about the mechanics of being an animal. The reason you stay hooked is its surrounding world. The game is set in a cyberpunk version of Kowloon Walled City, a Hong Kong settlement demolished in 1994. There's a police station, night club and hat shop for you to wander around. Those claustrophobic surroundings tease menace at every turn. Yet its neon colours and enticing streetlights add warmth and balance.

The future looks a little different in Stray. Robotic humans are the norm, but they're in danger.

Hopefully curiosity won't kill the cat. You don't have nine lives to play with in this game.

DLC

While there's no additional content for *Stray*, Steam users can grab the soundtrack as DLC. It's all penned by Yann van der Cruyssen, who plays Morusque!

The protagonist was voiced by a cat named Lala.

Check Out

Spirit of the North is available on every format going, and turns players into a spirit-powered fox who roams around stunning Iceland.

The cat is out of the bag. Your cat carries a backpack to store essentials.

Members of the Avengers, X-Men, Runaways and Midnight Suns unite to take Lilith down.

Marvel's Midnight Suns

Developer Firaxis Games **Publisher** 2K **Platform** NS, PC, PS4, PS5, XBO, XBX/S
Rating PEGI 12+

■ The studio behind *XCOM* shifts its turn-based skills to the world of Marvel. With superb results! Create your own hero called The Hunter and team up with the Midnight Suns to take down demonic matriarch Lilith. The Suns also get the chance to work with renowned superheroes Iron Man and Captain Marvel

Family Feud

Matriarch? Oh yes. Lilith is The Hunter's mum! You take a three-person team into each mission, armed with a customisable deck of eight cards. These are used to attack, support or heal. With thirteen playable characters to choose from, you will never, ever get bored across *Midnight Suns'* sixty hour campaign.

While there's plenty of strategy involved, luck plays a part too. The three cards unleashed from your deck in battle are chosen at random, meaning the best-laid plans don't always come off. On the plus side, that encourages you to make sure that every card in your deck is a star. If you want a complete change of pace from last year's *Guardians of the Galaxy* blaster, you need to give this a go!

DLC

The Midnight Suns season pass has added more playable heroes to the game – including Morbius, Storm, Venom and Deadpool!

Old foes are also back for more fun as Spiderman battles Venom.

Abbey Adventures

Turn-based battles are the focus, but there's lots more to do. Befriending superheroes never gets old, and throws up plenty of banter. Outside of missions you can explore your home of the Abbey, with spin-off mysteries to solve, like finding four heroic statues. You can even go mushroom picking, bird watching or watch movies – although sadly these tasks aren't interactive. Who wouldn't want a mini-game where you catch carp with Wolverine?!

Lilith is awakened by Hydra in this game. Lilith and Hydra combined? What could possibly go wrong?

The Hydra base is a dangerous place for a superhero to be lurking.

Wowzers! There are hundreds of cards in this game.

Noob Tip

Make sure you take a healer on every mission, to counteract the randomness of cards. Focus on Nico early in the game to aid this plan.

Family Roots

MCU addicts may be wondering who exactly the Midnight Suns are. So let's explain! In Marvel comics they're styled as the Midnight Sons. The original team of nine included Morbius, Blade and two Ghost Rider characters: Danny Ketch and Johnny Blaze. Their battles with Lilith were much more supernatural than standard Marvel tales. All these guys are likely to make MCU appearances eventually, but for now the only one confirmed is Blade. He's getting an upcoming cinematic reboot starring Mahershala Ali.

Ultimate Scream

The Hunter is the first ever customisable Marvel superhero. His or her abilities are split into three branches: light, dark and power. Each offers ten different cards, for a total of thirty.

The team talk tactics at the mirror table. Strategy is at the heart of this game as you prepare your best cards.

The Best Gaming Vinyl

Records have become cool again – and these are the hottest soundtracks for your collection!

The Vinyl Countdown

Other new releases which are well worth a listen include *Cuphead: The Delicious Last Course, Streets of Rage 4: Mr X Nightmare* and *Psychonauts 2*.

Animal Crossing:
New Horizons

This one is a mouthful. It's called the *Animal Crossing Totakeke Music Instrumental Selection*! Thankfully, the tunes are catchier than the name. There are 19 in total, spread across two sides. Side A is the Upbeat Side, while Side B is the Chill Side. A second collection of music is available separately. That one is a five-CD box set, with 110 songs!

Sonic Frontiers

Sonic games are legendary for their use of head-nodding electronics and catchy melodies. *Sonic Frontiers* continues that legacy, with some unique twists! Listen carefully for Iranian percussion, Celtic vocal samples and Armenian folk instruments. This one is a collaboration between Sega and vinyl experts Data Discs. Like the hedgehog himself, both records are blue!

Minecraft Volume Alpha

The theme music from Mojang's blocky sandbox sounds impeccable on vinyl. You don't even need to have played *Minecraft* to enjoy it. The soothing collection of tracks are pleasing whether you're seven or seventy! It was created by German composer and musician Daniel Rosenfeld. The collection is also easy to find on CD, if you don't own a record player.

Horizon Forbidden West

Aloy's amazing adventure mixes up the pace at regular intervals. That's reflected in the soundtrack! Its twenty-three tracks blend gentle instrumentals with heart-racing drum beats, meaning you're never quite sure what's coming next. Until you've learned it off by heart on the 33rd listen! This one comes in a deluxe case which looks gorgeous next to your record player.

Stray

This isn't just a record, but a work of art. *Stray*'s soundtrack is spread across two vinyl discs, with a holofoil front cover. Those who loved the mix of keyboards and drum beats from the Mega Drive era will be big fans! Yann van der Cruyssen had complete control of the project. He also plays musician Morusque in the game itself!

Glossary

Holofoil is a special type of material that displays a holographic image when you hold it up to natural light!

What in the Weird?

Wild and Weird Gaming Stories From Across the World

© dpa picture alliance / Alamy Stock Photo

The PS5 Electric Car

If you thought getting your hands on a PS5 was hard[...] imagine how quickly a PlayStation car will sell! Sony [...] Honda's new electric car is called the Afeela EV, and [...] features a widescreen strip that can play PlayStation [...] That's just in the front. There are two more screens i[...] back that provide PS4 and PS5 entertainment. The o[...] of the car is jazzy too. It has a media bar that can be [...] for custom images and animations. There's no co[...] price yet, but we can assume it [...] pretty steep!

Hogwarts' Magical Launch

Hogwarts Legacy had one of the biggest launches ever among the Twitch community! The first twenty-four hours saw streamers rack up $57,000 (£47,000), as 16.2 million gamers tuned in for wizarding wonders. The most-watched stream was by Fextralife. It scored 2.4 million viewers in the first day, earning him an estimated $8,400 (£7,000!) The most popular topics were inventory, combat, spells and new character Sirona Ryan. The Three Broomsticks owner is the first ever transgender character to appear in the Harry Potter universe.

Chilled Out Gaming

Gaming is the number one stress reliever, according to Xbox gamers! Microsoft ran a survey that asked Xbox players for their best way of reducing anxiety. Games finished first, with 54% of those polled saying that the likes of *Minecraft* and *Forza Motorsport* helped them feel better. Social media came second on 46%, and reading a book was third with 45%. It also revealed that 31% of gamers planned to play with (or against!) their family over Christmas — and 5% said it would be with their grandparents!

Elden Ring Mind Games

A Twitch streamer made it possible to control *Elden Ring* with her brain! Perrikaryal has a masters degree in psychology, and did it with clever use of an EEG headset. EEG stands for electroencephalogram. The headset uses small metal discs to measure electrical activity to the brain. She bound hers to *Elden Ring* and, after lots of experimenting, worked out how to control The Tarnished! Attacks were the first thing she figured out, and she's hoping to eventually enjoy complete hands-free play.

STATE OF PLAY
Console Catch Up
What's New With Steam?

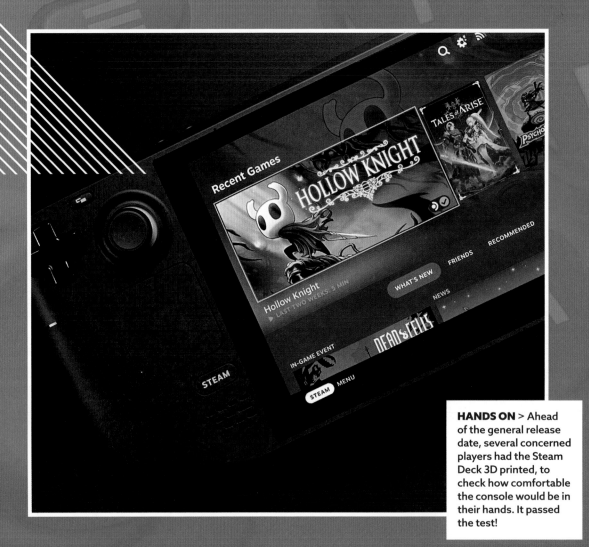

HANDS ON > Ahead of the general release date, several concerned players had the Steam Deck 3D printed, to check how comfortable the console would be in their hands. It passed the test!

■ Steam recently smashed an incredible record. It hit 32.1 million users online at once – with more than 10 million users actively playing games at the same time. It cemented the service as the home of PC and Mac gaming. Just in case anyone wasn't already sure!

Goose For Dinner
Unsurprisingly, most of its top played games of the year were eSports faves. *Apex Legends*, *PUBG Battlegrounds* and *DOTA 2* topped the list. But shooters didn't have it all their own way. Free-to-play card battler *Yu-Gi-Oh! Master Duel* snuck its way into the top ten. As did *Goose Goose Duck* – an *Among Us*-style multiplayer effort with loads of moreish modes.

Steam exclusives are hard to come by these days. Most of the newer releases are also made available on PS5 and Xbox Series X. Creators Valve have countered that with the new portable Steam Deck – offering triple-A gaming on the go. It's led to many console gamers switching sides, for good!

It isn't just triple-A games that are winning players over to the new handheld console. Steam is known as a haven for smaller games by boutique studios and crowd-funded indie hits. Giving gamers the chance to play their faves, like *Stray*, *FTL: Faster than Light* or *Coffee Talk*, is a huge selling point for the Steam Deck.

All Hands on Deck

Elden Ring, Stray and *Forza Horizon 5* on the move? Yup! Thanks to Steam's new handheld, you can now play almost every major game while sat on the bus (or hiding from your homework). The Steam Deck has a D-Pad, two sticks, four face buttons, a mic, a trackpad ... and an incredible engine underneath.

Seriously, you've never tried a handheld console like this one. *Elden Ring* plays even better this way than with a mouse and keyboard – to the point of earning 'Verified' status from Valve. All your existing Steam purchases play on it too. The only catch is the price: even the cheapest 64GB model will cost £349.

Top 3 Steam Exclusives

Songs of Conquest

This turn-based strategy sim is inspired by old-school fave *Heroes of Might and Magic*. You control one of four kingdoms and expand through tactical play – unleashing magicians called wielders in combat.

Aperture Desk Job

Legendary puzzler *Portal* gets a spin-off that showcases the Steam Deck's technical expertise. You write your name on the touchscreen, and use the gyroscopic controls to shoot stuff. It's short and sweet – and very funny too.

Did You Know?
Steam launched in 2003 as a way for Valve to offer automatic gaming updates. It now has a database of more than 50,000 games!

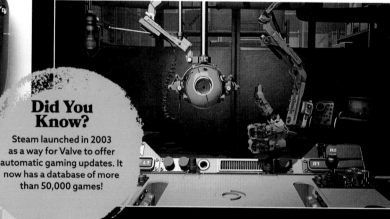

Albion Online

Free-to-play medieval MMORPG. It has over five million users, and has been translated into eleven languages. All equipment and items are made by fellow players, meaning your customisation options are genuinely endless.

Remakes & Remasters
Your Guide to the Gaming Genre

■ **The first console launched in 1972. It was called the Magnavox Odyssey and came with ten games like *Table Tennis* and *Volleyball*! In the five decades since, gaming has become the biggest form of entertainment in the world. That's led to favourites from the 1980s and 1990s making comebacks on modern machines!**

And Repeat

This trend started in the Super Nintendo era. Nintendo realised that many of its NES favourites could be upgraded and sold together. *Dragon Quest I* and *Dragon Quest II* were pulled into a single package. Even better was *Super Mario All-Stars*. It contained all three original *Mario* platformers, plus spin-off *Super Mario Bros.: The Lost Levels*!

We've enjoyed a steady stream of similar releases since the turn of the century. A remaster has tidied up an old game and given it state-of-the-art visuals. While a remake rebuilds it from the ground up. *Shadow of the Colossus* and *Tony Hawk's Pro Skater 1 + 2* are two incredible examples!

Sweet, Sweet Fantasy

The best recent set of remasters belongs to *Final Fantasy*. All six original RPGs were remastered for PC in 2021, and are now available on PS4 and Nintendo Switch too!

Top 5 Remakes & Remasters to Play Right Now

The Legend of Zelda: Link's Awakening

One of Switch's loveliest tales was originally a 1993 Game Boy game! It looks better than ever in colour. Link wakes up on the strange tropical island of Koholint. Its dungeons are littered with tricky traps and mean monsters – but it's still utterly charming throughout.

Sonic Origins

A collection of the games that made our fave hedgehog famous! *Sonic The Hedgehog, Sonic 2, Sonic 3 & Knuckles* and *Sonic CD* are all here. You can try them in their classic form, or with lives removed. Even better is playing all four in a row, with cut-scenes to bridge them together.

Final Fantasy VII Remake Intergrade

Many reckon *Final Fantasy VII* is the best RPG ever. So Square Enix remade it for PC and PS5! As Cloud Strife, you take on the Shinra Corporation in thrilling real-time battles. Characters get new voices, and the story changes too – including a different ending!

Shadow of the Colossus

All you have to do in this amazing PS4 remake is fight bosses. But it's tougher than it sounds! There are sixteen in total, all with unique behaviours and weak points. It's a game about trial and error, never giving up – and trying to enjoy its gorgeousness even when angry!

Live A Live

Want to try out a time-travelling RPG that Japanese gamers loved back in 1994? It took twenty-eight years for a Western remake! The end result is one of Switch's most unique experiences. Ancient China, Feudal Japan and the Wild West all throw up new characters, battles and twisting tales!

REMAKES & REMASTERS

Return to Monkey Island

Developer Terrible Toybox **Publisher** Devolver Digital **Platform** NS, PC, PS5, XBX/S **Rating** PEGI 12+

■ Point-and-click adventure *The Secret of Monkey Island* is considered one of the greatest games ever. This update brings back main man Guybrush Threepwood for more pirating fun. It also restores classic characters and locations, while introducing new places like Terror Island and the super chilly Brrr Muda! The aim of the game is to finally uncover that isle's big secret, after more than three decades. Its arrival was big news for fans. *Monkey Island 2: LeChuck's Revenge* had finished on a major cliffhanger, all the way back in 1991!

Arrrrr! Go toe to toe against LeChuck once again.

The Lookout spent his time watching out over Mêlée Island.

Did You Know
Monkey Island mastermind Ron Gilbert was inspired to create the series by Disney's Pirates of the Caribbean theme park ride!

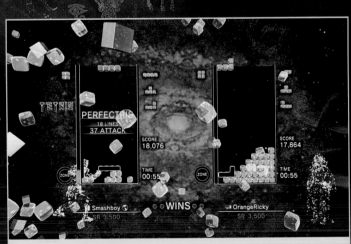
Go one-on-one against an opponent or the AI.

Tetris Effect: Connected *keeps players hooked with different modes.*

Tetris Effect: Connected

Developer Stage Games **Publisher** Enhance **Platform** NS, PC, PS4, PS5, XBO, XBX/S **Rating** PEGI 3+

■ Watched the Taron Egerton *Tetris* movie and wonder what all the fuss was about? Basically, there's never been a more addictive puzzler than this one! It started out in Russia in 1984, but went supermassive when it was packaged with Nintendo's groundbreaking Game Boy handheld. Since then, it's passed 495 million sales, making *Tetris* the second biggest gaming series ever after *Mario*. *Tetris Effect: Connected* is the most recent version, reinventing the puzzler with twenty-seven stages and up to eight players online. The PS5 version also supports PSVR2, placing you at one with the blocks like never before!

Mario Music

As well as updated graphics and Joy-Con controls, you also get a music player with the soundtracks to all three classic games!

Mario's ingenious way of travelling across large bodies of water is just as much fun as it looks.

Super Mario 3D All-Stars

Developer Nintendo, Monstars Inc. and Resonair **Publisher** Nintendo
Platform NS **Rating** PEGI 7+

■ This Mario collection remains one of the greatest remastering templates in gaming history! It groups together three absolute classics in one place: *Super Mario 64*, *Super Mario Sunshine* and *Super Mario Galaxy.*

Isle Be Back

Super Mario 64 made history in 1996 as the first game in the series to go 3D. Gamecube classic *Super Mario Sunshine* dropped Mario and pals onto the tropical Isle Delfino to face off with a mysterious villain called Shadow Mario. And *Super Mario Galaxy* catapulted him into space to rescue Princess Peach and collect 120 Power Stars along the way!

It's an especially exciting collection because of its rarity. *All-Stars* was only available for seven months on the Switch eShop, to mark Mario's 35th Anniversary. That means hunting down the physical edition if you're keen to revisit its delights. It sells for £50-70 on eBay. If this sounds like a wallet breaker, you know what to put on top of your next birthday list!

Delfino isn't the only isle in Super Mario 3D All-Stars. *Glide through the air to and from islands in the sky.*

Take on classic Mario *rival Bowser, plus all of his friends, including the mischievous Bowser Jr.*

JAH 53800

LEVEL 3

Check Out

Want a retro compendium with more familiar characters? *Grab Sega Mega Drive Classics* to enjoy *Sonic The Hedgehog* and *Streets of Rage*.

Atari 50:
The Anniversary Celebration

Developer Digital Eclipse **Publisher** Atari
Platform NS, PC, PS4, PS5, XBO, XBX/S **Rating** PEGI 16+

Background | This may be the greatest retro collection ever made! Atari was a gaming giant throughout the 1980s and 1990s, and ninety-six of its most memorable games feature here. Along with seven new ones, exclusively for this collection! Classics include *Pong*, *Asteroid* and *Millipede*.

Features | New games like *Haunted House* and *Neo Breakout* aren't the only fresh content. There's also an interactive documentary, meaning you can see video content, art and flyers from each game before or after playing them. It's like a gaming museum that you never have to queue up for!

Gameplay | The variety here is wild. There's racing (*Atari Karts*), sports (*RealSports Soccer*), adventure (*Dark Chambers*) and loads of retro shooters. Jaguar game *Trevor McFur in the Crescent Galaxy* is one of the weirdest blasters ever. You power through the galaxy while controlling an actual jaguar!

Lynx for Lefties
◉ Five games here were originally unleashed on the Atari Lynx. Released in 1993, it was the company's handheld rival to the Game Boy. You could flip it upside down to reverse the D-pad and button layout – a dream for left-handed gamers!

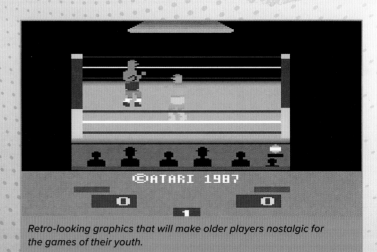

Retro-looking graphics that will make older players nostalgic for the games of their youth.

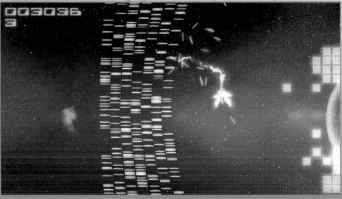

With over 100 games to try out, Atari 50: The Anniversary Celebration is out of this world.

Noob Tip
All four turtle abilities are needed to finish *Radical Rescue*. Donatello can climb walls, while Mikey hovers by using his nunchakus as a helicopter!

Teenage Mutant Ninja Turtles:
The Cowabunga Collection

Developer Digital Eclipse **Publisher** Konami **Platform** PC, PS4, PS5, XBO, XBX/S **Rating** PEGI 12+

Background | Just in case Digital Eclipse weren't busy enough remastering Atari classics, they also made this trip to half-shell heaven! Thirteen games are included, beginning with NES favourite *Teenage Mutant Ninja Turtles* from 1989. Three handheld Game Boy games even get console makeovers!

Features | Like *Atari 50*, there are loads of behind-the-screens treats to enjoy. It's the games that are the big deal, though. You can save when you like, re-map buttons and even rewind your progress. It's the perfect throwback set for any Leonardo nut or Donatello diva!

Gameplay | Most of the games here are beat-'em-ups, including legendary Mega Drive side-scroller *Hyperstone Heist*. In *Tournament Fighters*, however, the Turtles do battle *Street Fighter*-style. And *Radical Rescue* is a very green and amphibian Metroidvania!

Some of the games in the collection, like Turtles in Time, *aren't easily accessible anymore.*

Teenage Mutant Ninja Turtles II: The Arcade Game *is another hard-to-find classic included in the compilation.*

Collectors' Edition

➋ A limited-edition physical version of *Cowabunga Collection* was also released. Inside fans found a cloth poster, acrylic diorama, enamel pin set, twelve Tournament Fighters cards and a beautiful 180-page artbook.

Crisis Core:
Final Fantasy VII Reunion

Developer Tose **Publisher** Square Enix
Platform NS, PC, PS4, PS5, XBO, XBX/S **Rating** PEGI 16+

■ Sony's handheld PSP never reached the heights of Nintendo's Game Boy. But it did give us an incredible prequel to *Final Fantasy VII*. *Crisis Core* is set seven years before that classic RPG – and this remaster is even more memorable than the original portable version!

Zack Attack

You play as spiky haired soldier Zack Fair. When his pal Genesis goes missing, Zack is tasked with hunting him down. Sadly, Genesis has already turned rogue. He's created an army of clones to attack Shinra HQ, and you need to eliminate those evil forces. Battles take place in real time. You can 'fuse' attacks, abilities and magic to make them even more powerful!

Fighting is made unique by something called DMW. It stands for Digital Mind Wave. Two sets of spinning wheels, like a slot machine, cycle through the numbers one to seven and pictures of Zack. If the numbers read '777', Zack levels up. And if you see three pictures of him lined up, he gets a limit break attack that does extra damage! But these pictures can also summon random monsters, so it's not always good news ...

Clever Logo

The *Crisis Core* logo was designed to represent its main characters. The blue sky is for Zack. The white feather symbolises Angeal. And the water pays tribute to Aerith.

Cloud Forecast

The story of *Final Fantasy VII* makes much more sense after playing *Crisis Core*. This isn't just Zack Fair's tale. It also pulls in Cloud, Aerith, Tifa and main *FFVII* baddie Sephiroth! At one point Zack tells Cloud to be his living legacy, instilling the values that make him such a top lead character. While Sephiroth visits Nibelheim and discovers his mother wasn't human, but a Shinra experiment. That's the reason he went from elite goodie to planet-wrecking super villain!

Zack and former friend Genesis go sword to sword.

Final Fantasy VII enemy Sephiroth returns in this prequel.

Zack tries out the iconic buster sword.

The One Winged Angel before his poetic nickname is formed.

Genesis is known, and sometimes disliked, for quoting from a book of poetry, which has been adapted into a stage play within the game.

Ability gauges are a new mechanic in the game. Enemies have special abilities, and when activating them in fights, the gauge appears to show players how powerful they are.

Recurring character Tifa Lockhart in her cowboy outfit.

Giant robot arachno are one of the Shinra-created enemies to watch out for.

PSP Remembered

Sony's handheld gave us these cool games in addition to *Crisis Core* ...

Lumines

Amazing block-clearing puzzler. Like *Tetris*, you had to place falling blocks together to clear them – while tapping your feet to tunes from Gwen Stefani and Black Eyed Peas!

Wipeout Pure

The classic PS1 racer made a superb portable comeback. Set in 2197, you sped through space while unleashing rockets, missiles and plasma bolts!

Metal Gear Solid Portable Ops

Cool Solid Snake spin-off where members of your squad could die permanently! Cut-scenes were also cool. Unlike the main console series, they were drawn to look like a comic.

LocoRoco

Little jelly-like creatures had to be steered through levels to get to an end goal. Literally: to move them, you needed to tilt the environment using the shoulder buttons!

THE INSIDER TAKE

Developers Share Highlights from a Memorable Year

James Pearmain
Art Director on Cult of the Lamb

What's the best thing you played in the last year?
The scale and sense of discovery in *Elden Ring* made it an experience like no other. It felt like a true adventure that will influence games for years!

What element of *Cult of the Lamb* are you most proud of?
Making the combat and cult management work together in a fun way was a huge challenge for the team that took a lot of iteration. It finally clicked not long before launch – which was a huge relief!

What game are you most looking forward to?
I'm excited to see Naughty Dog's multiplayer game – it sounds like they are trying to bring narrative elements to a larger scale version of *Factions*. It could be something special!

Evan Nikolich
Senior Design Director on Apex Legends

What's the best thing you played in the last year?
Metroid Prime Remastered. Replaying it for the first time in twenty years and the first time as a developer, I appreciate so much more what they accomplished in that experience. Masterclass design!

What element of *Apex Legends* are you most proud of?
The team I get to work with. They have taken on tough challenges and consistently delivered season over season. Couldn't ask for a better crew.

What game are you most looking forward to?
S.T.A.L.K.E.R. 2: Heart of Chernobyl. I believe Eastern European devs bring such unique experiences to the games they touch and I am excited to see how they evolved *S.T.A.L.K.E.R.*

Dave Grossman
Co-writer of Return to Monkey Island

What's the best thing you played in the last year?
Probably *Immortality*. I like Sam Barlow's exploratory story soup approach. Normally when you watch a movie you have occasional moments of small revelation that make you feel good for noticing them, and Sam's games focus on those moments and make them the main attraction.

What element of *Return to Monkey Island* are you most proud of?
The life-truths and self-reflection lurking around underneath all the silliness. We take our comedy very seriously around here.

What game are you most looking forward to?
I'm hoping this is the year Daniel Benmergui will finally release *Storyteller*. It has a unique take on the mechanics of stories, and is also adorable.

Ron Gilbert
Director of Return to Monkey Island

What's the best thing you played in the last year?
Vampire Survivors. On one hand it's such a crappy game, but on the other it's so brilliant.

What element of *Return to Monkey Island* are you most proud of?
The relationship between Guybrush and his son (Boybrush) and the way he tells of his adventures, that might or might not be true. Warms me to hear about players who played as kids and are now sharing *Return to Monkey Island* with their children.

What game are you most looking forward to?
I'm way too spontaneous to look forward to games. I'm impulsive and hear about something new and exciting and rush to play it.

2014

What Games Were Big Ten Years Ago?

■ 2014 had a little bit of everything. With no new consoles, it was all about the games. Shooter fans cooed over *Destiny*, but handheld gamers were too busy playing *Shovel Knight* to notice. Until November, when *Super Smash Bros.* knocked all rivals out of sight ...

Super Smash Bros. for Wii U

Nintendo Wii U's definitive brawler had us tussling like mad to knock our opponents off screen. Up to eight players could compete in absolute carnage! One minute you were kicking a football in Luigi's face, the next you were unleashing a swarm of bees at Sonic. Yes, Sonic! The mainly *Mario*-based cast was expanded with Pac-Man, Mega Man and the blue blur. Whoever you played as, you were guaranteed a flurry of crazy moves, crushing knockouts and noisy requests for "just one more match!"

Shovel Knight

Many will tell you this is the greatest handheld game ever made. It's a breathtaking 2D platformer that pays homage to numerous classics like *Zelda* and *Castlevania*. You play as the knight of the title, engaging in tactical combat with memorable bosses. There are towers to climb, jumps to navigate and weapon and armour upgrades to consider. Brilliantly, you only ever need two buttons for all of them. Even its touchscreen elements were perfection.

Amiibo Instincts

Mario Kart 8 sped onto Wii U, but it wasn't Nintendo's only breakthrough in 2014. The company also released the first wave of amiibo – figures that could interact with games. *Super Smash Bros.* was the first to get toys.

Destiny

After years of wowing the world with *Halo*, developer Bungie unveiled its new bombastic blaster. Set 700 years in the future, it married great gunplay with addictive character progression. Classes were inspired by legendary sci-fi. Warlocks aped Gandalf from *Lord of the Rings*, while Titans blended *Star Wars*' stormtroopers with Bungie's own Master Chief! Three-player strikes and six-way raids kept us coming back, and inspired four DLC packs – before *Destiny 2* came along in 2017.

Biggest-selling Games of 2004

01. Call of Duty: Advanced Warfare
Publisher Activision

02. Madden NFL 15
Publisher EA

03. Destiny
Publisher Activision

04. Grand Theft Auto V
Publisher Rockstar

05. Minecraft
Publisher Mojang

06. Super Smash Bros.
Publisher Nintendo

07. NBA 2K15
Publisher 2K

08. Watch Dogs
Publisher Ubisoft

09. FIFA 15
Publisher EA

10. Call Of Duty: Ghosts
Publisher Activision

Breath of the Future

Anyone who tuned into the 2014 Game Awards was witnessing history. On a famous night, *The Legend of Zelda: Breath of the Wild*, *No Man's Sky* and *Super Mario Maker* all received world premieres. *Hearthstone* also turned heads as best mobile game.

Driveclub

An exclusive Sony racer not called *Gran Turismo*? Yep! The mega publisher switched things up on PS4 with this most classy of drives. The big pull was forming your own drive club – check the title – with five friends. Or strangers! Completing challenges together earned XP to unlock new cars and colour schemes. Bentley, BMW, Ferrari and Lotus all provided customisable vehicles. Sadly, it's too late to try it for yourself. The servers were shut down in 2020.

DANCE MASTERS

Ubisoft Paris

■ The publisher of *Mario + Rabbids Sparks Of Hope* has studios all over the world. But Paris will always be considered its home! It began as a business helping out French farmers. Soon it branched out into selling audio CDs, and eventually games! Its first was 1986 adventure *Zombi*, for Alan Sugar's Amstrad. These days it's more focused on *Tom Clancy's Ghost Recon* and the *Just Dance* series. 700 people work at the studio. Ubisoft Paris is just around the corner from the breathtaking Château de Vincennes!

Biggest Series: Just Dance

Ubisoft Paris innocently launched its motion-based rhythm game in 2009. While rivals like *SingStar* and *Guitar Hero* are long gone, it's still going strong! There's been a new edition every year since then. *Just Dance 2023 Edition* mixed things up, though. From now on games won't be released annually. Instead you get regular updates, with fresh tracks being added all the time!

Have You Played?

Red Steel

Ghost Recon Advanced Warfighter 2

Rayman Raving Rabbids 2

Just Dance 2023 Edition

FROM FIRE FIGHT TO FORTNITE

Epic Games

■ Epic by name, Epic by nature! These Carolina heavyweights hold the Guinness World Record for the most successful game engine. It's called Unreal, and is the tech behind loads of popular series like *PUBG Battlegrounds* and *Fortnite*. The studio began as Potomac Computer Systems in 1991. It made brilliant blaster *Fire Fight* for EA, and has been famed for shooter expertise ever since. It's also known for the Epic Games Store – one of the few rivals to Steam when it comes to PC gaming!

Big Boss

Epic is still run by the man who started it all back in 1991. Tim Sweeney's first game was a puzzler called ZZT. His dad kept sending out mail order copies until 2013!

Have You Played?

Jazz Jackrabbit 2

Shadow Complex Remastered

Fortnite Battle Royale

Fortnite: Save The World

Biggest Series:
Fortnite

Well, duh. Unleashed on the world in 2017, Epic's incredible trio of experiences continues to attract new players and keep older ones hooked. It won two Game Awards in its first year, and keeps on picking up nominations and adoration. There are more than 400 million registered *Fortnite* users, and around 3 million of those play it at any one time!

LOOKING FORWARD

»

The fun doesn't stop here. Stay tuned for all these massive newcomers in *Next Level Games Review 2025*!

Exoprimal

Developer Capcom **Publisher** Capcom **Platform** PC, PS4, PS5, XBO, XBX/S

A futuristic shooter, but with dinosaurs as enemies? Count us in! *Exoprimal* looks insanely fun. Its main mode is Dino Survival. Two teams of five square off against one another – while the deadly dinos want to wipe out anything that moves! Raptors, Triceratops and T-Rex are all out to get you. Along with mutated monsters called NeoSaurs, with special combat abilities. Other modes include Dinosaur Cull, where you have to eliminate a specific breed.

Helping you in battle is your armour, AKA the exosuit. Like all the best shooters, its abilities define how you play. Witchdoctors heal other players. Roadblocks are tank characters who carry a shield, while barrages are explosives experts. You can mix and match these abilities as you progress. *Jurassic Park*? More like Jurassic sparks!

Also Coming Soon

Switch owners have lots to look forward to. There's curious time loop game *Outer Wilds*, Metroidvania-style sequel *Hollow Knight: Silksong* and beautiful platformer *Disney Illusion Island*.

Kingdom Hearts IV

Developer Square Enix **Publisher** Square Enix **Platform** TBC

Long-time *Kingdom Hearts* hero Sora is back for more Disney-themed action-adventuring! He's trapped in a place called Quadratum, which is an alternate-reality version of Tokyo. Luckily, Sora has Donald Duck and Goofy on hand to help him escape. Unluckily, he has loads of dark monsters trying to halt his fairy-tale ending! Parkour plays a big part of the gameplay. The series' unique Keyblade weapon is also essential. You can now use it to grapple hook across massive distances!

Final Fantasy VII Rebirth

Developer Square Enix
Publisher Square Enix **Platform** PS5

Final Fantasy VII is one of the most acclaimed RPGs of all time. As a result, the project to remake it is being split into three games! Rebirth is the second. It'll pick up where *Final Fantasy VII Remake Intergrade* left off. Cloud has arrived at the village of Kalm, while Zack is entering the Sector 5 church in search of Aerith. You'll get to add party members, then explore the world beyond Midgar. Given the series' history of memorable places, scenery and characters, it's all guaranteed to be incredible!

Avatar: Frontiers of Pandora

Developer Massive Entertainment **Publisher** Ubisoft **Platform** PC, PS5, XBX/S

Nearly fifteen years after the classic movie, we're getting a proper *Avatar* game. It opens up a whole new region of Pandora. You control the Na'vi and must battle the evil RDA. It's an action-adventure with a first-person viewpoint, built on the company's slick Snowdrop engine. That was also used for *Mario + Rabbids Sparks Of Hope*. So you can guarantee it'll all look gorgeous, and throw up breathtaking areas to explore!

EA Sports FC

Developer EA Vancouver
Publisher EA **Platform** NS, PC, PS4, PS5, XBO, XBX/S

FIFA is gone forever. No, really! After thirty years, EA's footballing series has been turned into *EA Sports FC*. It still has all the biggest names from across the globe. There are more than thirty leagues, 600 teams, 100 stadiums – and 19,000 players. Real Madrid, Liverpool, Manchester City and Spurs were especially keen to announce their involvement in the game. They all confirmed their spots in *EA Sports FC* before *FIFA 23* had even been released!

The Hottest New Gaming Movies

Gran Turismo
Orlando Bloom
2023

Borderlands
Cate Blanchett
2024

Five Nights At Freddy's
Matthew Lillard
2024

It Takes Two
Dwayne Johnson
2024

Metal Gear Solid
Oscar Isaac
2023

Minecraft
Jason Momoa
2024

Sonic The Hedgehog 3
Idris Elba
2024

Also Coming Soon

There'll be no slowing down! *Civilisation VII* is yet another epic turn-based RTS. *Lost Soul Aside* brings sword-wielding Kazer and a shapeshifting dragon pal to PS5. All your annual sports faves, like *WWE 2K24*, too!

Transformers: Reactivate

Developer Splash Damage **Publisher** Splash Damage
Platform PC, PS5, XBX/S

Reactivate had one the most secretive announcements when it was unveiled at The Game Awards. That hasn't stopped us getting excited for it! It's an online action game for up to four players. There are crazy vehicular sections, and spectacular sky-based shootouts. Bumblebee was the first robot confirmed for it. It's been nearly a decade since the last truly great game featuring these mechanical faves: *Transformers Devastation*. If this is 75% as good, fans will be happy.

Crash Team Rumble

Developer Toys For Bob
Publisher Activision **Platform** PS4, PS5, XBO, XBX/S

All your *Crash Bandicoot* favourites go head-to-head in this chaotic battle arena! Teams of four buddy up to grab more Wampa Fruit than their rivals. You need to get the delicious treats into your drop-off zone, while preventing opponents from reaching theirs! Playable characters include Crash, Cortex, Coco, Brio, Tawna and Dingodile. It's guaranteed to be total mayhem!

WHAT'S NEXT? »»

Still looking for more games to try out? Check out these incoming releases and stick them on your to-play list.

Pikmin 4

It's been a decade since the last *Pikmin* came out! Players who are new to the game can expect cute creatures to befriend and a beautiful planet to explore in this real-time strategy.

Samba de Amigo: Party Central

Similar to *Beat Saber*, players must hit rings in time to the tune to earn points. It's packed with catchy hits and mini-games, and comes with an online mode!

Professor Layton and The New World of Steam

Solve riddles with your favourite professor in the newest game of the popular

Tekken 8
This fighting series prides itself on being the longest running video game story of all time. In the newest release, players can delve into the father-son rivalry of Kazuya Mishima and Jin Kazama.

INDEX

CREDITS

All rights in the games, consoles, licensed characters and events within these pages and on the cover, including rights in the images taken from within the game, are owned by the copyright owners. This book is an unofficial guide to gaming. This book is published by Expanse, an imprint of HarperCollinsPublishers, neither this book nor Expanse is associated or affiliated with the following games, movies, franchises, albums, consoles, licensed characters and events:

2K, A Plague Tale: Requiem, The Addams Family 2, AEW Fight Forever, Albion Online, Alien: Isolation, Altered Beast, American Idiot, Among Us, Andrew Shouldice, Animal Crossing Totakeke Music Instrumental Selection, Animal Crossing, Animal Crossing: New Horizons, Animaniacs, Anthem, Aperture Desk Job, Apex Legends, Arcane, Armored Core: For Answer, Assassin's Creed: Valhalla, Asteroid, Astro's Playroom, Atari 50: The Anniversary Collection, Atari Karts, Atari, Avalanche Software, Avatar: Frontiers of Pandora, Batman: Arkham Asylum, Batman: Arkham City, Bayonetta 3, Beat Saber, Bendy and the Dark Revival, Bendy and the Ink Machine, Berserk, Big Brain Academy: Brain vs. Brain, Blast Brigade vs the Evil Legion of Dr. Cread, Bloodborne, BlueTwelve Studio, Bolt, Borderlands, Brain Breaker, Breakers Collection, Breakers Revenge, Breakers, Burnout 3: Takedown, Call of Duty 2, Call of Duty, Call of Duty: Advanced Warfare, Call of Duty: Ghosts, Call of Duty: Modern Warfare 2, Capcom's Soccer Shootout, Cars 3: Driven to Win, Castlevania Anniversary Collection, Castlevania III: Dracula's Curse, Castlevania, Castlevania: Symphony of the Night, Civilisation VII, Coffee Talk, Confessions of a Drama Queen, Costume Quest 2, Counter Strike: Global Offensive, Crash Bandicoot, Crash Team Racing, Crazy Taxi, Creed: Rise to Glory, Crime Crackers, Crisis Core: Final Fantasy VII Reunion, Cult of the Lamb, Cuphead, Cuphead: The Delicious Last Course, Dakar 18, Dakar Desert Rally, Dance Dance Revolution, Dark Chambers, Dark Souls 3, Dark Souls, Darwin Project, Deadpool, The Death and Return of Superman, Demon's Souls, Destiny 2, Destiny 2: Beyond Light, Destiny 2: Cult of Osiris, Destiny 2: Lightfall, Destiny 2: The Final Shape, Destiny 2: The Witch Queen, Destiny 2: Warmind, Destiny, Devil May Cry, Diablo II: Resurrected, Diablo III: Reaper of Souls, Diablo IV, Diablo, Dicey Dungeons, Dirt 5, Disney Dreamlight Valley, Disney Illusion Island, Disney Infinity, DNF Duel, Donkey Kong Country, Donkey Kong Jr., Donkey Kong, Door Door, DOTA 2, Dotemu, Dragon Ball, Dragon Quest II, Dragon Quest Treasures, Dragon Quest VIII, Dragon Quest XI S, Dragon Quest XII, Dragon Quest, Dreamscraper, Driveclub, Dungeon Fighter Online, Dungeons & Dragons, EA Cricket, EA Rugby, EA Sports FC, EA Sports MMA, EA Sports PGA Tour, Earthworm Jim, Ecco The Dolphin, Elden Ring, Elder Scrolls IV: Oblivion, Elder Scrolls V: Skyrim VR, Elder Scrolls VI, Encanto, Enix, Enter The Gungeon, ESPN NFL 2K5, Evolution Studios, Exoprimal, F-Zero, F1 2021, F1 22, FA Premier League Stars, Fable 4, Fall Guys, Far Cry, FIFA 06, FIFA 07, FIFA 09, FIFA 11, FIFA 19, FIFA 2000, FIFA 2005, FIFA 22, FIFA 23, FIFA 25, FIFA 97, FIFA 99, FIFA International Soccer, FIFA Manager, FIFA Street, FIFA, Fight Night, Final Fantasy VI, Final Fantasy VII Rebirth, Final Fantasy VII Remake Intergrade, Final Fantasy VII, Final Fantasy XIV, Final Fantasy XIV: Endwalker, Final Fantasy XIV: Heavensward, Final Fantasy XIV: Shadowbringers, Final Fantasy XIV: Stormblood, Final Fantasy XVI, Final Fantasy, Fire Fight, Five Nights at Freddy's, Five Nights at Freddy's: Security Breach, Football Manager 2023, Fortnite, Forza Horizon 3, Forza Horizon 4, Forza Horizon 5, Forza Horizon 5: Hot Wheels, Forza Horizon, Forza Motorsport , Forza Motorsport , Forza Motorsport (2005), Forza Motorsport (2023), Forza Motorsport 2, Forza Motorsport 4, Forza Motorsport 5, Friends, Frozen, FTL: Faster Than Light, Fueled Up,

Game of Thrones, Gangan, Genshin Impact, Ghost Recon Advanced Warfighter 2, Ghost Trick, Ghostbusters II, Ghostbusters, Ghostbusters: Afterlife, Ghostbusters: Rise of the Ghost Lord, Ghostbusters: Spirits Unleashed, Ghostbusters: The Video Game, Gilded City, God of War, God of War: Ragnarök, Golden Axe, Goldeneye, The Golf Club, Goose Goose Duck, Gotham Knights, Gran Turismo 3, Gran Turismo 4, Gran Turismo 7, Gran Turismo, Grand Theft Auto 5, Grand Theft Auto 6, Grand Theft Auto, Grand Theft Auto: San Andreas, The Great Ace Attorney Chronicles, Grid Legends, Grounded, Guardians of the Galaxy, Guitar Hero, Hades, Half-Life 2, Half-Life: Alyx, Halo 2, Halo 4, Halo 5: Guardians, Halo Infinite, Halo, Halo: The Master Chief Collection, Haredevil Hare, Harry Potter and the Philosopher's Stone, Harry Potter and the Prisoner of Azkaban, Harry Potter: Quidditch World Cup, Harvestella, Haunted House, Hearthstone, Hello Neighbour 2, Hero Quest, Heroes of Might and Magic, Hitman 3, Hogwarts Legacy, Hollow Knight, Hollow Knight: Silksong, Honor of Kings, Horizon Call of the Mountain, Horizon Forbidden West, Hyrule Warriors: Age of Calamity, Immortality, Islets, It Takes Two, Ittle Dew, Jak & Daxter, Jak & Daxter: The Precursor Legacy, Jak 3, Jazz Jackrabbit 2, Jurassic Park, 46, Jurassic World: Aftermath, Just Dance 2023 Edition, Kid Dracula, Killzone: Shadow Fall, Kingdom Hearts III, Kingdom Hearts IV, Kingdom Hearts, Kirby & The Amazing Mirror, Kirby and the Forgotten Land, Kirby's Return to Dream Land Deluxe, Kukoos: Lost Pets, The Last of Us, League of Legends, Legend of Mana, The Legend of Zelda, The Legend of Zelda: A Link to The Past, The Legend of Zelda: Breath of the Wild, The Legend of Zelda: Link's Awakening, The Legend of Zelda: Majora's Mask, The Legend of Zelda: Ocarina of Time, The Legend of Zelda: Skyward Sword, , The Legend of Zelda: Tears of the Kingdom, The Legend of Zelda: Wind Waker, LEGO Dimensions, LEGO Harry Potter Collection, LEGO Star Wars: The Skywalker Saga, LEGO Star Wars: The Video Game, Like a Dragon 8, Like a Dragon: Ishin, The Little Mermaid, , Little Town Hero, LittleBigPlanet, Live A Live, LocoRoco, Looney Tunes, Lord of the Rings, Lord of the Rings: Return of the King, Lost Soul Aside, Luigi's Mansion 3, Luigi's Mansion, Lumines, Madden NFL 15, Madden NFL 2005, Madden NFL 23, Madden NFL 24, Madden NFL 25, Madden NFL 95, Madden NFL, Mafia: Definitive Edition, Mahjong Goku Sky: Atsushi, Mario & Sonic At The Olympic Games, Mario & Yoshi, Mario + Rabbids Kingdom Battle, Mario + Rabbids Sparks of Hope, Mario Family, Mario Golf: Super Rush, Mario Is Missing, Mario Kart 64, Mario Kart 8 Deluxe, Mario Party Superstars, Mario Party, Marvel Snap, Marvel's Iron Man VR, Marvel's Midnight Suns, Marvel's Spider-Man 2, Marvel's Spider-Man, Marvel's Spider-Man: Miles Morales, Mass Effect, Mega Man 11, Mega Man, Mendel Palace, Metal Gear Solid , Metal Gear Solid 2: Sons of Liberty, Metal Gear Solid 3: Snake Eater, Metal Gear Solid Portable Ops, Metroid Dread, Metroid Prime 2: Echoes, Metroid Prime Remastered, Metroid, Michael Jackson: The Experience, Mighty Morphin Power Rangers, Millipede, Minecraft Legends, Minecraft Volume Alpha, Minecraft, Minecraft: The Movie, Mischief Makers, MLB The Show 21, MLB The Show 22, MLB The Show 23, Mojang, Monkey Island 2: LeChuck's Revenge, Monster Hunter Rise: Sunbreak, Monster Hunter, Monster Hunter: World,

Moonbreaker, Mortal Kombat II, Moss: Book II, MultiVersus, My Little Pony, NASCAR 2005, NBA 2K15, NBA 2K23, NBA Jam, NBA Live 19, NBA ShootOut 98, Need for Speed Underground 2, Need for Speed, Neo Breakout, Neon White, New Star Soccer, NFL GameDay, NFL Head Coach, NFL Street, NHL 23, NHL FaceOff, Nick & Norah's Infinite Playlist, Nintendo Switch Sports, No Man's Sky, Ori and the Will of the Wisps, Out Run, The Outbound Ghost, Outer Wilds, Overcooked, Overwatch 2, Overwatch, Oxenfree II: Lost Signals, Oxenfree, Paper Mario, PC Zone, Periscope, Peter Jackson's King Kong, Peter Pan, PGA Tour 2K21, PGA Tour 2K23, PGA Tour 98, Phantasy Star IV, Pikmin 4, Pilotwings, Pitch Perfect, Plants Vs. Zombies, Pokémon Emerald, Pokémon FireRed/ LeafGreen, Pokémon Legends: Arceus, , Pokémon Let's Go: Pikachu/Eevee, Pokémon Red/Blue, Pokémon Scarlet/Violet, Pokémon Sun/Moon, Pokémon Sword/Shield, Pong, Population: One, Portal, Prince of Persia: The Sands of Time, Princess Remedy in a World of Hurt, Pro Evolution Soccer 4, Pro Evolution Soccer 6, Pro Evolution Soccer, Professor Layton and the New World of Steam, Project Gotham Racing 3, Project Gotham Racing, Project Zomboid, Psychonauts 2, Psychonauts, Psyonix, PUBG Battlegrounds, Quake, Ratchet & Clank, Ratchet & Clank: Rift Apart, Rayman Raving Rabbids 2, The Real Ghostbusters, RealSports Soccer, Red Dead Redemption 2, Red Steel, Resident Evil Village, Resident Evil, Resistance 3, Resistance, Respawn Entertainment, Return to Monkey Island, Returnal, Ridge Racer, Ring Fit Adventure, Roblox Corporation, Roblox, Rocket League, Rockstar, Rogue, Rollerdrome, Rory McIlroy PGA Tour, Rugrats: The Movie, Rune Factory 5, S.T.A.L.K.E.R. 2: Heart of Chernobyl, S.T.A.L.K.E.R., Sackboy: A Big Adventure, Salt and Sanctuary, Samba de Amigo: Party Central, Scars Above, Scooby Doo, Sea of Stars, Sea of Thieves, The Secret of Monkey Island, Sega Mega Drive Classics, Sega, Segasonic The Hedgehog, Sekiro: Shadows Die Twice, Shadow Complex Remastered, Shadow of the Colossus, Shin Megami Tensei, Shovel Knight, Show do Milhão Volume 2, Shredders, Sifu, The Simpsons, The Sims, SingStar, Slap City, Slap-up Party: Arad Senki, Songs of Conquest, Sonic & Knuckles, Sonic Adventure 2, Sonic CD, Sonic Colours, Sonic Frontiers, Sonic Mania, Sonic Origins, Sonic The Hedgehog 2 , Sonic The Hedgehog 3 , Sonic The Hedgehog, Sonic Unleashed, South Park, Spelunky 2, Spelunky, Spider-Man: No Way Home, Spirit of the North, Spiritfarer, Splatoon 3, Splatoon, Spyro The Dragon, Star Ocean: First Departure R, Star Ocean: The Divine Force, Star Trek, Star Wars Jedi: Fallen Order, Star Wars Jedi: Survivor, Star Wars, Star Wars: Tales From The Galaxy's Edge, Star Wars: The Bad Batch, Star Wars: The Force Awakens, StarCraft II: Wings of Liberty, StarCraft, Stardew Valley, Starfield, Storyteller, Stranger of Paradise: Final Fantasy Origin, Final Fight, Stranger Things, Stray, Street Fighter 6, Street Fighter Alpha, Street Fighter II, Street Fighter II: Return to the Fujiwara Capital, Street Fighter III, Street Fighter IV, Street Fighter V: Arcade Edition, Street Fighter, Streets of Rage 2, Streets of Rage 4, Streets of Rage, Subnautica, Subnautica: Below Zero, Sunset Overdrive, Super Animal Royale, Super Mario 3D All-Stars, Super Mario 64, Super Mario All-Stars, Super Mario Bros., Super Mario Bros.: The Lost Levels, Super Mario Galaxy, Super Mario Kart, Super Mario Odyssey, Super Mario Party, Super Mario Sunshine, Super Mario World, Super Metroid, Super Monkey Ball, Super Smash Bros. for Wii U, Super Smash Bros. Melee, Super Smash Bros. Ultimate, Superman 64, Superman Returns, Table Tennis, Ted Lasso, Teenage Mutant Ninja Turtles II: The Arcade Game, Teenage Mutant Ninja Turtles, Teenage Mutant Ninja Turtles: Hyperstone Heist, Teenage Mutant Ninja Turtles: Radical Rescue, Teenage Mutant Ninja Turtles: Shredder's Revenge, Teenage Mutant Ninja Turtles: The Cowabunga Collection, Teenage Mutant Ninja Turtles: Tournament Fighters, Teenage Mutant Ninja Turtles: Turtles in Time, Tekken 8, Tekken, Tetris Effect: Connected, Tetris, Tiger Woods PGA Tour 14, Tiny Tina's Wonderlands, Tom Clancy's Ghost Recon, Tomb Raider, Tony Hawk's American Wasteland, Tony Hawk's Pro Skater 1 + 2, Top Gun: Maverick, 187, Toy Story 3, Transformers Devastation, Transformers: Reactivate, Trevor McFur in the Crescent Galaxy, Tunic, Twisted Metal 2: World Tour, Two Point Campus, Two Point Hospital, Ultimate Mortal Kombat III, Ultra Street Fighter II: The Final Challengers, Uncharted 2: Among Thieves, Uncharted 3: Drake's Deception, Uncharted 4: A Thief's End, Uncharted, Uncharted: Drake's Fortune, Uncharted: Legacy of Thieves Collection, Uncharted: The Lost Legacy, Uncharted: The Nathan Drake Collection, Undisputed, Valorant, Vampire Survivors, Virtua Fighter 4, Volleyball, Warcraft III: Reforged, Warcraft: Orcs & Humans, Warhammer, Warhammer: Chaos Bane, Wild Hearts, Wipeout Pure, Wipeout, The Witcher, World of Warcraft, World of Warcraft: Dragonflight, WRC 10, WRC 5, WRC Generations, WRC Shakedown, WRC, WWE '12, WWE '13, WWE 2K14, WWE 2K19, WWE 2K20, WWE 2K22, WWE 2K23, WWE 2K24, WWE Battlegrounds, WWE Smackdown vs Raw 2008, WWE Smackdown vs Raw, WWF No Mercy, WWF Smackdown, XCOM, Xenoblade Chronicles 3, Yu-Gi-Oh: Master Duel, Yuke's, Zombi, ZZT

Picture Credits

Front Cover Blizzard Entertainment, CAPCOM, Epic Games, Nintendo, SEGA, Sony Interactive Entertainment, Square Enix

Back Cover Finji, Nintendo, Warner Bros. Games

Photography
046 Andrew Leung
094 Andrew Leung
112 © Album / Alamy Stock Photo
113 © LANDMARK MEDIA / Alamy Stock Photo
      © Album / Alamy Stock Photo
      © Everett Collection Inc / Alamy Stock Photo
138 Andrew Leung
172 Andrew Leung
194 © dpa picture alliance / Alamy Stock Photo
208 Andrew Leung

⊶⊙EXPANSE

Acknowledgements

The Expanse team would like to thank the following people for their help and contribution towards Next Level Games Review 2024:

Alysia Judge, Ben Wilson, Craig Jelley, Jase Wan, Kris Doorga, Louise Blain, Russ Seal, Will Porter

LEVEL 2 COMPLETED

DO YOU WANT TO CONTINUE PLAYING?
> YES   NO

NEXT LEVEL

The
Art of
Golf
ANTIQUES

The
Art of

Golf
ANTIQUES

An Illustrated History
of Clubs, Balls, and
Accessories

by Gilbert King
Photographs by Bruce Curtis

In cooperation
with the USGA
Museum

COURAGE
BOOKS

An Imprint of Running Press Book Publishers
PHILADELPHIA • LONDON

© 2001 by Running Press
All rights reserved under the Pan-American and International Copyright Conventions
Printed in China

This book may not be reproduced in whole or in part, in any form or by any means, electronic or mechanical, including photocopying, recording, or by any information storage and retrieval system now known or hereafter invented, without written permission from the publisher.

9 8 7 6 5 4 3 2 1
Digit on the right indicates the number of this printing

Library of Congress Cataloging-in-Publication Number 00-135499

ISBN 0-7624-0990-8

Photographs © 2001 by Bruce Curtis

Cover design by Bill Jones
Interior design by Rosemary Tottoroto
Edited by Molly Jay and Victoria Hyun
Typography: Palatino

This book may be ordered by mail from the publisher.
But try your bookstore first!

Published by Courage Books, an imprint of
Running Press Book Publishers
125 South Twenty-second Street
Philadelphia, Pennsylvania 19103-4399

Visit us on the web!
www.runningpress.com

The author would like to thank the United States Golf Association for its participation and assistance in making this book possible. Particularly, Andy Mutch and Nancy Stulack of the U.S.G.A. Museum in Fair Hills, New Jersey, who were extraordinarily generous with their time and efforts. Rand Jerris at the U.S.G.A. Library was also of invaluable assistance in the research stage of this project. —*Gilbert King*

I would like to acknowledge Andy Mutch and Nancy Stulack of the United States Golf Association; John Foster; Tara Dalrymple; John Wheatley; W.W. Carrath, Sr.; Jay Morelli; Graham Lenny of the St. Andrews Golf Links Trust; and Jay Nieporte of the Winged Foot Golf Club. — *Bruce Curtis*

Anything from antique golf trophies to scorecards
from noteworthy tournaments or courses will get
the attention of the serious collector.

INTRODUCTION

An assortment of woods and irons from 1900–1906 when hickory shafts were the standard shaft on most clubs.

The game of golf has traditionally surged in popularity from time to time in its glorious history. Sometimes it was because of a lapsed edict. In 1457, King James II of Scotland banned golf because the country was at war with England, and it appeared that his soldiers were neglecting their archery practice to partake in the ancient Scottish game of golf. When James IV demonstrated a significant addiction to the links courses himself, and the war with England ended, the Scots took to the game with a vengeance and never looked back.

Sometimes golf surged in popularity because of a ball, such as when the inexpensive gutta percha was developed in the mid-nineteenth century. Gutties replaced the expensive feathery balls and enabled the masses to play rather than just the royal and wealthy. The game expanded into the countrysides and clubmaking became an industry.

But sometimes, the surge in golf could be attributed to a man. In 1900, a British golfer by the name of Harry Vardon crossed the Atlantic for a nine month barnstorm-ing tour of America. Vardon was already an Open Champion and legend in Europe, but the soft-spoken Brit caused a sensation ("Vardonmania") in the United States upon his arrival. His every round was front page news, and when his tour brought him to New York City they closed the Stock Exchange in his honor. It was a British invasion of a different sort, and the impact on the younger generation of Americans was deep and lasting.

A year after Vardon returned to Europe, a golf prodigy named Robert Tyre Jones, Jr. also known as Bobby Jones,

Hickory was primarily used in making shafts from 1900–1906.

was born in Georgia. Jones would ultimately achieve unprecedented success on the golf course and his dignity and grace made him the most revered athlete of his era—an era that included Babe Ruth, Jack Dempsey and Red Grange. Upon his death in 1971, the famed sportswriter Grantland Rice wrote, "Whatever any future giant of the links does to par, no one will ever replace Bobby Jones in the hearts of those to whom golf means more than a game."

The integrity and aura of Bobby Jones also had a lasting impact on the sport, an even greater contribution than his extraordinary Grand Slam conquest. Later on, great golfers such as Ben Hogan, Arnold Palmer and Jack Nicklaus would give golf another jolt, bringing the game to new levels of popularity and increasing the lure and mystique of golf.

The full effect remains to be seen, but it goes without saying that the most current surge in the popularity of golf can be attributed to Tiger Woods. Woods burst onto the golf scene as a child prodigy, laughing it up with Bob Hope on television at the age of three, hitting balls inappropriately long and straight for a child of his age. He would go on to win three straight amateur championships before turning professional at the age of 20 in 1996, and just four years later his accomplishments, particularly in golf's major tournaments, have created a "Tigermania" the sport has not seen in perhaps a century.

With public interest in golf at such a fever pitch, it is no surprise that antique golf collectors are thrilled as well, as they see the value of their collections growing by leaps and bounds. Like the gutty ball which brought golf to the masses, the internet has made it possible for anyone to do an eBay search for antique golf collectibles and begin collecting themselves! A recent "eBay" search by the author revealed an Old Tom Morris putter selling for $1,400 and a few Tiger Woods golf cards listed for over $3,000. Novices can start their collections on a shoestring budget and still find their own piece of golf history. From the Schenectady putter to the next yet-to-be-discovered "Troon Clubs," there's a great deal of the game's past out there somewhere. The intent of this book is to give both serious and novice collectors an understanding of some of golf's most treasured collectibles and how they came to be.

Novices can start their collections on a shoestring budget and still find their own piece of golf history.

Golf trophies are still popular collectibles because they display well on any collector's shelves.

A BRIEF
HISTORY
OF THE
GAME

*Ben Hogan wore these shoes, noted for the extra spikes, in 1951
when he won the U.S. Open at Oakland Hills.*

Perhaps you've seen the commercial. Tiger Woods blasts his golf ball across the streets, buildings and parks of New York City, and ultimately sinks a putt into a paper cup on the Brooklyn Bridge. It might seem like nothing more than some ad man's contrived attempt to urbanize golf and market the game as exciting and explosive, rather than one which generally takes place in a more pastoral setting.

In fact, Tiger's "street" game in Manhattan is closer to the origins of golf than one might imagine. In the late 13th century, the Dutch were actually playing a game called golf where players would hit hard wooden balls toward targets such as the doors of windmills, courthouses and castles around town. (Casks of beer to the winner, too!) In their passion for long and challenging matches, they would march through cemeteries and centers of town, often having to clear pedestrians from their target sights, much to the dismay of the citizens, who sometimes suffered broken windows and even bones as

a result of errant shots! What could be more exciting and explosive than that?

To effectively pinpoint the exact origin of golf as we know it today, it is important to take into consideration history's proliferation of stick and ball games. There may indeed have been hundreds of variations on games that bear some resemblance to golf. There are ancient Greek murals portraying men engaged in games that appear to be closer to what we now consider field hockey as far back as the 5th century B.C. And in fact, the Romans used a ball that was very close to the feathery, a pagani-

An assortment of smooth-faced irons pre-1895.

ca, which was a leather ball stuffed with feathers or hair in a game that appears to be related to handball.

If a ball such as the paganica existed in those ancient times, it seems entirely possible that someone thought to use it in a stick and ball game as well, perhaps even in some early form of golf itself. Yet, without knowledge of the types of clubs or rules of these games, we can only speculate. There are records as far back as the year 872 when King Alfred of England was coronated in which some sort of game was made of "driving balls wide over fields." Clearly, at some point, a man with a stick in his hand and a stationary ball must have had the imagina-

tion to test his strength and accuracy by hitting the ball to some distant target without some type of "defender" present to impede his stroke. And perhaps this early "feathery" ball took flight in a way not unlike a golf ball of today, and the thrill of a solidly struck shot excited this man. Perhaps he hit the sweet spot, immediately took notice, and set about looking for ways to make his shot better. Maybe he discovered that a lofted clubface produced more height on his shot. The speculation is endless. But it does not seem beyond the realm of possibility that some form of golf was probably being played long before history can document its existence.

Clubs used by Walter Hagen in the 1919 U.S. Open.

Ben Hogan's driver, used in U.S. Open competition.

Photographic portraits of golfers are another popular collectible.

THE
GAME
OF
GOLF

Since almost every major tour player has written one, golf instruction books
have always been popular collector's items.

The main reason there is any documentation at all of golf is because the game apparently created a great deal of havoc among the Dutch citizenry. There was so much collateral damage caused by golf players (windows of houses and churches were broken, not to mention sometimes significant injuries to pedestrians) that city and country officials were forced to put laws on the books curtailing the more harmful aspects of the game.

The game of golf apparently went like this: four players from each team took turns hitting a wooden ball toward the intended target, with the winner determined by the fewest number of strokes needed. The earliest game on record, a match on Boxing Day in 1297, took place at the Castle of Kronenberg, near the town of Loenen aan de Vecht. The targets were the door of a windmill, a kitchen door, the door of a castle and the door of a courthouse. Incidentally, the game continued to be played annually on Boxing Day for nearly 550 years until 1831, when the Castle of Kronenberg was demolished, and so vanished one of the holes!

At some point, because of the above described collateral damage, the game of golf was moved to open grounds to steer clear of buildings and bystanders. Games were played on a rectangular court with grass apparently kept short by the archers who also made use of the grounds. A tree appears to have been the target the players worked toward, now that castle doors and the like were prohibited. Golf became a more peaceful and pastoral game, rather than the noisy and destructive version villagers had come to know and be bothered by.

Still photos of Byron Nelson's swing at impact in 1949, as well as swing sequence photos of Julius Boros in 1959.

By the 15th century, golf must have exploded if the amount of ordinances noted on public records are any indication. Orders about compensation for damages relating to mishit balls show up in many towns and cities, as do laws prohibiting the game being played near churches and churchyards. If you were caught in Amsterdam in 1480, for example, playing golf near a street named Nes, you'd have to forfeit your clothes right there on the spot!

In the beginning of the 16th century, golfers were likely to be the subject in portraits and sketches by Dutch painters. In the *Book of Hours* located in the British Museum, a golfer is portrayed in the act of putting while he is kneeling amidst three other players. It is also interesting to note that the game was most popular during the seasons other than summer, since that is the time of year that the grass grew to be the longest. In fact, golf was often played on ice, and many drawings and paintings depict the game in this fashion.

At around the same time in the 16th century, portraits of children with a golf club and ball became a popular form of depiction, further indication that the game was quite popular at the time. We also know that the demand for clubs and balls was increasing, as villages such as

In 1588, during the Spanish war, the village of Tilburg was held ransom for 12,000 balls!

Goirle and Delft were commonly described as "ball-stuffers" since their output of golf balls was so significant. In fact, on record in 1588 during the Spanish war, the village of Tilburg was held ransom by an army commander (Sebastian van Warendorp of the Duke of Parma) for 12,000 balls! Tilburg was unable to produce that many balls on such short notice. But their neighbors in Goirle were able to provide a 6,500 ball installment, preventing Tilburg from being burned to the ground!

It is also of note to mention that there is, on record, something of an environmental concern the Dutch had regarding their prolific golf ball production. The end of the 16th century saw the city fathers of Delft doing their best to stem the tide of pollution caused by washing the hair used to stuff balls in the city's water supply.

By the 17th century, golf is popping up in references everywhere. Dutch painters themselves seemed to have developed an affinity for the game, as they began traveling to Rome to paint, towing along their clubs and balls! The game even traveled across the Atlantic Ocean, and we know this because of similar ordinances prohibiting the game being played in public places such as Albany, New York, where many Dutch settled. Yet, stick and ball games were not just confined to Europe. There are artistic refer-

Golf art, especially paintings depicting golf's early days, have particular appeal to collectors.

A special rasp for putting fine grooves on wooden faces.

A caddie bag with clubs from 1915 – 1920.

ences to such games in many cultures, including China, South America and the Pacific Islands dating as far back as the middle ages. What is known is that there are still early records that acknowledge the existence of games very similar to modern golf as far back as the middle ages.

Chole, Jeu de mail, paille maille, pila malleus, etc.

Historians believe that the Roman game of paganica, or pila malleus, was imported to France by Roman soldiers with a fondness for the game. The French version was called paille maille, and the game was played in a court. However, an offshoot of paille maille called jeu de mail a la chicane was born and more closely resembled golf, since it was played along the roads and fields of France, and similarly had trees or doors as the target. Ultimately, jeu de mail made its way to Holland where golf appeared and grew in popularity.

After the battle of Hastings in 1066, in which the noblemen of Flanders gave their support to the victorious William the Conqueror, they were rewarded with extensive land masses in Britain, most notably Lincolnshire and the East Midlands. When an important

Golf cards have become valuable collector's items in recent years.

Flemish widow named Maud was married off to David I of Scotland, the Flemings migrated north to Scotland and took root, becoming an influential and important part of the Court. Descendents of this Flemish family ultimately formed a significant portion of the great nobles of Scotland.

Naturally, the Flemings imported their games of chole or croisse across the English Channel, and many golf historians believe the English game of cambuca was simply the British version of croisse. By the time the game found its way to Scotland, it was probably a version of jeu de mail or croisse. There is no documentation of when these games in Holland may have formed into Scottish golf, but by the 17th century, there are references to Fleming players "holling the ball," so we can be sure it had arrived by then.

Alas, however, the game of golf seems to have died out by the end of the 17th century, and the reason is not entirely clear. Some historians have gone so far as to claim that the 18th century was a more effeminate and refined century, and gentlemen took toward the indoors to pursue such games as billiards. Some historians believe golf was then transformed into or replaced by kolf which, in the 18th century, was played in a small enclosed court and under a roof, with walls and a smooth floor similar to a modern gymnasium. The balls ultimately became larger and heavier, and the game is still played in Holland today.

The rules of golf were quite similar to early versions of the French game called mail, and the game became very popular right up to the 19th century. Records show that by 1769 there were nearly 200 kolf courts around and within a short distance of Amsterdam. But although the game of kolf did not die out completely, neither did it merge or transform into the game we know as golf today.

In medieval times, Scotland too had its share of stick and ball games. Once again, ordinances on public record in the 15th century show that the authorities were concerned enough with the more dangerous elements of the game to prohibit or at least curtail "golf-like" activities. On Sundays, and mostly during the winter, townspeople would gather near the church for drinking before and after services, and the entertainment was likely to involve golf and shinty—another stick and ball game which was closely related to golf, but more team oriented.

Records show that by 1769 there were nearly 200 kolf courts around Amsterdam.

Bookends from the 1930s.

THE RULES OF GOLF

Since golf seems closely related to the popular Dutch game of golf, it's worth pointing out the rules. The object of the game of golf was to strike a ball with a club toward a target in the distance. Matches were either scored in hole-to-hole accounts with the lowest number of strokes taken per side during match play, or for striking the longest distance for an agreed number of strokes, which was known as flag match. As early as 1500 or so, golfers began to use a hole in the ground as a target, or when playing on ice, a small, painted post. A player would keep score by making a notch in a stick carried by each player.

The rules mandated that a player may use only one club, and generally there were four types of clubs used at the time. The earlier versions of golf consisted of play with all wooden clubs before yielding to forged iron heads since at least the year 1429. Ash and hazel-shafted clubs were then used, and it was common for clubmakers at the time to use personal stamps on the heads, noting the city and name of the manufacturer. Eventually, Scottish cleeks (wooden-headed clubs) imported from Scotland in the early 17th century and made of box-wood weighted with lead, became the club of choice.

The earliest balls used for golf were generally made of boxwood or beechwood before giving way to the more expensive leather balls stuffed with cow's hair. The lower cost of making boxwood balls, however, allowed them to be quite popular among golfers well into the 17th century.

The U.S.G.A. Museum displays scorecards from some of the most dramatic U.S. Opens in history.

BLUSH HILL COUNTRY CLUB

	4	3	3	4	4	4	4	3		33
267	182	170	373	282	385	353	245	188		
1	2	3	4	5	6	7	8	9		2445

	4	3	3	4	4	4	4	3		66
267	182	170	373	282	385	353	245	188		
4	8	9	3	5	2	1	6	7		
10	11	12	13	14	15	16	17	18	IN	2445

TOTAL 4890 · HANDICAP · NET SCORE

Competition ....

M.....................

No. of Hole	Name	Yds.	Stks.	Bogy.	Markr.	Playr.
1	Hope Grant	440				
2	Nest	280	4	5		
3	The Spinney	176	7	4		
4	Blockade	294	13	3		
5	Heather	394	17	4		
6	Windmill	308	2	4		
7	Elcho	236	10	4		
8	Big Ravine	260	15	4		
9	Long Butt	304	6	4		
Out		2692	11	36		

This Card measures 6 inches diagonally

SSS 13th Hole 4
SSS Course 71

Replace it

Competition.....................

Date.....................
Signed.....................195.....

No. of Hole	Name	Yds.	Stks.	Bogy.	Markr.	Playr.	Result
	Running Deer	346	1	4			
	Queensmere	250	16	4			
13	Sand Pit	302	9	4			
14	...rise	400	8	4			
15	Ca... Well	284	12	4			
16	Caesar's C'mp	136	18	3			
17	Long Hole	316	6	4			
18	Plateau	460	5	5			
In		420	14	3			
Gross Score		2714		36			
Less H'cap		...					
Net Score						Bogey Result	

Competition.....................

	SCORE	HOLE	YARDS	PAR
9		10	324	4
11		11	314	
		12	437	
			201	
			323	
			42	

	2690
5380	66	TO...

HANDICAP
NET SCORE

REPLA...

Hole	Ya...
1	324
2	378
3	123
4	312
5	486
6	260
7	141
8	417
9	325
Total	2766
	35

	HOLE	YARDS	PAR	INDEX	SCORE
	10	324	4	10	
	11	314	4	12	
	12	437	4	2	
	13	201	3		
	14	323			
	15	425			
	16	230			
	17	276			
	18	160	3		
		2690	33		
		2690	33	OUT	
		5380	66	TOTAL	
	HANDICAP				
	NET SCORE				

..... Competition.....

THE
RISE OF
SCOTTISH
GOLF

*The Scottish golf union shield—given to golf clubs that
hosted the British Open.*

The beginnings of golf in Scotland portray a game that was clearly one of royals, and tracing the history of the game is to understand the bloodlines and rulers of Scotland. For example, we know that in 1457, James II banned "fute-bal" and "Gouff" because the games were distracting the military from its most important archery practice. By 1501, the Treaty of Glasgow was signed, signaling an end to the conflict between Scotland and England. This led to a less strident mandate on archery practice, and ultimately, the ban on golf was no longer enforced.

Perhaps one of the earliest aspiring and ultimately obsessive golfers was the Stuart King, James IV, who seems to have waited patiently for the ban on golf to end before he took up the game with a passion. In fact, there is documentation that the King's High Treasurer was given orders to pay for his Master's "clubs" from a bow-maker in Perth.

Golf was fast becoming the sport of kings, and by the early 1600s, appointments to the Court included the title, "Royal clubmaker." It was common now for Royals to travel to England, with clubs in tow. However, the Court's fondness for the game made it an expensive endeavor for commoners, who were basically shunned from golf. During the nearly two hundred years from the Peace of Glasgow in 1502 to the Revolution in 1688, every single reigning monarch of the Stuart line, which included two kings and one queen of Scotland and four kings of England, played the game of golf.

Perhaps the most legendary anecdote of early golf centers around Mary Stuart, Mary Queen of Scots, who,

Here at St. Andrews, golfers have attempted to break par with everything from long nose woods to titanium drivers.

at her trial in 1586, played golf "in the fields beside Seton" just a few days after the murder of Dranley, her husband. On other occasions, it was known that Mary Queen of Scots played with Mary Seton of Seton Palace, and the two once wagered on a game, with Mary Seton winning a necklace and a Holbein picture.

There are countless other historical references to the royal practice of golf as well. In 1642, Charles I was playing the game at Leith when his noblemen approached with news of the Irish Catholic Rebellion—the beginning of a very troublesome time for the king. There are accounts of this match as well, with one version stating that the king decided to finish off the game. The other, of course, is that Charles was being soundly beaten at the time, and hurried away to avoid having to pay his bet! It is interesting to note that the next account of Charles playing golf finds him a prisoner in the hands of the Scots, playing a game outside the walls of Newcastle-upon-Tyne.

When Charles Edward Stuart, the "Bonnie Prince Charlie" was exiled to Rome after his defeat at Culloden in 1745, he was noted to have relieved his boredom by playing golf in the Borghese Gardens! But the true history of modern golf is generally conceded to have begun in

The early development of golf societies and clubs in Scotland shows the active involvemen of Freemasons.

the mid-18th century with the forming of the first Scottish Golf Clubs. This was significant in that for the first time, there appeared to be a committee or community of golfers to regulate the rules of the game and maintain the courses. It was entirely possible that different communities played golf under different rules and methods of scoring. The game was played on natural grounds, on links courses.

In 1744, we know that The Honourable Company of Edinburgh Golfers was holding meetings, as the first minutes to these gatherings are documented. There is no indication how many meetings may have preceded the 1744 meeting, however, it is generally thought to be, by scholars, the oldest golf club. The purpose of the meeting was to establish a Silver Club competition on the Links of Leith, and the magistrates agreed to provide a trophy. The Silver Club's trophy would be awarded after a tournament similar to an Open Scratch Competition in Edinburgh. The winner would be deemed the "Captain of the Golf" (today it is the Champion Golfer!) and would therefore become something of an arbiter of the game, interpreting rules and generally all matters concerning golf.

Although only ten golfers actually took part in the

The seaside links at St. Andrews have also produced some of the most prolific clubmakers, ncluding Old Tom Morris and Tom Stewart.

tournament, John Rattray, an Edinburgh surgeon, emerged victorious. (He went on to defend his championship the following year.) More importantly, Rattray won the Silver Club itself, the oldest golf trophy in the world.

Ten years later in 1754, twenty-two gentlemen put their signatures on a document to play a championship from the Society of Golfers at St. Andrews. They were men who held golf in high regard as exercise, and though not all of them actually played for the championship, Bailie William Landale, a merchant in St. Andrews was the winner. In this tournament, however, the winner did not become Captain of Golf, but rather simply the winner of a local golf championship. This was the beginning of the Royal and Ancient Golf Club of St. Andrews.

The early development of golf societies and clubs in Scotland shows the active involvement of Freemasons. Although competition was intended to be open to all golfers, it was soon apparent that these clubs were designating the competition only for St. Andrews Gentlemen and Gentlemen at Leith. In effect, a closed competition. Politically, the City of St. Andrews had demonstrated some Jacobite leanings, and Scottish Masonic golfers are believed to have formed secret "clubs within a club" and the Freemasons took pains to keep the game private. In fact, it is generally conceded that golf may not have actually survived without the

secrecy and thoroughness in which the Freemasons regulated the game of golf.

By 1853, the Union Club of St. Andrews agreed to build a new clubhouse for its archers, and also accommodate golfers as well. Although they were housed under the same clubhouse, the Union Club and the Royal and Ancient Golf Club of St. Andrews maintained separate identities. By 1877, the golfing membership had enjoyed a significant increase in members, and archery began to subside. It was in May of that year that the two clubs agreed to merge. It was no doubt attributed to the influence of the Freemasons that archers and golfers shared a common clubhouse, and the two "sports" are linked tightly in Scottish history.

Although competition for the Silver Club generated a certain amount of public interest, it dimmed in comparison to the excitement generated by a high-stakes match between well-known amateurs. Betting was common, and in a match between two golfers of equal skill, it was more likely that, instead of handicapping by conceding strokes during a round, odds were put into place. Eventually, the revered age of private match play games was basically done away with by the implementation of the first Championships in the middle 1800s.

On April 6th, 1857, members of the Prestwick Club sent a letter out proposing a match between the eight

From Old Tom Morris to Tiger Woods, many of the greatest names in golf have crossed the stone bridge over Swilcan Burn on the Old Course at St. Andrews on their way to victory.

prominent golf clubs. The match would be comprised of the best four golfers from each club, with the game to be played in double matches or foursomes drawn randomly. The winning pair would be awarded a medal, and they would compete against each other in a single match, the winner's club to become the possessor of the medal.

The Prestwick letter was such a success that four other clubs asked to join in the competition, and it was determined that the matches would be held at St. Andrews, with the winner receiving a silver claret jug. In the end, the Royal Blackheath Golf Club trounced The Royal and Ancient St. Andrews Golf Club. The following year, the Claret Jug would be awarded to a single golfer rather than a club, and were it not for a heated rivalry between Willie Park and Old Tom Morris, the Championship may have faded. In the first eight singles competitions, Morris would win four Championships to Park's three.

Old Tom Morris spent his early years as a clubmaker's apprentice, and in 1851, he became the custodian of the Prestwick Club's links course. Playing out of Prestwick, Morris established himself as the best golfer in the world, and he was ultimately hired (after repeated pleas on the part of the R & A) to be head greenskeeper at St.

Scottish links golf was aesthetically pleasing, infinitely challenging, and perhaps most importantly, easy to maintain.

Andrews—a position he held for forty years.

His fame, however, owes more to his spirit as a presence at St. Andrews rather than his accomplishments on the golf course. One of the pioneering Scots of professional golf, Morris was not only regarded as the first of the great players, but a character and institution. He retired in 1904, but held the honorary position for four more years until his death. Old Tom Morris' funeral was a day of mourning in St. Andrews, and his reputation and spirit continue to linger in the game today. His pro shop beside the 18th green, as well as his portrait, which hangs inside the clubhouse, help to immortalize the man and his influence on the game of golf.

Great Old Tom Morris was an extraordinary player, but it is universally acknowledged that his son, Young Tom Morris, reached an even higher plateau. At the age of 16, Young Tom won a big tournament at Carnoustie from a top level professional after winning a playoff with Willie Park and Bob Andrew, another elite player from Perth. That same year, Young Tom finished fourth in the Open Championship, but the next year he began a string of four straight championships which has not been equaled yet. Most impressive is the fact that Young Tom didn't just emerge victorious in these Championships,

A #4 iron from the 1860s, from the Geo Nicoll Leven Club in Scotland.

rather he won them in convincing fashion, by as many as 12 strokes over his contemporaries in 36 hole contests.

Young Tom was so strong a player that his scoring records were never equaled while in the gutta percha ball era. Sadly, Young Tom was just finishing a match in 1875 when he received a telegram that his wife and new-born baby were very ill. He was just about to board a boat to return home when he received another message that his wife and baby had died. It was said that the great golfer never recovered from this tragedy, and he died of a broken heart on Christmas Day that same year.

Eventually, the St. Andrews Club superseded the

Honourable Company as the true arbiter and overseer of the game of golf. The quality of the turf at St. Andrews, along with the quality of golfers and the beauty of the course itself, was the reason more and more golf clubs turned to the R & A for leadership. It didn't hurt that the older Honourable Company changed its site and lost ground to St. Andrews as well. In 1897, the Royal and Ancient club agreed to become the governing authority on the rules of the game. But one could not count out the impact both Young and Old Tom Morris had on the game of golf at St. Andrews. The charm and spirit of these two men continue to add mystique to the Old Course today,

Left to right:

Noted St. Andrews clubmaker Tom Stewart designed this iron pre-1900.

Scottish clubs were the choice for many professional golfers around the turn of the 20th century.

Spalding made clubs in Scotland, such as this iron from the late 1800s.

as thousands of golfers across the world visit the "Home of Golf" each year.

Many theories abound as to why golf took hold in Scotland with such passion. One reason is as clear as day. The country's beautiful coastlines seem to be made for the game. In lowland parts of Scotland, the "links" between the beach and land that is ripe for farming are hilly grassland areas where nature created seemingly perfect hazards and fairways. The term "links" is derived from the Scottish word *lynk's*, meaning "ridges, hummocks" and also "rough open ground." In general, it referred to a tract of low-lying seaside land on the east coast of the Lowlands which was held by a town and used during the Middle Ages for sports such as archery and golf. The land is characteristically sandy and treeless, with undulating turf, wind-swept dunes and natural pot bunkers. The turf was typically comprised of bent grass, with gorse bushes quite prevalent.

In short, the land must have tantalized and tortured the country's earliest golfers. The grassy areas were kept short by nature's natural greens keepers—Scotland's grazing animals, creating near perfect links fairways. The growth of fescue throughout the links land also provided a natural penalty for golfers who missed the short grass.

Scottish links golf was esthetically pleasing, infinitely challenging and perhaps most importantly, easy to maintain. Yet, Ireland and Britain also have similar landscapes that are ideal for golf, and the game was being played in both countries around the same time golf reached Scotland. So clearly, the land alone did not enable Scotland to make the undisputed claim of being the home of golf. For that to happen, it is important to look not to the land, but the people of Scotland.

While forms of golf died out in other parts of the world, such as Holland and France, the intractable, hard-headed Freemasons of Scotland, despite their secret, closed societies, stubbornly kept the game alive, and indeed, enabled it to take root into the popular world game that it is today.

Early golf societies took great pride and careful measures to preserve the game they so boldly took claim to, while golf and other forms of the game simply transformed into other games (such as kolf in Holland) or faded away completely.

Mallot and center shafted putters were once banned by the Royal and Ancient Golf Club.

THE AGRIPPA
GOLF BALL COMPY

VENTRY

Thoroughly
Seasoned
"Woodley Flier"
Golf Balls

TRIANON
MILLS

"Woodley Flier" Embossed on every ball.
Guaranteed made from new material.

EARLY
GOLF BALLS

Golf ball boxes from 1890–1900.

THE BOXWOOD

Trying to determine the exact origins and characteristics of the boxwood ball is a bit like trying to pinpoint the precise moment in time when the game of golf began. The earliest golfers are said to have played the game with a hardwood ball very similar in nature to the balls used in pall mall and chole in England and Belgium respectively.

Believed to be made of beech or boxroot, these hardwood balls were handcrafted on a carpenter's lathe in many estimates, between the 13th and 17th centuries. While the balls were not very sophisticated and tended to indent, split and become misshapen during the course of the game, they were balls that were inexpensive to construct and generally permitted common folks to play. For this reason, they remained popular for centuries of play, despite advances in ballmaking.

Another downside to the boxwood ball is that it had a tendency to stray dramatically if not struck cleanly by a club. Wild, hardwood projectiles naturally led to broken windows and worse, injuries to those in the general vicinity. However, the upside was that in the early 14th century, medieval laws began to appear on the books in prohibiting the playing of certain "stick and ball" games in areas that were more populated, thus enabling historians to track and date the origins of the game.

THE FEATHERY

There is also a bit of uncertainty as to when the feather ball period of golf truly began, given what we know of the paganica in ancient Roman times. Some historians suspect the ball may have been around Europe and used in golf-like games as early as the 1400s, while others believe it wasn't until 200 years later when the ball was introduced. What is clear is that because of the more expensive nature of the feather ball's construction, the game of golf stopped expanding in the early 1800s.

Feather balls.

A century earlier, the cheap boxwood ball enabled the game to spread to the masses. But in the early 17th century, the feathery began to gain in popularity. Here was a ball that required more finesse than power and rewarded the cleanly struck shot rather than brutal strength. However, the ball was much more expensive to make and it had a lasting effect on the game. Golf became a sport only for the wealthy and privileged because they were the only ones who could afford to pay for the feather ball.

Not only were the feather balls expensive to make, but the average golfer was not likely to finish a round using just one. The earliest feather balls were actually leather cased balls stuffed with wool or hair. In most cases, these balls had three pieces of leather about $\frac{1}{16}$ inch thick and made of either bull or horse hide.

Two end pieces (often soaked in alum water) were joined together by a rectangular middle piece— $\frac{5}{32}$ of an inch thick leather flap. The flap had tiny holes perforating it, enabling twine stitching to form a hollow case, and the pouch was simply turned inside-out through a small hole that was used for the stuffing of the ball.

This inside-out turning of the casing protected the wax twine under the edge of the leather cover. Then, the case was stuffed very tight (using a "brogue," a blunt-edged iron spike) with either chicken breast feathers or wet goose down and stitched shut with twine. More

important to the ball's performance was the manner in which the ball was prepared after it was stuffed. The wet leather would ultimately shrink once it dried, thus tightening around the feathers, which actually expanded when they became dry.

The result of these two opposing factors eventually produced a very hard, fairly resilient ball, which was hammered round by the ballmaker and then painted to add further protection from the elements.

The ball was capable of flying 200 yards in the air by better players, but more importantly, it proved to be very workable. Finesse ball strikers were able to control it and the game of golf was reaching a new stage in its evolution. Ballmaking was becoming an art.

But the feathery was not without its problems, cost being the most noticeable. The best ballmakers were incapable of making more than four a day, and it was generally assumed that anyone making more than that in a single day was simply not making a ball worth owning. Featheries cost more than ten times what the old boxwood balls cost, and adding insult to injury, they weren't nearly as durable.

In spite of its resilience and the golfer's ability to have more control over the direction and trajectory of the feathery, even the finest golfers were unable to avoid water from time to time. Even though featheries would

A long nose spoon with feather ball.

float and it would take days of exposure to water to saturate, a waterlogged feathery would often come out of play until the leather cover had time to dry and be treated again. But that was the least of a golfer's problem. Skull an iron shot with a wet feathery ball and there was a good chance the stuffing would be knocked out of it. Therefore, even a decent player would have to carry a half-dozen featheries in his bag for a round of golf.

The expense of the feathery ball naturally produced varied quality in the balls produced. There does not appear to be any standardization of the size or weight of a feathery ball, but most seemed to be about 1.6 inches in diameter, which is close to what today's balls measure. Feather balls were usually about 1.5 ounces, but ballmakers varied the weight by the method in which they stuffed them. A golfer might prefer a lighter ball, say 1.32 ounces, for downwind shots, and a heavier ball closer to 2 ounces when playing into the wind. (The rules of golf in the early 1800s permitted the golfer to change balls at the start of a new hole.)

Ballmakers also made different grades of balls—the highest quality balls, and culls, which were generally sorted out because they weren't perfectly stuffed or had some kind of stitching flaw. As a result, culls were often used as practice or range balls, or maybe carried deep in a golfer's bag for those days when his swing was not in

sync and he didn't want to risk skulling a shot on a good ball before finishing his round.

A good player could make a feathery last for many holes by striking it cleanly on the harder sides. After time, though, the ball would soften and ultimately become unplayable. What many don't realize is that the feathery was never really round. In fact, the looser stuffed balls were more round than the properly packed featheries. Yet, despite their oblong characteristics, featheries did fly and roll quite true on the courses of the day.

THE GUTTA PERCHA

While the introduction of the expensive feathery was unable to render obsolete the boxwood ball, (and nearly the game of golf itself) the invention of the Gutta Percha golf ball in the early 1850s soon established the featheries as collectors' items. For the game to survive, a ball would have to come along that would be cheaper, less vulnerable to the elements, more durable and yet workable for the finesse player. Round would be nice, too.

The Gutta Percha accomplished just that. Arriving from East Asia in around 1848, the ball enjoyed over 50 years of prosperity and managed to attract more people to the game of golf because of its affordability. No longer was golf merely a game for the wealthy and royal.

The exact origin of the Gutta Percha is not clearly

An autographed golf ball by Bobby Jones from one of his four U.S. Open victories.

defined. One disputed, albeit romantic saga revolves around the Reverend James Paterson of Dundee who, it is claimed, made the first Gutta Percha ball in 1845. Paterson, a Scottish missionary working in India shipped a Hindu statue to his brother, Robert, a ministry student back home in St. Andrews. Inside the crate used to ship the statue were chunks of rubbery gutta percha used as packing material, which Robert attempted to resole his boots with. At some point, he gave up on the boots, but then tried to make a golf ball, which he took to the Old Course in April 1845 for a test round. He either liked what he found, or gave up on the idea completely, because a third Paterson brother who lived near Edinburgh began manufacturing gutta percha balls. Under the name of "Paterson's Patent" the gutty ball was originally made to resemble the feathery, with a smooth surface and lines engraved to mimic the seams on feathery balls.

Made from the dried sap of sapodilla trees of East Asia, the substance was sent to Scotland in sheets, which ballmakers then cut into patches or strips, softened them in hot water, and rounded them by hand into a ball. Once the desired shape and size was achieved, the balls were then dipped into cold water for hardening.

Soon after Paterson, other Scots joined in the gutta percha movement. While some golf "purists" argued that featheries were the superior ball, transition to the gutty

was fairly swift and unanimous, making it the standard equipment of play. Still, the first gutties were not without their own set of problems.

Smooth as marbles or billiard balls, gutties had little aerodynamic stability. They tended not to get airborn with much consistency, and would often dive or bore down in flight. In fact, some professionals became so disappointed with the poor performance and trajectories of the gutties that they gave them away, often to their caddies to play. Not long after that, professionals noticed their caddies were achieving the kind of ball flight they themselves desired with beat up, secondhand gutta balls.

So it was quite by accident that an experiment with physics and aerodynamics led to the second generation in gutta percha golf ball design. Players noticed that the nicks and scratches on the surface of the ball caused a truer, more stable trajectory. Robert Forgan, a club and ballmaker from St. Andrews is credited with selling the first gutta percha balls with surface patterns. Forgan placed each ball in a mount and indented the surface with the claw end of the hammer, attempting to simulate cuts and scratches made by a golf club. For twenty years to follow, Forgan's method became the standard on gutta balls, and the practice became known as "hand hammered."

Now golfers had a ball that traveled further, rolled more consistently, and was significantly less expensive to

"THE DEVELOPMENT OF THE GOLF BALL"

| WOODEN | FEATHERY | GUTTA PERCHA | MACHINE GUTTY | HASKELL |
| c.1590 | c.1790 | c.1850 | c.1880 | c.1900 |

The evolution of the golf ball dramatically changed the shape and design of golf clubs as well.

make than the feathery. People were coming back to golf in droves and the game enjoyed a rebirth among the common people. Forests in Asia were being gutted to satisfy the demand for the new gutta percha ball, and ballmakers were able to significantly increase their production of golf balls.

As a result, golf began to grow at a rapid rate outside of Great Britain. Toward the end of the 19th century, markings on the gutta ball were being applied in the mold, with the earliest patterns appearing to be circular marks emanating from the poles of the ball. Experimentation was now the rage, and manufacturers continued to design, redesign and create molds, all promising improved ball flight. The amount of unique pattern designs is actually what makes the gutty ball the sought after collectibles that they are today. One can find circles and triangles among the many geometric shapes that were used as marking patterns for these balls at some time in their history.

One of the most well known balls to emerge from the gutta percha period was the A. G. Spalding & Bros. Vardon Flyer, which Harry Vardon, the soft-spoken Englishman who, many believe, took the golf craze in America to new levels during his nine month tour of the States in 1900.

The process of making featheries was an art form. Ballmakers would take over three hours to make a single ball, and a mistake could cost them half their day. If you were a maker of featheries, you didn't have much time to learn the art of clubmaking. However, once gutties became the golf ball of desire, clubmakers easily shifted into ballmaking mode by purchasing molds and substantially increasing their incomes by meeting the demand for gutties.

Gutties were not without their share of problems, though. In cold weather, the gutta percha could become brittle and when struck, actually break apart. This problem was even addressed in the rules at the time. If a gutty ball broke, a player was allowed to drop another in the spot next to the largest remaining piece of the broken ball.

In hot weather, the gutty could become soft, lose it's compression and not fly nearly as far as it would in mild weather. Still, none of these problems were enough to send the golf world scurrying back to featheries.

Before long, every serious clubmaker had his own brand of gutty ball, and by the end of the century, there were hundreds of brands on the market, creating the kind of competition for market share that golf enjoys today. Collectors also benefit from the variety of gutties manufactured then.

The gutta percha ball ranged in weight from about 1.4 ounces to 1.7 ounces. The average guttie traveled about 30 yards farther than the feathery, and because of it's stability, tended to last much longer as well. When

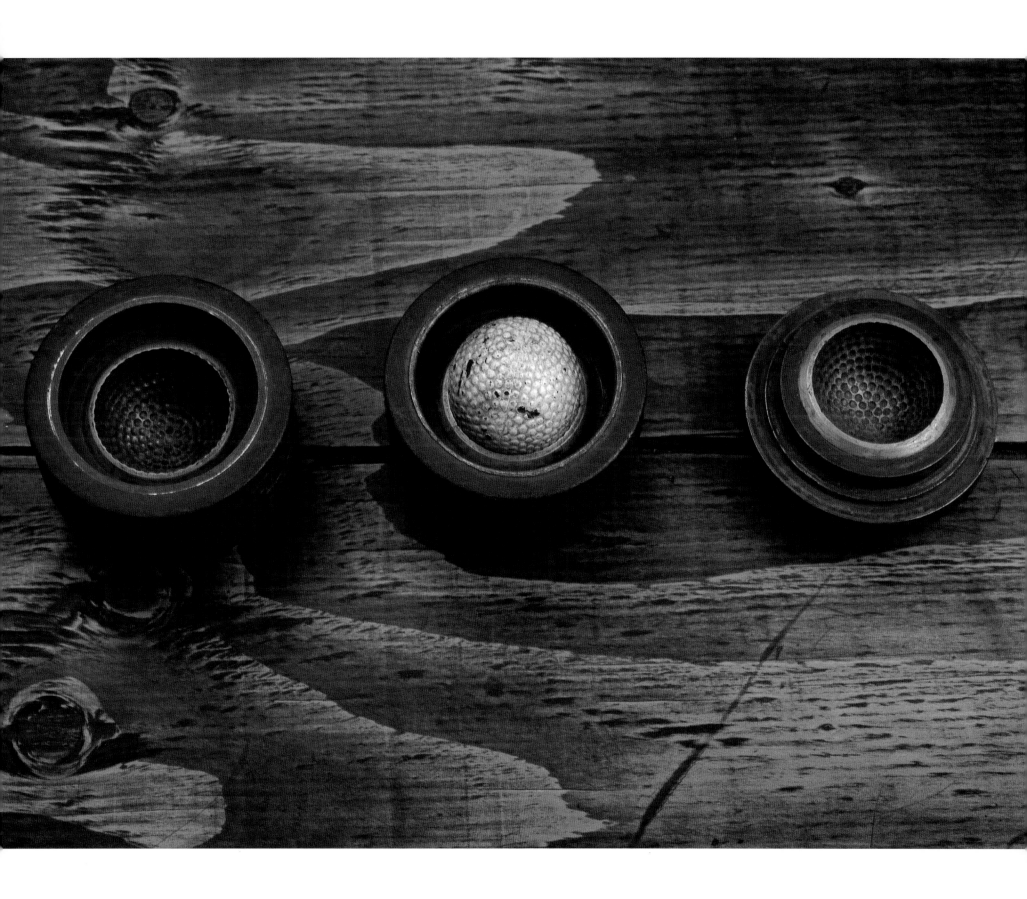

Golf ball molds with golf ball, 1880–1900.

struck, the gutta percha generally made a clicking noise at impact. Aged gutties are often dark brown and nearly black, but sound and color are not enough to tell if a ball is pure gutty, as some early rubber core balls often had a gutta percha cover.

Collectors of gutta percha balls will often come across balls that were remade, or with several layers of enamel and paint. This was a common way gutties further brought golf to the masses. Old balls found or purchased from golfers were remade and resold back into the market. And while finding a retouched gutty generally doesn't diminish the collectibility of the item, there are few things more scarce than finding a gutty with its original paint and markings intact.

THE RUBBER CORE OR MODERN BALL

By the time Harry Vardon returned to England after his whirlwind tour of the states, his Vardon Flyer was quickly becoming obsolete. A few years before Vardon arrived in America, an entrepreneur from Cleveland, Ohio was thinking of ways to improve his own game. The shortest hitter in his foursome, Coburn Haskell happened to be visiting a friend of his at the B.F. Goodrich rubber company in Akron when he discovered some elastic threads of rubber sitting in a bin. He returned home with the strips and attempted to wind them into a

ball, but his early attempts would often end in frustration as the ball would slip from his hands and unwind furiously as Haskell chased it around the room.

Eventually, Haskell persuaded Goodrich to help him find a way to wrap the balls with high tension and put a gutta percha cover around the wound rubber ball. It would ultimately become America's greatest contribution to the game of golf. The Haskell ball immediately flew a good 25 yards further than the gutta percha ball in the air, and it rolled even further than the gutties.

The first Haskell balls were a bit wild. Nicknamed "Bounding Billy's" by players, these early balls virtually exploded on impact because of irregularities in the winding process. The balls did not land on greens as softly as the gutties, and ballmakers began to experiment with the thickness of the gutta percha covers in an attempt to solve some of the Haskell's trajectory inconsistencies.

By the turn of the century, molded covers quickly yielded to raised, round nubs of the bramble pattern, and a thicker gutta cover was becoming the norm. This helped to reduce the "jacked-up" liveliness of the ball.

Accordingly, the game of golf began to change as dramatically as the ball itself. The added distance most golfers enjoyed with the new Haskell balls completely altered the strategy players used on the course. Par fives were reduced to par fours in many cases, and balls that

A Willie Park mid-iron from 1886, as well as two feathery balls from 1850, and two dimpled rubber-core balls from 1940–1950.

no longer landed softly on the greens led to the increased employment of bump and run shots.

As might be expected, there was a great deal of resistance to the Haskell ball, especially in Europe. Prominent British golfers urged fellow professionals not to use the ball, describing it as unfit, and even unmanly because of the added distance. But in a game where everyone is constantly searching for the slightest advantage over their opponents, it wasn't long before even the most vocal critics of the ball had to eventually accept the fact that the Haskell ball was here to stay and there would be no turning back. The modern ball had a very deep impact on the game, most noticeably the clubs. Although golf courses themselves were altered and strategies rethought, the actual tools used to strike the rubber core balls were the most dramatic. At first, rubber core balls were more expensive to produce than the gutta percha balls, but once free market competition emerged, the costs were greatly reduced.

It is interesting to note that the first golf ball patent (No. 3428) was issued in England in 1876 to a Captain Duncan Stewart of St. Andrew's, Scotland, who invented a ball that combined gutta percha with cork and metal fillings in an effort to prevent the ball from splitting open. The ball Stewart attempted to develop was not successful, but he persisted with various other rubber threads within a gutta percha cover.

In 1905, Stewart testified in the defense of a patent violation case where the Haskell Company sued British ball manufacturers for developing their own rubber core balls. Stewart's testimony about his own experiments ultimately enabled the British to void the Haskell patent in the UK.

In 1907, an English engineer by the name of William Tyler was given a patent for developing a dimple-covered golf ball, which the A.G. Spalding & Bros. company purchased U.S. rights to. The next year, Spalding began to produce dimple covered balls until 1912, when mesh and lattice (square or fishnet) became the pattern most golfers favored, and they lasted well into the 1930s.

The early 1900s saw a great deal of experimentation with golf balls. Frank H. Mingay of Berfield, Scotland was given a British patent for his use of incompressible liquid centered golf balls. Mingay used water, treacle, castor oil, honey and even mercury in his research, hoping to invent the ball which would receive and transmit club-head impact energy at a minimal loss of total energy. Again, A.G. Spalding stepped in to purchase the rights to Mingay's patent and ultimately introduced the "Witch," Spalding's first liquid center golf ball. By that time, however, the "Witch" was but one of several liquid center balls already available to golfers.

In 1931, the United States Golf Association recog-

Winged Foot imprinted balls, along with various antique clubs, including the Schenectady putter.

nized that the advances in ball design needed to be regulated, and ruled that no ball weighing more than 1.55 ounces or smaller than 1.68" in diameter could be played in their championships. While Americans did not seem to mind much, players from England and Scotland did not take much comfort in this ruling. Links golf was a different game, they argued, and with the heavy winds they were accustomed to, a smaller and heavier ball was needed. After much back and forth, the USGA and the Royal and Ancient Golf Association reached a compromise.

Beginning on the first day of 1932, the R & A set their measurements—an official 1.62 ounces was maximum while 1.62 inches for a diameter was now the rule for a ball. The USGA agreed with the 1.62 ounce maximum weight, but maintained 1.68 inch as the minimum diameter of a ball. Ballmakers since then have attempted to improve performance by experimenting in several areas, while still maintaining approved status by the USGA. Balata balls, wound balls, two piece and three-piece balls, and liquid center balls have all come into fashion since.

Another important development was the implementation of a surlyn cover which proved to be more durable than balata. Surlyn balls last longer, generally don't lose their shape, or suffer disfiguring cuts from bad swings or skulled shots, and even cost less to produce. Many surlyn balls are often designed to impart low spin rates, lessening slices and hooks—another factor that has helped make golf more enjoyable for the high handicapper.

Olin Dutra, fighting severe stomach cramps, won the 1934 U.S. Open at the Merion Cricket Club in Ardmore, Pennsylvania, using this ball.

EARLY
GOLF CLUBS

Various antique putters.

THE WOODS

It is telling that, in terms of golf club invention, the iron clubhead is a relative newcomer to golf. Golf historians generally believe that wood clubs preceded irons by centuries. How many centuries is still a topic of debate, since the origin of the game of golf has never been proven. There is an old myth of golf being invented by the shepherd boy who, passing time while minding his sheep, hits a stone with his staff, only to see the stone drop into a distant hole. No one knows if that myth has any truth to it, and it doesn't seem too far fetched to be possible. But one thing is for sure. The shepherd boy was probably not hitting an iron.

The oldest documented golf clubs, unfortunately, can only be found in old paintings and descriptions from centuries ago. However, Sotheby's, the noted auction house, sold a club in 1992 for over $150,000 which is currently displayed in the museum in Spain's famed Valderrama Golf Club. And it is with a touch of irony that this old club is an iron! Historians date the club to about 1680, and it was found centuries later in a shed in Edinburgh and well kept by its owner. Leave it to a Scotsman to be astute enough to wrap the club in a cloth soaked with linseed oil for over 40 years, for the club is in excellent condition today.

One of the problems historians and collectors are faced with is the deterioration of wood over time. Unless effort was made over time to preserve wooden clubs, they simply disappeared, which explains the prevalence of early irons.

Among the oldest clubs in existence are the "Troon Clubs" which were found inside a boarded-up closet, along with a newspaper dated 1741. It turned out the clubs were actually much older than the newspaper. Some golf historians estimate the Troon Clubs were made in the early 1600s, and quite possibly the 15th cen-

Long nose woods from 1850–1900.

tury. The clubs are comprised of six long nose woods (drivers and spoons) and two irons. Determining the exact age of golf clubs prior to the mid 19th century is quite difficult since the markings clubmakers often stamped on clubs cannot be documented or attributed to specific craftsmen so far back in time. The Troon clubs are very valuable in that they add a great deal of perspective toward the dating of other early clubs.

Long Nose Woods and Spoons

Since feathery balls were susceptible to damage from a poorly hit iron, the clubs of choice in the feathery era were long nose woods and spoons. With long, slim heads, a concave face and shallow clubfaces, the long nosed woods were characterized according to the desired shot. It was not uncommon for a player to carry with him eight to twelve clubs, including two "play clubs", a grassed driver, three or more spoons, a baffy spoon, a wooden niblick and a wooden putter.

Prior to the mid 1880s, a golfer standing on the first tee would be very likely to hit with his play club which was the driver of the era. With a long shaft and low loft, the play club was the club of choice for hitting the ball the greatest distance possible. Another long nosed wood that was quite useful was the "grassed driver" which had more loft than play clubs and helped the golfer get the ball in the air. The grassed driver was used from the tee as well as the fairway, but it would still require a good lie from the short grass.

Instead of having irons that ranged from long to mid to wedges the way a golfer today does, the 19th century golfer was mostly likely to employ either a "long spoon," a "middle spoon," a "short spoon" or a "baffy spoon" depending upon his distance from the green. Long spoons generally had longer shafts than middle spoons, even though the middle spoon might be stiffer in shaft flexibility. Short spoons and baffy spoons had more loft to them.

The baffy spoon was early golf's version of the wedge, as it was often employed to achieve a high trajectory over a hazard, and to land softly on the green with minimum roll. Collectors note that the baffing or baffy spoon are more rare, as long nose era golfers began to move toward the iron lofter instead. Even more difficult to come across are the wooden niblicks from the latter part of the 19th century. Used to advance the ball from out of a trouble spot, the wooden niblick features a smaller, but heavily lofted clubface. These clubs never achieved the durability of other long nosed woods and were ultimately replaced by irons.

Historians believe that the Scottish clubs of the 15th century were remarkably similar in design to the clubs a player might carry today, with the exception of the tech-

Mixture of play clubs, including spoons and grass drivers.

nology and the adjustments to the modern ball. A typical 15th century club had a very sturdy shaft, a weighted head and a handle gripped with hide from a pig, sheep, cow or horse. A chamois grip might also have been a possibility.

When the long nosed woods came into fashion in the 18th century, golfers typically used a flatter swing to advance the ball with a low trajectory but a great distance because of roll. But play clubs were also likely to crack or split upon impact, the reason why many golfers of that period usually carried a couple of play clubs.

These early woods were made from a sturdy, straight-grained shaft which tapered to a long flat wedge. The wedge was then joined to a taper on the socket of the clubhead and glued before finally being held into place by tightly wrapped twine around the tapering splice in a process known as "whipping." There was a great deal of variation in the choice of wood used to make these clubs. Clubmakers generally preferred to use the fruitwoods, such as apple, pear, cherry and plum to make long nose heads, as well as dogwood, hornbeam, thornwood and beech. Whatever the wood, it was important for the club-head to have the grain running up the neck of the club so as to limit its vulnerability to splitting upon impact with a golf ball. This was accomplished best by having a natural bend in the wood.

The earliest form of wood used in a clubhead was the "thorncut" which was made of wood from a blackthorn tree. It was apparently important to have the grain running up the neck of the clubface, so the manner in which the blackthorn tree was cut (with wedges to make a stronger piece of wood) appears to have been vital. Cut this way, the blackthorn was less likely to split upon impact with a golf ball. Therefore, putting a natural bend into the clubface was highly desirable.

Beech was also a popular wood for clubheads, and the quality of this wood was used until the turn of the 20th century. Clubmakers were careful with beech, choosing only from trees that grew on hills rather than in the valley.

The reason—valley wood had a tendency to be softer. Along the way, other woods were tried, such as apple, dogwood and holly, but beech appeared to be the most popular choice among early clubmakers.

For about the first 400 years or so of the game's development, wooden clubheads were joined to a shaft in roughly the same manner. That is, basically strapping the shaft to the back of the head in a flat join which would be glued and then whipped with twine. The twine was generally used to either conceal the join at the head and shaft, or to add strength to the joining. Twine was simply flax derived from the linseed plant and covered with hot pitch to protect it.

Some clubmakers, in an attempt to avoid having to

The development of modern woods. From left to right, a modern Persimmon with brass insert made by Wheatley Golf, a MacGregor Jack Nicklaus driver, and a Taylor Made metal wood from 1987.

fasten a clubhead to a shaft, experimented with a one-piece club. But they never became as popular as separate woods for both clubhead and shaft. One problem was that once a one piece club was broken, there was no chance to fix it. Most of the breaks from clubs prior to the one-piece were centered in the area where the shaft and clubhead were joined, and this was not an uncommon occurrence in a round of golf. There was simply no way to reshaft a one-piece club. It wasn't until nearly the beginning of the 19th century when splice fixing became the preferred method of linking the shaft and the clubhead.

Early long nose woods were heavy, and designed to swing through the long grass that the golfer of the times often encountered. It was also not uncommon for a clubmaker to fasten lead as a backweight on long nosed woods prior to the 1800s. The earliest clubmakers were often bowmakers and carpenters who already had a fine understanding, passed down from generations of bowmakers and carpenters before them, of the different qualities of wood. Before the arrival of machine tools, clubmakers prior to the late 1800s had to make clubs by hand. A playclub would be made by forming a block of wood into a shaped head with a curved socket which would taper into a splice so that it could be fitted to the shaft. The process would generally involve filing, spokeshaving, and chiseling, before the club was leaded,

boned, glasspapered down to the require length, usually stained with a keel (red keel was a popular finish) and ultimately treated with a hare's foot dipped in a mixture of oil and varnish.

The tools used for this work would be the usual tools of any woodworking craftsman of the time might use, namely hammers, saws, files, planes and drills. A clubmaker would also use a Bunsen burner to melt lead, which was then ladled into a groove on the back of the club to provide the desired weight and balance.

The earliest long nosed woods are long and shallow faced with a slight hook or spoon bend to them. In clubs made before 1860 or so, there do not appear to be any with a face deeper than an inch on play clubs. Only in baffing spoons and other, more lofted clubs does the face exceed an inch or so in deepness.

Ultimately, the demand for golf clubs became so great that there became a need for specialization. Clubmakers were often men who were employed at specific golf courses as rangers or supervisors. They may have regulated play, repaired members' clubs, maintained the course and even play the game. In short, the game was becoming more popular and bowmakers were no longer the men golfers turned to for quality golf clubs.

Many times, ram's horn (or ramshorn) was used as an insert in the sole or face of the club to reduce damage

Photographic portrait of a golfer.

done to the clubs by struck rocks and stones in the course of a player's swing. These plates were made by cutting the horn of either a ram or cow, then softening the pieces by boiling them in water. The softened horn was then made flat by squeezing it in a vice. The plate was then inserted into the sole, fastened with pegs, and could be easily replaced when worn.

Another way of protecting and adding weight to a clubhead was by heating lead, then pouring the molten liquid into a cavity placed in the back of the clubhead. Soft lead was generally used for this process, and when poured down the cavities, the lead would become solid again. This was also another way a clubmaker could customize a club, weighing it differently to alter its swing characteristics. Fixing a soleplate to a clubhead was another important step that a clubmaker would take to both protect the wood and add weight to the club. Most of the early woods featured a brass soleplate, fixed to the club with brass screws.

Early golf grips were usually made of sheepskin or cowhide and were obtained from a sheet of leather cut with a chisel. Before a grip was fastened, it was likely that an undergrip of cloth, called "listings" was applied so that the leather grip would adhere better to the club. This also resulted in a much thicker grip.

Early clubmakers used keratin, a mixture of sheep and cattle horn and hooves, which, when crushed and heated, formed a natural fixative. It was very effective, unless it became wet, so the whipping process with twine was more than just decorative. It served to protect the glue.

Eventually, clubmakers found persimmon, a dense and straight-grained wood that was imported to Scotland from North American forests. The quality of persimmon woods was so great that persimmon became the wood of choice deep into the modern era of golf.

Shafts

In the late 17th century, it is generally believed that hazel was a popular choice of wood for a club's shaft. Scholars have noted that hazel would have made a rather whippy shaft, which may explain why clubmakers seemed to have turned to ash at some point, since ash would make a stiffer shaft than hazel.

Ash shafts became the wood of choice for clubs until hickory came along around 1820 and demonstrated considerable lasting power because it had a steely spring to it and was deemed far superior to any other woods for making a shaft. The shaft revolutionized the game of golf.

Hickory quickly established itself as being superior to ash, because it has a great deal of strength, is light and absorbs shock. Originally in abundance in the southern regions of the United States, particularly the Tennessee

Assortment of antique clubs, balls, trophies, and scorecards guaranteed to draw the collector's eye.

hickory belt, the popularity of this shaft contributed greatly to an eventual shortage of the prized wood. Ringed hickory shafts cut from the center of the trunk were the most desired, since they were much tougher than hickory cut from other portions of the tree.

Clubmakers determined that the most effective shafts were made of a variety of red hickory, preferably cut from the center of the tree. Center cut hickory grain had a circular look to it, and shafts made from this part of the tree were noted to have "ring" hickory. The death of the hickory shaft resulted from an increasing demand in relation to a decreasing supply of hickory trees. Clubmakers were basically forced into finding a replacement for the well regarded hickory shaft.

The Bulger

When the gutta percha ball arrived toward the second part of the 19th century, the long nosed woods were found to be more easily damaged by the harder and heavier gutty. The result was that by 1880, wooden head clubs were designed to reflect the changes in the game because of golf's new ball. Clubheads were moving toward a shorter, broader shape, with a deeper face. In short, the "Bulger" was born.

The bulger's design was so scientifically sound that modern clubs are still produced in this mold. Credit for this design usually goes to Willie Park Junior and Henry Lamb. Park claimed he invented the club in 1883, but gives Lamb the credit for conceiving the name, "bulger." Whatever the origin, scientists concede that a ball struck with the type of convex surface such as the face of a bulger will produce less hook or slice than the concave surface of a long nose wood. The results on the course were even more convincing, and the long nose driver with the hooked face had seen its day.

That is not to say that clubmakers completely gave up on long nose woods. Some experimented with clubs that maintained the long, narrow aspect of the clubhead, but employed a convex face. But it was too late, of course, and the bulger shaped clubs became the club of choice for the golfing public.

The new bulger-shaped wooden heads permitted the clubmakers to improve the method by which shafts were now attached to the clubhead. The bulky, wider head on the bulger made it easier for clubmakers to drill a hole for a tapered shaft to be inserted into. Other techniques of the times were the mortise, the twin-splice and V-insert, but the bore-through socket design was so sound, that it is still used today, even on steel shafted woods. With the advent of the socket head wood came new methods to replace whipping. Some clubmakers replaced the twine with brass bands which, they claimed,

Array of bulgur clubs.

strengthened the neck of the club as well as improved it from a visual perspective.

Clubmakers also began experimenting with inserts on the bulgers, and everything from glass, rubber, elephant hide and ivory were used to protect the bulger's face from striking the hard gutta percha. Ultimately, strips of metal, coil springs, and even ball bearings were tested to improve distance and trajectory. While most of these inventions and experiments failed, some proved scientifically sound and are used in the design of clubs even today.

Once golfers committed to the bulger design, it wasn't long before the baffy came along to replace the baffing spoon. The baffy was a small headed, highly lofted wood which, despite the popularity of irons at the end of the 19th century, enjoyed a great deal of popularity because of the distance the club produced and the ease of which the club lofted the ball off the fairway.

The bulger design also paved the way for the brassie, a wood with more loft than a driver, but not quite as much as the baffy. The brassie was used off the tee quite successfully because its shorter shaft and higher loft made it easier to hit straight.

Golf clubs with aluminum heads began to appear in the game at the end of the 19th century as well. One of the most popular metalwoods designers was William Mills of England who developed a very successful putter,

and by 1892 began experimented with various aluminum clubheads. In his early metalwood clubheads, Mills would insert three wooden inserts so that the gutty ball would be met with wood on impact. But by 1900, Mills was the first clubmaker to make an aluminum wood that did not feature inserts made of wood or any other material for that matter. Mills manufactured the clubs and marketed them as unbreakable and economical, since they would not be damaged by water and did not demand constant cleaning. Yet the aluminum clubs, while popular, did not replace the more traditional woods, which flourished well into the 20th century.

THE IRONS

The earliest clubmakers, who were by trade carpenters and bowmakers, were already experts on the implementation of wood in their designs of golf clubs.

But when an iron clubhead was desired, it was the blacksmiths who picked up the ball, so to speak. However, the demand for irons was relatively minute in golf's early days. With the feathery ball, a wood club was still the desired club of choice, since an iron was more likely to do damage to the leather cased featheries.

Still, there were certain types of shots that the average Scottish course required. Chiefly, shots from the tall gorse, or sand bunkers or general hardpan surfaces

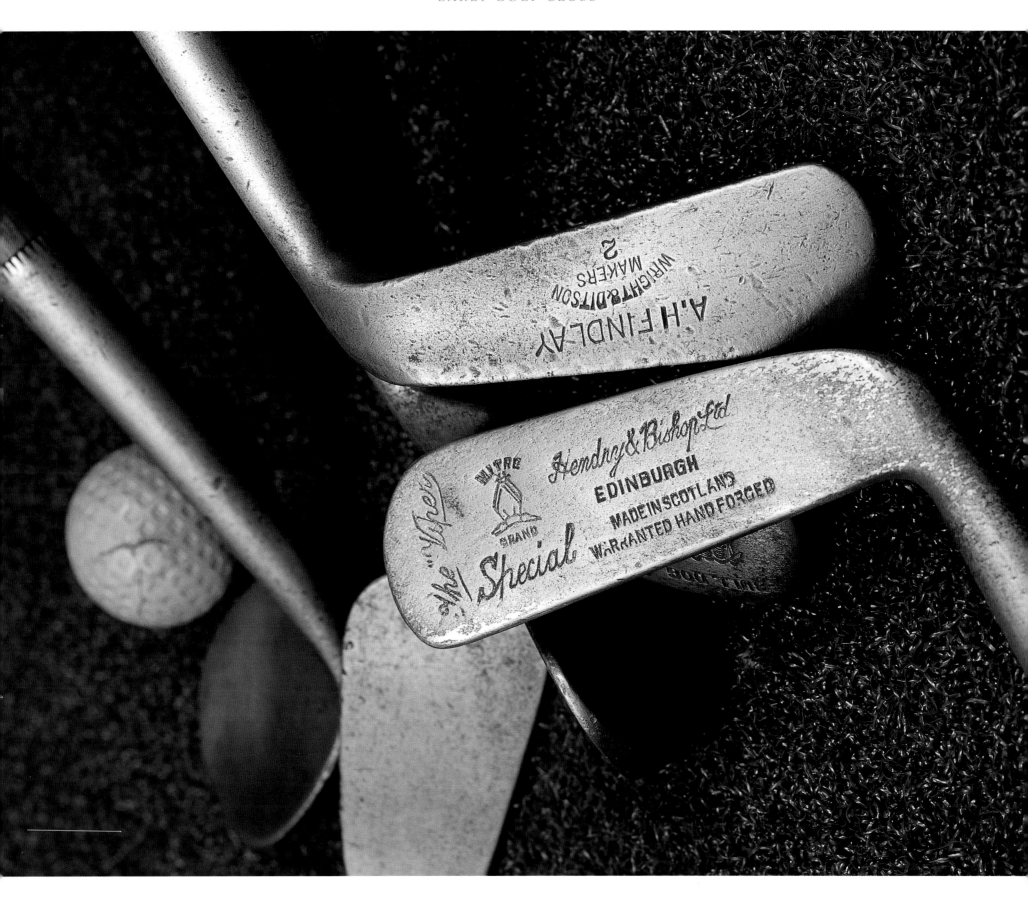

Assorted smooth-faced clubs pre-1900.

where a wooden club might likely be damaged. Therefore, it is believed that the earliest irons were made exclusively for hazard shots.

Blacksmiths, whose work mostly comprised of shoeing horses and making farm implements, were only too happy to pick up extra work they picked up from wealthy golfers in search of improving their game. Early irons were often large and heavy and players were discouraged from using them on the course because of the giant divots they often left in their wake. They were also expensive to make—twice the cost of a wood, so there weren't a lot of them around. In fact, an "early iron" is still considered by collectors to be any iron made prior to 1850.

To make an iron, a blacksmith would begin with a flat piece of iron a few inches wide and nearly a foot long. After heating it, he would flatten half of the strip so that it was twice as thick as when he began. The thin part was then wrapped around to form a hosel, then hammered again to create the desired loft and lie. The face was hammered to give it a concave face and left plain. Once the blacksmith did this, the head would be given to a clubmaker who shafted and gripped the club.

These early irons had names like "heavy iron," "bunker iron," and "spade." They were often crude in appearance, but they served their purpose, which was to advance the golf ball from hazardous places. Playing a ball from where it lies, in Scotland, often meant hitting through mud, cart tracks, driftwood and grass so thick that it may have occurred to golfers at some point to bring along a sword. The clubhead had to be quite heavy because the golfer needed mass behind his swing to clear the ball from the hazards. Collectors often note that early irons have significant denting because of the manner in which these clubs were used.

These heavy-headed irons also demanded strong shafts, like ash, as well as a very thick grip to execute the shots required of them. The early 17th and 18th century irons were held into place on the shaft by a joining method with serrated knopping at the top of the hosel. Later into the 19th century, rivets began to be used to firmly hold the shaft and the iron head together.

By 1850, iron niblicks and track irons, also known as general purpose irons, became more popular. The term "track" referred to the many cart tracks that appeared on links courses of the time, since farmers used to transport seaweed from the shore to their farms for fertilizing purposes. The wheels, with their wet loads, would sink down into the turf about two inches thick. The Scottish, with no affinity for winter rules or free drops, were faced with lies that would be difficult, if not downright unfair, to say the least. To play out of such lies, the blacksmith made a special iron with a small enough head to get behind the ball.

From left to right, a track iron pre-1890, a heavy soled niblick from 1900, a smooth faced sand iron from 1935, and Young's sand iron from 1929.

Such rut irons were either simply round, small headed irons, or sometimes a rut iron with a cut-off toe.

Rut irons or "rutters" came to be used in bunkers as well, but because of their small faces, they did not always produce the desired intent. With the feathery ball sitting in sand, an explosion shot was the shot of choice, since a skulled or topped shot with an iron was likely to render the feathery useless. Therefore, not too many irons were found in a player's bag. The damage to the expensive feather ball being the reason.

By the time the gutta percha ball arrived in 1848, golf became available to the masses because the expense of a golfball had dropped considerably. Most importantly, iron clubs did not destroy gutties, so more people began carrying more and more irons. This increased demand for irons enabled blacksmiths to set aside some of their other metal work and focus their efforts on the world of iron clubmaking. These new "cleekmakers" soon found themselves specializing in certain iron heads and many of them produced clubs for different clubmakers. The more renown they became, the more likely it was for them to begin stamping their names or marking the backs of the iron heads as a signature.

By the late 1800s, irons began to flatten out and the heavy track irons began to fall by the wayside. Cleekmakers were soon hiring dozens of men to meet the demands of golfers, and a cleekmaking company often had certain specialists. The bigger and stronger men were often "hammer men" who did all the heavy and more physical work. Others worked with dies for the stamping and grooving of patterns on the face of the club so that golfers could put spin on the ball.

One of the major problems a clubmaker faced when assembling an iron was to ensure that the shaft was tapered perfectly to fit the hosel of the club. If there was any give or action at the hosel, the club would be useless, so they took great pains to ensure that cleekmakers extended the hosel to the very heel of the club, enabling the clubmaker to drive the shaft down to the sole of the club. This ensured a very tight fit and made it possible for the cleekmaker to make an even shorter hosel, creating a lighter club, and balancing the clubhead so that there was more weight behind the ball on impact.

With the advent of these less clunky irons, golfers began using "cleeks" on parts of the course that were formerly taboo for irons. Now, cleeks were being used for approach shots to the green, as soft, lofted shots were possible with these irons. Golfers were finding out that lofted shots were more playable with these lighter irons than the old baffing spoon, and "mashies" and "niblicks" were born.

Serious collectors have learned the names of the clubmakers who stamped their names on the clubs they

Niblicks from 1935–1945.

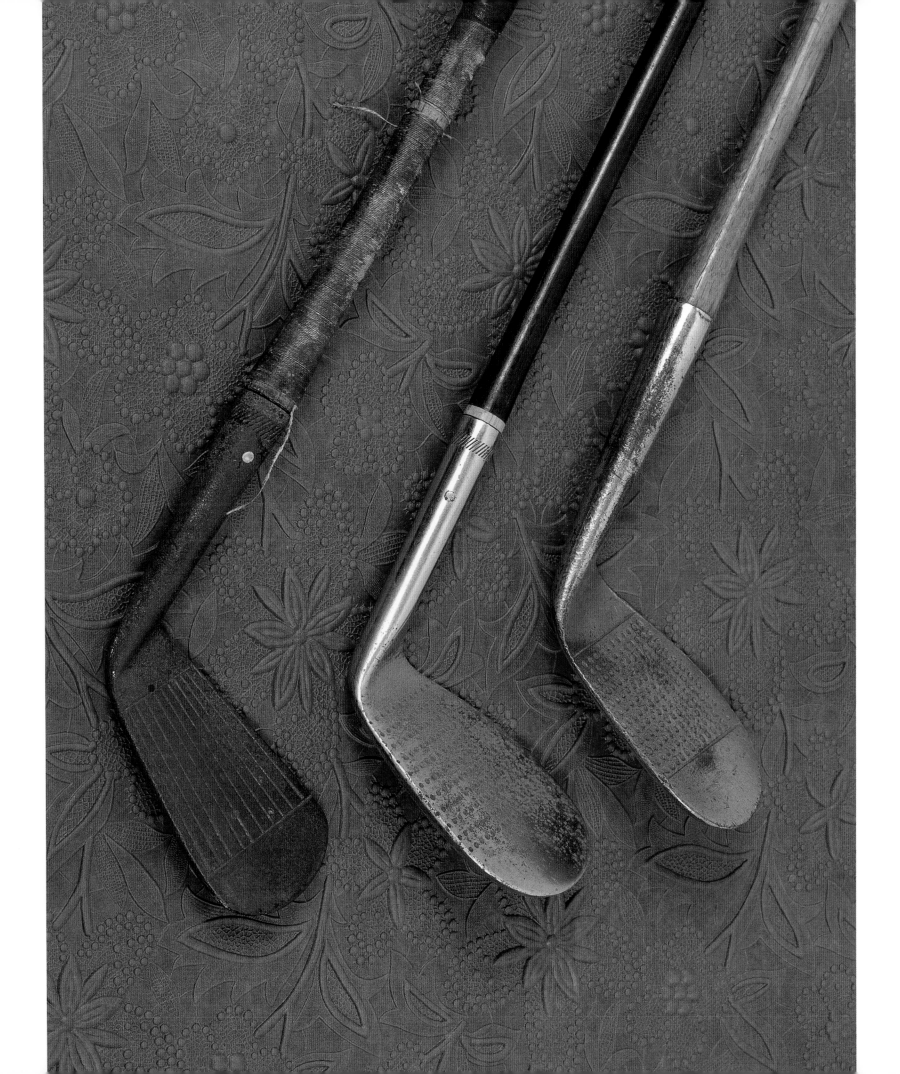

produced, since families and individual clubmakers often had certain specialties that golfers desired. Blacksmiths who worked alone generally did not put their named on the clubs they made, but there are some cleekmakers who were renown for their quality and collectors continue to seek out these clubs.

One noted cleekmaker from Musselburgh was the Carrick family, which formed F.& A. Carrick in 1840. Carrick's irons were the first known irons to carry trademarks, which were marked with a simple "X", sometimes with the Carrick name stamped on the head. The family continued to produce clubs of a very high quality right through the turn of the century.

The Anderson family at Anstruther in Fife had a very successful cleekmaking company which, by the end of the 19th century, was producing 40,000 iron clubheads a year. The company was probably best known for developing the patent on the Carruthers Cleek, an iron with a short hosel in which the shaft was brought right through the hosel down to the sole, forming one of the sturdiest irons to date. On early clubs, the Anderson family stamped their name, but later switched to a trademark "Arrow."

Old Tom Morris, working out of St. Andrews, stamped his name on many irons, and the name familiarity has always drawn collectors to his work. By 1880, golfers now had several irons in their bag, but the one club making the most noise seemed to be the mashie, and by the end of the century, the club was in wide circulation among golfers. Comparable to a 5 iron today, the mashie achieved a great deal of attention when J.H. Taylor began to hit it with great success in several Open victories. Taylor, known for his control of his iron shots, had a strong, short swing and seemed to stop his balls on the green with remarkable skill. When it was known that Taylor was playing a mashie, golfers went to the club in droves.

The success of the mashie led to driving mashies, deep-faced mashies and even the mashie-niblick. Eventually, the mashie spun off other clubs, such as "the glory iron," the "spade niblick," the "sky iron," the "jigger," and the "sammy." The result was that greenskeepers now had a new problem. Divots were tearing up their courses!

It wasn't until the 1920s when the idea of a clubmaker selling a matched set of irons took hold. Until then, a golfer might carry a small set of irons, or perhaps an assembly of mismatched irons made by different clubmakers, according to either his specialty or the golfer's desire. But in the mid 1920s, manufacturers such as A.G. Spalding began offering a matching set of irons rather than individually priced ones.

One of the most popular Scottish cleekmakers was Tom Stewart, who gained even more fame when the world's greatest golfer, Bobby Jones, used irons Stewart

Mid-irons from the early 1900s.

had made for him. Stewart then sought to cash in on Jones' success by offering "R.T.J. Model" clubs until Jones, also an attorney, asked him to cease. It wasn't until after Jones, who kept his amateur status throughout his playing career, retired in 1930, that he entered into an agreement to allow Spalding to market his golf clubs under the Jones signature. Once matching sets became the norm, the modern era of irons was born.

Ironically, steel shafts had been experimented with in the late 19th century, but the top clubmakers couldn't seem to make them work. They were simply too heavy to replace hickory shafts. However, the golf world was beginning to exhaust the supply of quality hickory for shafts, and golf manufacturers were worried. They referred to their problem as the "hickory famine," and began lobbying both the USGA and the R & A to consider making them legal. Curiously, there were no rules specifically against using steel shafts, and by the time manufacturers had begun to make hollow, tapered steel shaft which were not quite as heavy as their predecessors, both governing golf associations became worried and barred their use.

But by 1925, the USGA had fully recognized the problem, and in 1929, the R & A followed suit. Steel shafted clubs had become highly desired and there was no turning back. The hickory shafted clubs were now collector's items.

THE PUTTERS

Long nose putters

The putters used in the long nose era were usually quite versatile clubs, especially on Scottish links courses. Beyond putting, these clubs were often called upon for long bump and run shots from off the green, as well as lag putts over undulating grounds just off the green. To understand putters as equipment it is important to understand what role putting played in the early days of golf. The old links courses were very difficult to play around the hole. In fact, one of the earliest rules of golf states that a player, upon holing out, must tee up his ball within one club's length of the hole just played. One can only imagine what the area around the hole must have been like.

However, in the early days of golf, putting was not as important as it is today. It was possible to post a fine score by doing particularly well in the long game, and putting was often considered more a matter of luck. Golfers might complain about the unfairness of a missed putt, but it was probably with good reason. They often had to contend with "cupped lies" on the green.

The old wooden long nose putters looked quite similar to drivers of the times, and even had the same type of hooked face. However, putters were heavier, with shorter shafts and maintained a more vertical lie. Because the summer months in Scotland often produced

An assortment of early putters from left to right, a Schenectady putter, a wooden head win skeet brass face,
a smooth face putter, a rye neck putter, and a Mills of Sunderland aluminum case putter.

dry, unwatered and hard, dusty fairways, stopping the ball on the green to set up a putt was a tricky matter. Fortunately, the architects of golf had designed courses which had the hazards off to the sides of the greens, allowing players to use bump and run shots to the green.

These types of required shots on links courses led to the development of specialty putters, such as the driving putter. The driving putter was designed for the purpose of making long bump putts, and for hitting the ball low against a heavy wind. This club was basically a long, stiff shaft attached to a putter head. Not as popular as spoons and regular putters, these clubs were often used to skim the ball across the terrain. Scotswomen of the day might play an entire round with a driving putter, since the ground was often so dry, a ball could be advanced 100 yards easily with a driving putter.

Because of the way the game was played in Scotland on the links courses, it was necessary to have several putters to use for different shots. Putters for short putts and holing out were entirely different than the putters used to, say, advance the ball onto the green. The approach putter was another club that saw heavy use in the early days of golf. Similar to the driving putter, the approach putter was often used after a drive, depending

Golfers might complain about the unfairness of a missed putt, but it was probably with good reason.

on the length of the hole, to play a running shot to a desired area of the green. Depending upon how the ball was struck, the putt might bounce along the ground, or behave like a chip shot before settling down to a roll.

Upon the arrival of the gutta percha ball, the game experienced a dramatic increase in iron play because irons were not as hazardous to the life of a gutty ball as opposed to a feathery. Since it was easier with an iron to loft a ball onto a green and impart spin to control the way it landed, it was generally thought that it might also be a good idea to use an iron for putting as well.

The first iron blade putters had a little loft to them and putting cleeks became quite popular. By 1885, the wooden putter pretty much disappeared from the scene, and when Willie Park Junior patented the "Bent neck putter" (also referred to as a "wry-necked putter") around this time, a new design in putting technology was reached, and many of Park's original designs are still used today.

The bent neck putter had a bend in the hosel (similar to an offset) which had the effect of putting the ball in direct line with the shaft. Once this design was in place, clubmakers began to experiment a great deal with putters, and because of the increased importance that putting now has in golf, putter designs are, to this day, con-

Faces of mid-irons.

stantly reworked and redesigned in an attempt to improve a golfer's scores.

In 1895, William Mills of Sunderland, England who would eventually become the most prolific designer of aluminum headed golf clubs, produced an aluminum clubhead frame which was filled with wood. Five years later, he would produce a clubhead made entirely of aluminum, and a golfer by the name of James Braid, who had never demonstrated much prowess as a putter, began winning Open Championships using a Mills aluminum putter. That same year, Harold Hilton used a Mills putter to capture the British Amateur, and aluminum putters became enormously popular.

Around the turn of the century, golfers had a wide variety of putters to choose from, provided they had the patience to experiment. Drilled face putters with holes punched through a deep, offset blade, apparently to reduce the distance a putt will travel, became just one of many unusual looking clubs designed for putting. Tom Morris produced a cylinder head putter, also called a drain pipe putter, in the early 1890s and it led to a series of cylinder designs and convex blades which followed.

In 1900, Willie Dunn Jr., winner of the open American championship received a patent on August 14th that covered a putter which was designed especially for the Haskell ball. The putter featured a negative loft convex faced put-ter, enabling it to strike the ball above its center and give it forward spin, similar to the way a ball is struck in billiards. The result was Dunn's Rotary mallet head putter, which achieved some popularity at the turn of the century.

However, in 1902, a man by the name of Arthur F. "Bill" Knight of a small city in upstate New York called Schenectady, set out to improve his own putting game by designing a putter he thought would answer his putting woes. He got the idea to try a putter with a flat head, but with the shaft inserted in the center, and with his engineering bent, decided to tackle the invention himself.

Knight tried a few versions with lead, hoping to achieve the kind of balance he felt was needed to give the club proper feel and weight distribution. The lead putter apparently did not work out too well, and Knight quickly relegated his prototype to the scrap heap. But when he attempted to fill the same mold with aluminum this time, he stumbled onto the putter that would eventually become the most renown putter the game of golf has ever known.

Scientifically, Knight believed that by placing the shaft in the center of the head, a golfer would produce less torque on impact, resulting in more consistency. He also felt that the shape of the Schenectady improved alignment and sight lines to the ball. While playing at his country club in Schenectady, Knight met with Devereux

Two mid-irons from the late 1890s.

Emmet, who happened to be a friend of the great Australian-born amateur golfer, Walter Travis. Emmet tried Knight's Schenectady putter, liked it, and showed it to Travis a few days later. It wasn't long afterwards when Knight received a telegram from Travis himself, ordering a putter just like Emmet's. Knight made two putters for Travis, one with slightly more loft, and Travis quickly proclaimed it the best putter he'd ever used.

Travis used the putter in the 1902 U.S. Open and finished second, prompting hundreds of orders for Knight's Schenectady putter. Knight recognized the demand for the putter and wanted to give it the name "Travis" putter, but Travis, perhaps out of modesty, declined, stating that he felt "Schenectady" would be a better name for the putter.

Knight applied for and was granted a patent for his putter, and the date of the patent, "March 24, 1903" was marked on most of the Schenectady putters. The next year, Walter Travis became the first person outside of the United Kingdom to win the British Amateur. He beat Edward "Ted" Blackwell in a showdown between golfers who demonstrated different skills. Blackwell was a long hitting power golfer and Travis simply outputted him in the end, adding a great deal of mystique to the Schenectady putter.

Today, the Schenectady putter is still a prized collector's item even though they are available in relative abundance.

Upon news of Travis' victory in Britain, demand for the Schenectady putter went through the roof. Spalding was now manufacturing the putters, and cleekmakers in St. Andrews were also flooded with demands for the new club. Unfortunately, there was a great deal of resentment toward Travis' victory, as many influential British golfers felt the putter gave Travis an unfair advantage.

In 1910, the R & A finally ruled on the fate of the Schenectady putter, making it an illegal club. Thousands of clubheads in production in Scotland had to be dumped, and many felt the ruling body overreacted when banning the putter. The controversy was further flamed when, in 1911, the USGA ruled the Schenectady a legal putter, and many felt the strain between the two governing bodies of golf would not be good for the game. But as it turned out, the two bodies were able to work together, despite their differences. Finally, in 1951, the R & A lifted their ban against the Schenectady putter, as well as the other many center-shafted putters that had come into prominence. Ironically, Walter Travis, after igniting the world on fire with his putting prowess using the Schenectady, was never able to recapture the magic with the infamous putter again. Today, the Schenectady

Early 1900s clubs from the collection at Winged Foot Golf Club in Mamaroneck, New York.

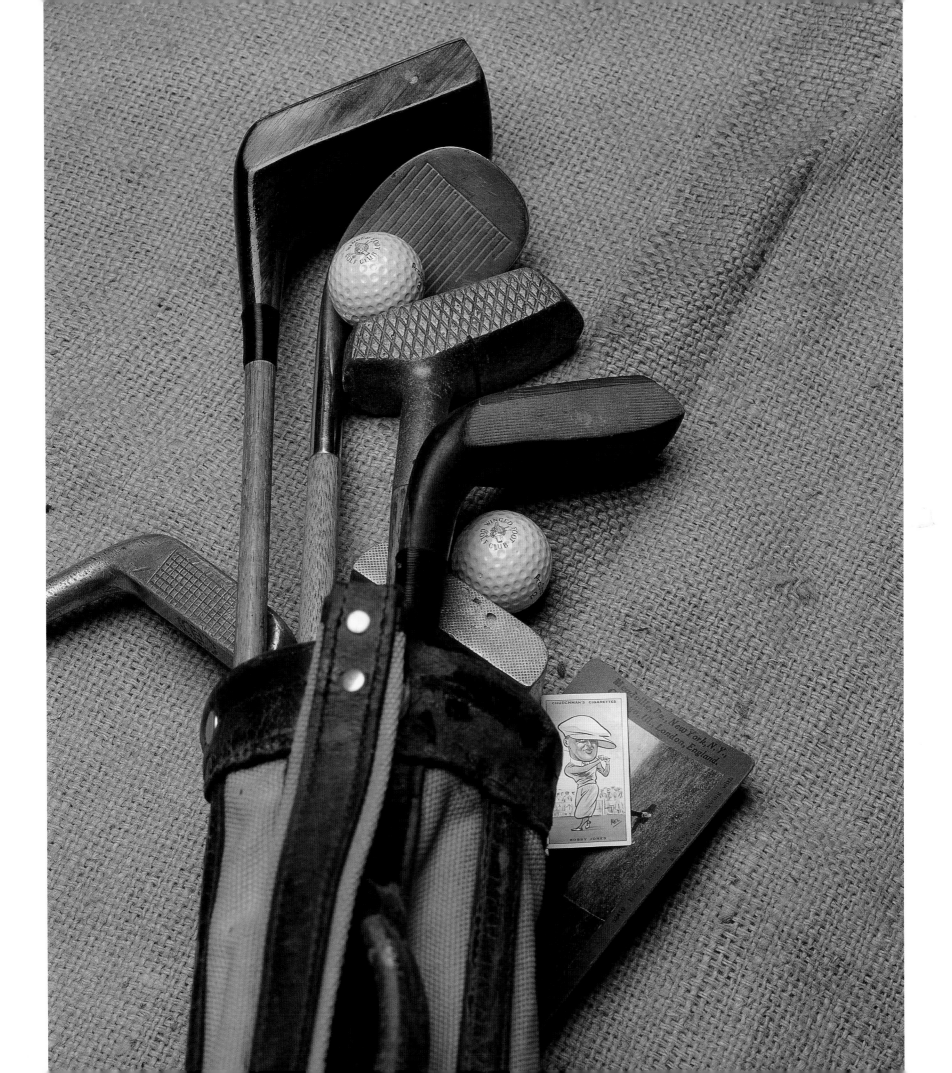

putter is still a prized collector's item even though they are available in relative abundance—a true reflection of their popularity at the time

Patent Clubs

There were several factors which led to the proliferation of patent clubs around the beginning of the 20th century. Perhaps the most significant was that interest in golf was reaching new heights. Golf courses were being built around the world quite rapidly to meet the growing legions of aspiring golfers in need of a place to play. Meanwhile, the industrial revolution enabled manufacturers to use new techniques which were not possible in earlier times. Hand forging was beginning to be replaced by mass production, and manufacturers looked for ways to cash in on the golf craze by pouring money into research and development of new clubs. All these factors contributed to the production of some of the oddest clubs imaginable, and collectors have this era to be quite thankful for.

While collectors of long nose woods and early irons are mostly drawn to a club's age and condition, the collector of patent clubs is generally inspired by a designer's creativity. Many collectors believe that patent clubs act as something of a bridge between the ancient and the modern clubs. If nothing else, they reflect the spirit of a golfer's neverending quest to improve his game. They also serve as a reminder of how the game has developed and how and why certain rules came into effect as well.

A patent is a legal document which is granted to an inventor, allowing him to produce and develop his idea for several years without competition. While nearly every golfclub ever made was patented, the term "patent club" to collectors, means any unusual club that may or may not have even been patented.

Patent clubs are generally very different in either their appearance or their construction from other collectible golf clubs. In many instances, patent clubs were prototype clubs which never made it to production. But they were well made and the intent to have them produced was genuine. The first patent golf club was granted in 1876 to Thomas Johnston, who intended to make long nose clubs from an Indian rubber called "vulcanite" or "ebonite." Not many of these clubs have ever been seen, and apparently, most of them were putters. From then on, inventors put a great deal of emphasis on patenting their designs, and it was not uncommon for clubmakers to mark clubs with either the patent date or "patent applied for" on the heads.

Among the most interesting patent clubs that turned up in the midst of patent club craze were the clubs which featured intriguing face treatments. The "Water" irons are

Assorted sand irons from 1880 to 1935.

among the most unusual. Water irons were designed at a time when many gutta percha balls on the market actually floated in water. Subsequently, it was not uncommon for a golfer to find his ball sitting atop a puddle of standing water, either on the fairway or in a bunker. The early golfer would therefore have to play the ball as it lied or suffer penalty strokes. One such water club was the "President" which was designed by W.G. Roy and featured a gaping hole right through the middle of the iron's clubface.

Also known as the ring mashie, the President performed well enough for Tom Morris to try his hand at the design of the club. But ultimately, it had inefficient balance and weight, and most troubling, four potential hitting surfaces to create further havoc. It wasn't surprising that the club eventually disappeared.

But other clubs with similar claims were quick to follow. "Rake" irons, which had slots and perforations that resembled a wide-toothed comb or rake came along, promising golfers an advantage in the sand, deep grass or water. Theoretically, the club, when swung, would allow obstructions such as water, sand and grass to pass through the clubface, while striking the ball unimpeded toward the target. Still, despite the apparent backing of some of the best golfers in the world at the time, rake irons did not gain much popularity. The prongs or teeth could easily become ensnared in the grass or ground and cause the clubhead to veer off line. Still, despite their uselessness on the course, downward pronged rake irons maintain high collector value because of their scarcity. Brown rake irons are particularly desirable because the teeth and perforations were surrounded with decorative engravings.

Despite the lack of popularity of Brown's rake irons, other noted cleek makers responded at the time with rake and water irons of their own. John S. Pearson produced mashies and niblicks with open slots in the back running horizontally across the clubface. His clubs also had another purpose beyond rescuing a ball from a lethal hazard. Pearson's irons were designed to create maximum backspin. But it seems that not many were actually made, since the clubs became illegal shortly after their introduction, and apparently, they were prone to break if swung at full force.

Also interesting from a visual perspective were the William F. Reach "waterfall" irons. These irons were designed to impart backspin on the ball, and the designs on the faces resembled waves of deep grooves. They were just one of many backspin irons to come along. Among them, ribbed and gridded irons, deep-dimple irons, and vertical-grooved irons, all of which were ultimately banned by both the R & A and the USGA. By 1924, slotted, ribbed, waffle faced or punched clubs with lines more than a given width were barred from competition, and the clubs ultimately disappeared. Apparently, these backspin clubs were well loved by the game's top golfers of the time because at the 1924 Southern California championship, bags were examined on the first tee and over 200 clubs had to be removed! Such was infiltration of backspin irons at the time.

Other designs, such as the anti-shank clubs, lifted the hosel connection to the top of the club and hoped to appeal to golfers with a case of the dreaded shanks. And flanged niblicks were designed to help players explode a ball out of a soft sand hazard.

Perhaps best known and desired by collectors are the adjustable or mechanical clubs which came into prominence at the end of the 19th century. The best known and most famous adjustable club is the Urquhart. A member of the Honourable Company of Edinburgh Golfers, Robert L. Urquhart came up with several patents for clubs which could be adjusted to many different lofts, both right and left handed, by simply pressing a button on the rear of the hosel and simultaneously pulling out and twisting the head of the club.

This was accomplished by a spring which was inserted into the iron socket at the end of the wooden shaft. The socket was something of a cog-wheel arrangement which prohibited the head from moving or even becom-

ing loose. Ideally, a player would need only to carry one iron with him during a round.

Countless adjustable irons followed, with various means of adjusting the loft on the clubs, such as "all-in-one" clubs as they were called, or "emergency" clubs. Even metal shaft adjustable woods never amounted to much on the golf course and the were ultimately banned from competition. But that doesn't stop the average collector from delighting in these rare finds. Face inserts were used by some clubmakers to protect the area of impact on the ball, and some of the materials they used resulted in patent woods that are every bit as interesting as the irons of the patent era.

Brass, ivory and steel were some of the more common inserts on woods at the time. Then clubmakers began to experiment with the actual clubheads, with the most common being aluminum. Some clubmakers used molded and compressed synthetics in their efforts to come up with heads that could withstand the elements. But the most interesting patent woods clearly revolved around the shapes of the clubs themselves. At the turn of the century, most woods were descendants of the bulger design and all of them looked fairly similar. That is, until MacGregor unleashed the "Streamliner." The Streamliner looked like a bullet going backwards, and it was MacGregor's attempt at increasing clubhead speed through experimentation with aerodynamic properties. As a bonus to collectors, the Streamliner featured one of the earliest chromed steel shafts. Other patent woods featured unique designs to the neck, such as the Scott patent fork splice and the Spalding triple splice, which were designed to increase strength between the head and shaft.

If ever a club was designed and redesigned throughout golf history, the putter was it. No stroke in golf is quite so temperamental and streaky as the putt, and golfers are renown for their willingness to try something new on the putting green. One popular patent putter design revolved around the hosel and neck of the club.

Designers did everything they could to move the hosel back and away from the blade striking area, and bending the hosel back was the preferred method. Weighting the putter head for balance and feel was another popular form of patents on putters. Aside from the infamous "Schenectady" putter and other center shafted or forked hosel designs, the most interesting patent putters were the many adjustable putters that, like adjustable irons, could be changed to alter lie or loft on approach putts, or even left or right handed putts.

All in all, the early part of the 20th century produced a gold mine of patent clubs that are every bit as enjoyable for collectors as the era of long nose woods and early irons.

Assorted irons from 1870–1910.

GOLF
ACCESSORIES
AND
COLLECTIBLES

Credential buttons from golf tournaments worldwide.

Clubs and balls are the only thing a golfer needs to play a round, but collectors are well aware that rarely can a collection end there. The game of golf has produced too many interesting accessories, artifacts and odds and ends for the collector to turn his back on. The more familiar one becomes with the history of the game, the more golf memorabilia and collectibles will gain in appeal. And like the appeal of the patent clubs, the more interesting the design or invention, the better!

TEES

The golf tees used today are basically all the same. Cheap, disposable wooden tees which barely get a player's attention should he, after a drive, notice that his tee has split into two pieces. However, 500 years ago, golfers were looking to elevate the ball on the turf, and an evolution in the design of golf tees followed. The earliest tees were most likely tees created by a golfer's heel imprint in the ground. This method raised the ground behind the heel and a player was able to create a desired lie from which to hit the ball. In fact, there are still tour players who do this from time to time off the tee, especially on par three holes where an iron would be the club of choice.

The next stage in golf tee design centered around the formation of small mounds of dirt or sand which a ball could be rested upon to create elevation. Golfers (or caddies) would do this by hand until the invention of the sand tee mold captured the imagination of the golf world shortly before the turn of the 20th century. Since making a tee by hand was a very time consuming and dirty practice, the sand tee mold enabled golfers to begin forming consistent tees without the mess.

Since golf tees are relatively inexpensive, they're a great way to start a golf collection. There are literally hundreds of different tee brands from the 1930s alone.

Made of various shapes and sizes, sand tee molds were often made of aluminum or stainless steel, and usually featured some type of spring plunger. A golfer would scoop up some moist sand or dirt, pack it into the mold, then depress the "button" or plunger to form a consistent sand or dirt tee. Sand tee molds were considered a great improvement over existing tee making by hand, but the golf invention craze that occurred in the early 1900s with clubs and ball patterns also affected the design of the golf tee.

Self-adjusting golf tees which resembled giant tweezers, cupped-dome tees made of plastic, rubber tees with round weights on one end, and brass tees with rubber arms that swiveled after impact were all inventions that made their way into golf by the 1930s. Tees were also being made of every material imaginable, such as aluminum, steel, paper, wire, rubber and zinc, to name a few. In fact, greenskeepers had the most to say about the abolition of wire tees, which would often entangle their mower blades.

The shape of tees was also a great experimental ground for inventors, as triangles, stars, tethers and spinners all saw their day in the sun. Ultimately, however, the plain wooden peg emerged as the cheapest, simplest and least cumbersome method of elevating a golf ball. When this was realized, manufacturers turned to packaging to set their tees apart from the rest. The packaging and marketing of tees beginning in the 1920s is something that the sport no longer enjoys.

Walter Hagen endorsed "The Yello Tee," a simple wooden peg, which he famously left in the ground after every tee shot. Once the last player in his group left the tee box, a scene not unlike the aftermath of a foul ball hit into the stands at a baseball game would follow, with fans and collectors scrambling for Hagen's tee!

Packaging concepts for tees included cloth bags, boxes of all sizes and matchbook-like packets with ornate designs and often outlandish claims, guaranteeing lower scores. To many, a tee is just a tee in today's game, and manufacturers wouldn't waste a penny trying any marketing strategy beyond keeping the cost low. In the roaring '20s, the golf tee was an accessory that collectors today are quite thankful for.

GOLF BAGS AND CARRIERS

Awkward as it might have been, for centuries, golfers and their caddies carried golf clubs under their arms without the benefit of any devices or contraptions. One of the reasons it wasn't necessary to carry some kind of bag or carrier is because players rarely played a round with more than seven clubs. And if they did, it was generally the caddie who bore the brunt of the extra load.

In the late 1800s, bags or covers came into usage so

A caddie bag from the 1870s.

that golfers could keep the grips from getting wet in the traditionally damp Scottish weather. The earliest bags were made of cloth but had no handles or straps. Only sacks, really, with the sole purpose to keep clubs dry rather than make carrying them any easier. Usually made of brown sack cloth or canvas, these simple sacks are the rarest of golf bags. Eventually, bag designers turned to leather to cover the base of golf bags so that the cloth would not become soaked when rested on wet grounds. Circular rings were then added to make the insertion and removal of clubs easier. Before long, handles and shoulder straps were added, as well as three and four stays, which kept the bags stiff and prevented them from folding or collapsing. Ball pockets as well as pockets large enough to carry golf clothing were added along the way, as leather became the material of choice for golf bag design.

Called "caddy bags" at the turn of the century, they began to have the manufacturer's name lettered on the side, as well as the golfer's name in many cases. The bags were getting larger and larger and heavier as well, due to the increased usage of leather on the entire bag. Earlier bags had circular openings with smaller diameters such as three or four inches, but as the size of the

bags increased, so did the number of clubs golfers wanted to carry!

Smaller "quiver" bags, called such because they resembled the holders that archers would use for their arrows, were now giving way to large leather bags, up to eight inches in diameter and made of different grades of hide, such as elk, kid leather and suede.

Unfortunately for collectors, leather, unless oiled and treated on a regular basis, has a tendency to deteriorate after half a century or so. Broken straps and handles are the most common problem, followed by deterioration or rotting of the leather itself. Wicker bags and other patent bags are considered rare finds among collectors.

The other less common devices were the club carriers, which featured dozens of different designs, ranging from stands, satchels and rings. Bipod legs, common on bags today, were actually in use in the late 1800s as golfers sought ways to play the game without the help of caddies. The most renown carrier equipment is referred to as "Osmond's Patent" and commands the highest value among collectors. But other makers, such as George Bussey of London, were well known at the time for high quality carriers which collectors still seek today.

In the roaring '20s, the golf tee was an accessory that collectors today are quite thankful for.

Golf-themed whiskey bottles from the 1920s.

OTHER COLLECTIBLES

There are countless golf collectibles from decanters and cocktail sets to ashtrays and match safes, all with golf themes and valued at whatever someone is willing to pay for them. Visual appeal or historical significance are often what makes these collectibles desirable. Golf scene ceramics, pins, badges, and figurines are just a few of many different areas of golf memorabilia that exist, and the amount of variety is limited only to the maker's imagination.

Some collectors are drawn to the numerous trophies and medals in existence, all of varying quality and significance, and, of course, price. Still, if a collector wants a British Open medal won by Bobby Locke, and has upwards of $50,000 to spend, he might very well be able to add such a medal to his collection. On more modest terms, collectors are often drawn to smaller medals demanding considerably less on the open market, but each with a story behind it.

The same goes for trophies, goblets and cups. Often, the esthetic value is more important to collectors, since hand-craftsmanship at the beginning of the 20th century, when these golf artifacts flourished, was the rule of the day. Bronze golfers atop elaborate marble bases and sterling silver loving cups, often with a golfing scene depicted, are popular golf objects for collectors because of the ease of which they can be displayed. They just look nice on a mantle or bookshelf!

Golf art is another category of collectibles which many collectors delight in because the nature of collecting golf art often entails research and study. In the 17th century in Holland, Dutch painters were drawn to winter scenes, and it was not uncommon for them to depict golf being played on frozen ponds. Drawings by Avercamp, which are displayed in the Royal Collection at Dresden and believed to be done in the year 1610, show golfers in remarkably modern poses such as lining up putts, where, were it not for the fashions depicted, it would be difficult to date them. Unfortunately, the Scots did not have any versions of "Dutch Masters" to paint the game of golf as they saw it in Scotland at the time. But toward the end of the 18th century, portraits of golfers with caddies and clubs begin to appear. These paintings have been translated to elaborate mezzotints which were famous in their day, and their depictions of various baffies and spoons were of great value to historians.

Some early depictions of Scottish golf, such as John Smart's *St. Andrew's Hell Bunker* and Garden G. Smith's *The Black Shed at Hoylake* are considered tremendously valuable watercolor paintings from the late 1800s, not to mention beautiful from a visual perspective as well.

Many collectors enjoy collecting rare, out-of-print golf books.

GOLF BOOKS

Golf books don't always command the kind of respect and value that other collectibles such as gutty balls and long nose woods do, but that's not an indication of the amount of pleasure a rare golf book can provide. After all, you can only look at a gutty for so long, but a book can be perused and studied for hours and days on end.

W.W. Tulloch's, *The Life of Tom Morris* is a rare and valuable book written as an 87th birthday present to Old Tom by a fellow member of the Royal and Ancient Club of St. Andrews in 1908. Tulloch painstakenly recounts the rich and bittersweet life of the legendary Scot, and the book is packed with poetic tributes to the man who captured the spirit of golf like no other.

Another charming and collectible book is Francis Ouimet's *A Game of Golf*, where Ouimet, the miraculous young winner of the 1913 U.S. Open at Brookline, documents his life, including his dramatic and unlikely victory against the likes of Harry Vardon and Ted Ray. If for no other reason than the cover art, these rare books make great collectibles because, once found, they can continue to be used and enjoyed by the collector. You wouldn't think about throwing a long nose wood in your bag and testing it on the range, but the golf book collector is almost sure to read the books he collects!

ODDS AND ENDS

With baseball card collections demanding record prices, it's no surprise that golf cards have taken a ride on baseball's coattails. Beginning in around 1880, tobacco companies needed some kind of stiff cardboard to prevent a pack of cigarettes from being bent or crushed. Since men made up the majority of smokers, companies often featured military and sports-themed cards in their packaging. Tobacco's success with these cards quickly spread into the packaging of magazines, cereals and chewing gum, and lo and behold, an industry of collecting was born. The American Tobacco Series of Champion Athletes and prize fighters of 1910 released the Mecca cigarette set, which included six American golfers who were among the top players at the time. The British also released a series of golf cards in their Guinea Gold cigarette packs, including Old Tom Morris and Harry Vardon.

While most single golf cards don't command values comparable to that of a Babe Ruth rookie card in baseball, there are several complete golf sets of cards, such as the Burline sets from 1910 in England, which are valued at over $20,000 in mint condition. Still, you might want to hold onto that Tiger Woods card!

Cigarette cards from 1910 to 1935.

COLLECTOR'S
GLOSSARY

"In the Rough" cocktail, a popular post-round drink for golfers in the 1920s.

Baffing spoon or baffy spoon: A wooden club which was the shortest, stiffest and most lofted club in a set of spoons. A golfer would use this club primarily for an approach shot. The modern equivalent is a wedge.

Baffy: A small headed, steeply lofted wooden club developed from the baffing spoon.

Balata: A hard, resilient substance derived from the gum of a bully or balata tree in either South America or the West Indies. Balata has been used in the making of rubber-cored golf balls, and is still popular among better golfers today who prefer "feel" balls rather than the more durable surlyn-covered balls.

Bap-headed: In the late 19th and early 20th century, these wooden clubs were more rounded in shape as opposed to the long nose woods made earlier.

Blade putter: A putter with the blade and neck of the same form of a golfer's standard irons.

Boxwood: The earliest known and rarest golf balls, these balls were often made of beech or boxroot.

Bramble: The small molded bumps on the surface of late gutta percha balls as well as early rubber-core balls, intended to improve the aerodynamic properties (similar to dimples) of a golf ball.

Brassie or brassy: Various lofted woods in the late 1880s were fitted with a brass sole plate. It is also a term for a wooden club which is lofted more than the driver but less than the spoon, and made with a brass sole plate. Later, a brassie became a term for a two wood.

Bulger: A wooden club, usually a driver with a slightly convexed face rather than just a flat surface.

Calamity Jane: A putter modeled on the Calamity Jane hickory-shafted blade putter made famous by Bobby Jones.

Chipper: A club used for chip shots, which often resembles an ancient mashie, i.e. a short shafted club.

Cleek: Derived from the Scotch word "click" meaning "hook," a cleek can be any of the numerous narrow-bladed irons, which can be used for long shots as well as approach shots or even hazard shots. The main characteristic of a cleek is that they are narrow-bladed and generally light. The cleek can also be a term for the one iron, as well as the four wood. Generally, the word is used today to describe a lofted wood with a shallow face.

Clubhead: The part of the club where the ball is struck. Usually made of wood or iron before the 20th century. The clubface is the actual surface on the clubhead which strikes the ball.

Golf tees used from 1900–1920.

Compression: The degree of resilience of a golf ball. A ball's compression is generally a measure of its hardness. The harder the ball, the less it will compress. The average compression of today's balls are 90 and 100.

Deep-faced: A club which is relatively thick when measured from top to bottom. Today's oversized drivers are deep-faced.

Dimple: The roundish depression on the surface of the golf ball.

Driver: The club that is one of the two longest hitting woods in a player's bag. Usually the number one wood, the modern drivers have an average loft between 8.5 and 12 degrees and a length over 43 inches.

Driving iron: A low lofted long iron, usually the 1 iron, this club is usually the most difficult club to hit well.

Driving mashie: An iron club with less loft than that of the mashie-iron, used for driving and for long shots to the green.

Driving putter: A straight faced wooden club used for driving low shots against the wind, this club was used in the early 19th century as a bump and run-type club.

Face or clubface: The striking surface of a clubhead.

Fairway wood: A wooden club that was used typically on the fairway or light rough and generally not the driver.

Featherie or feathery: A feather-stuffed, leather-covered ball used prior to the gutta percha ball in 1848. A feathery was usually stuffed with wet cow hair or feathers, and stuffed into a leather casing, also wet. When the feathers or hair dried, they would expand, and when the leather casing dried, it would shrink. The result was a very hard, round golf ball that lasted for centuries, until ultimately replaced by the cheaper, more durable gutty ball.

Flange: A projecting part on the back of an iron, the flange helps prevent the club from digging too deeply into the grass or sand. Thinner flanged clubs have less bounce and enable a golfer to cut down and under a ball, while sandwedges have a larger flange, adding bounce to the club. Putters may also be flanged.

Flip wedge: A highly lofted wedge, much like today's lob wedge.

Goose-neck: The neck of a club that is curved so much that the heel becomes slightly offset from the line of the shaft.

Grass club: A driver with slightly more loft than a straight-faced driver or play club. Usually with a stiffer handle and heavier head, a "grassed" club generally meant the club was "lofted."

An assortment of grass clubs from the mid-1900s.

Grip: The part of the shaft of a golf club which the player holds. In early golf, the grip was usually made with leather or pigskin, and later, rubber or some other synthetic material. The grip is also a term for the manner in which a golf club is held by a golfer.

Groove: This term refers to the linear scoring on a clubface. Clubmakers have long experimented with different types of grooves on clubfaces, similar to the way ballmakers have experimented with dimples on a golf ball.

Gutta or Gutta Percha: From the Malayan getah-percha sap tree, gutta percha was a resilient, easily molded substance from which golf balls were made beginning in 1848 until the early part of the 20th century. Some clubmakers also experimented with gutta percha to make clubheads, but the practice was quickly abandoned. The gutta percha was less expensive to make than its predecessor, the feathery, and therefore opened golf up to a broader section of the population.

Gutty or guttie: A gutta percha ball.

Gutty-perky: The Scottish variant of the gutta percha ball.

Head: See clubhead.

Heel: The near end of a clubhead directly below the neck.

Hickory: The wood from a North American tree from the Carya genus, hickory was used beginning in the early 19th century to the 1920s for making the shafts of golf clubs because of its toughness.

Hosel: This is the neck or socket in an iron clubhead.

Iron: A golf club with the head made of iron, or in modern times, an iron may be made of steel or titanium. An iron made prior to 1850 was likely to be heavily lofted and used mainly for playing out of trouble. Players had heavy irons and light irons and possibly even an iron putter, and all may have been referred to as irons. By 1890, irons were being classified as cleeks, mashies, niblicks and putters, according to the desired shot.

Jigger: A moderately lofted, shallow-faced and short-shafted iron that was designed for approach shots in the early 20th century, specifically chip shots.

Lie: The angle in which a clubhead is set on a shaft. This angle is measured between the shaft and the horizontal, when the club is properly soled by a golfer at address.

Links: Generally referred to as low-lying seaside land on the east coast of the Scottish Lowlands. Because of the short bent grass and natural windswept dunes and undulating turf, the land was the perfect setting for the earliest golfers. Today, links courses have been constructed all over the world to simulate the terrain of the earliest Scottish golf courses.

An assortment of early grips.

Loft: The degree to which a clubface is tipped back from vertical. This angle is measured as the angle between the face and a line parallel to the shaft.

Lofted: A club that has a relatively steep loft on the face.

Lofting Iron: A club used in the late 19th century for approach shots, ultimately replaced by the pitching mashie.

Long Irons: Generally considered to be the 1, 2, and 3 numbered irons, these clubs are typically used for long approach shots from the fairway, or for shots off the tee where it was desired to keep the ball low and below the wind.

Mallet or Mallethead: A putter which has a head that is significantly wider and heavier than that of a blade putter.

Mashie: A lofted iron club that was introduced around 1880 and used for imparting spin on a pitch shot. The club quickly became the most popular approach club in a golfer's bag. The mashie later became a term for the 5 iron.

Mashie-iron: An iron club which was less lofted than a mashie and used mainly for full shots to the green or off the tee. The mashie-iron also became a name for the 4 iron.

Mashie-niblick: An iron club that had a loft between that of a mashie and a niblick. Used for pitching, a mashie-niblick could also refer to a 6 or 7 iron.

Matched Clubs: Clubs that were designed and made in a graded and numbered series with consistent specifications, characteristics and swingweights.

Middle Spoon or Mid-spoon: A wooden club used in the late 19th century, and having a loft between those of a long spoon and a short spoon.

Mid-iron: An iron club which had more loft than a driving iron. It was also an alternate name for the 2 iron.

Mid-mashie: An alternate name for the 3 iron.

Neck: The tapered projecting section of a wooden clubhead where the shaft is fitted.

Niblick: Of the Scottish word meaning "short-nose" the niblick was a short-headed, highly lofted wood, used for trouble shots and tight lies and much shorter in the nose than any other wooden club. An iron niblick was a deep-bladed club that was more steeply lofted than a mashie and used mostly for playing from the sand and rough. The niblick is also an alternate name for the 9 iron.

Nose: The toe of a wooden club.

Offset: A crooked neck or hosel which sets the clubhead slightly off the line of the shaft. This is done on some putters to improve sight lines to the ball. It is also done on irons and woods to help golfers square the clubface at impact.

Assorted irons, including from top to bottom, a scored face iron from the early 1900s, a back stop mashie from 1917, a dot iron faced club from the early 1900s, and a smooth faced iron from 1905.

Peg: A tee.

Pimple: See bramble.

Pitching irons: The short irons.

Pitching wedge: An iron club used mainly for playing pitch shots to the green. These clubs are highly lofted and have less bounce than that of a sand wedge.

Play club: The earlier name for the straightest-faced, longest hitting wood which was later called the driver.

President: This was an iron club that had a steep loft similar to that of a niblick, with a hole through the face. It was a club that was used for playing out of the water.

Putter: A golf club designed for putting on or near the green. A putter usually has a very upright lie as well as a short shaft. Up until the 1850s, putters were made of wood until iron became the preferred putter clubhead.

Putty: The Eclipse ball, which was softer than the gutta percha.

Rake: A lofted iron club which had vertical slots in the face, (resembling a comb) used for water and sand shots in the late 19th century.

Ribbed: An iron club which was used in the 1920s and 30s, marked with scored ribs and grooves on the face. The feature was eventually banned.

Rubbercore: A rubber-cored ball.

Rubbercored: A ball which has a core of rubber. First manufactured by Coburn Haskell and J.R. Gammeter in 1898, the rubbercore ball featured an interior formed of strip rubber wound around a center and covered with either balata or some similar material. The rubbercored ball replaced the gutta percha.

Rut iron: Alternate names for the iron niblick or track iron, a rut iron was initially used to play out of ruts left by cartwheels.

Sammy: An iron club similar to the jigger, but with a rounded back, used for approach shots.

Sand blaster: A sand wedge.

Sand iron: A heavy, lofted stiff-shafted iron that was designed for play in bunkers.

Sand wedge: An iron club used mostly for "explosion" shots from bunkers. These clubs have a good amount of flange behind and below the leading edge, preventing the clubhead from digging too deeply into the sand. They also have more bounce than other wedges.

Scare: The spliced joint where wooden clubheads were fastened to the shaft before the introduction of drilled sockets near the end of the 19th century.

Arthur F. Knight's infamous Schenectady putter. This putter was banned by the Royal and Ancient Golf Club after Walter Travis used it to win the British Amateur in 1904.

Schenectady or Schenectady putter: This was a center-shafted putter with an aluminum head that was patented by Arthur F. Knight of Schenectady, NY on March 3, 1903. Walter J. Travis used this putter when he won the British amateur championship in 1904, eventually leading to the putter being banned by the Royal and Ancient.

Scoring: The markings of a clubface with grooves, punchmarks, etc.

Scraper: A lofted wood club.

Shaft or clubshaft: The long thin part of a golf club which is attached to the clubhead. Generally made of various woods until the 20th century, when steel replaced wood.

Shallow: A shallow-faced club is relatively narrow from top to bottom, in stark contrast to deep-faced clubs.

Short irons: The higher lofted irons.

Socket: The hosel of an iron clubhead.

Sole: The bottom surface of either an iron or a wooden clubhead.

Soleplate: A metal plate which was screwed to the sole of wooden clubheads.

Spade or spade-mashie: A deep-faced iron club which was more lofted than a mashie.

Spoon: Any group of early wooden clubs which had graduated lofts greater than that of a grassed driver, and accordingly, shorter shafts. The loft on many early clubfaces was usually concaved and resembled the bowled part of a spoon. It is also a term for a wooden club which featured more loft than a brassie in the early 20th century.

Spooned: Lofted.

Spring: Generally referring to the flexibility of a shaft.

Straight-faced: A club with very little loft on the face.

Sweet spot: The perfect spot on a clubface from which to strike the ball.

Swingweight: The measure of the weight of the club in which the shaft and the head are correlated. It is generally desirable to have consistent swingweights in a set of clubs. Clubs generally range from the lightest swingweights A-0 to the heaviest at E-9.

Tee: A tee is a small device, usually made of wood or plastic or rubber, but most commonly wood, on which the ball is placed for driving.

Toe: The end of the clubhead at the point farthest from the shaft.

Torque: The tendency of a clubshaft to twist from the impact of a shot.

Clubmakers and golfers used wax to weatherproof wood shafts.

Track iron: An alternate name for a rut iron or the earliest iron niblick.

Trolley: A British term for a two-wheeled pull cart on which a golf bag is placed and pulled around the course during a round.

Upright: A club having a wide angle of lie where the shaft at address stands relatively close to the vertical position.

Water club: Various patent clubs most popular between the 1880s and the 1930s, which were specifically designed for playing a ball out of the water. These clubs are now banned.

Wedge: A pitching or sand wedge. High lofted clubs used for approach shots to the green.

Whip: The flexibility of a shaft.

Whipping: The binding of thread around the neck of a wooden club. Nylon was later used on the areas where the neck and shaft meet.

Wood: Any club which has a wood head, or material other than wood but the same design characteristics of wooden clubs.

Wry-necked: A British term for a club with a crooked neck or hosel, making the club offset.

Top to bottom: a long-nosed spoon from 1850, a scared bolgin driver from 1885, a bored-through fairway wood from 1903, a bored-through driver from 1903.